EAST-CENTRAL EUROPE AND THE USSR

BOOKS BY RICHARD F. STAAR

Arms Control: Myth versus Reality (editor)
Aspects of Modern Communism (editor)
Communist Regimes in Eastern Europe
East-Central Europe and the USSR (editor)
Foreign Policies of the Soviet Union
Future Information Revolution in the USSR (editor)
*Long-Range Environmental Study of the Northern Tier of
    Eastern Europe in 1990-2000*
Poland: Sovietization of a Captive People
Public Diplomacy: USA versus USSR (editor)
Soviet Military Policy Since World War Two (co-author)
United States-East European Relations in the 1990s (editor)
USSR Foreign Policies After Detente
*Yearbook on International Communist Affairs: Parties and
    Revolutionary Movements* (editor)

EAST-CENTRAL EUROPE AND THE USSR

EDITED BY

Richard F. Staar

Senior Fellow
The Hoover Institution on War, Revolution and Peace,
Stanford University

St. Martin's Press
New York

The quality of this book was enhanced through interaction with the following participants at the workshop: John H. Brown (United States Information Agency and former American consul in Kraków, Poland); Andrew Goodman (officer-in-charge of East-West Relations, U.S. Department of State); John P. Hardt (associate director for research coordination, U.S. Congressional Research Service); James R. Hooper (deputy director for southern tier countries, U.S. Department of State); Robert L. Hutchings (director for European political affairs, National Security Council staff); Nicholas R. Lang (INR division chief for Eastern Europe, U.S. Department of State); Cameron Munter (desk officer for Czechoslovakia, U.S. Department of State); Jack R. Perry (director of the Dean Rusk Program in International Studies at Davidson College and former U.S. ambassador to Bulgaria); Beth E. Sanner (analyst on Balkan Affairs for INR, U.S. Department of State); Jeffrey Simon (senior fellow at the Institute for National Strategic Studies, National Defense University); James W. Swihart, Jr. (director, Office of Eastern European and Yugoslav Affairs, U.S. Department of State). Their policy perspectives added an invaluable dimension to the discussions. The editor wishes to express his gratitude to the United States Institute of Peace for a grant award which enabled him to organize the workshop and for that organization's gracious hospitality in allowing participants to convene in its conference room. He also thanks the John M. Olin Program on Soviet and East European Studies at the Hoover Institution for its generous support. Preparation of the book for the publisher could not have been accomplished without the able assistance of Joyce Cerwin and Margit Grigory.

Richard F. Staar
Stanford, California

Note: The term "Eastern Europe" is used in this book when discussing the Soviet sphere of domination until the revolutionary changes that commenced in 1989. "East-Central Europe" refers to the same region after the momentous transformation of the region had begun.

CONTRIBUTORS

JOHN D. BELL (Ph.D., Princeton) is professor of history at the University of Maryland in Baltimore and president of the Bulgarian Studies Association of North America. His latest book, *The Bulgarian Communist Party: From Blagoev to Zhivkov*, appeared in 1986.

CHARLES Z. JOKAY (Ph.D., Illinois), a research fellow at the Hudson Institute in Indianapolis, studies the relationship of the European Community and Germany with East-Central Europe, and is developing regional integration alternatives for Hungary, Poland, and Czechoslovakia.

CHRISTOPHER D. JONES (Ph.D., Harvard) is an associate professor in the Henry M. Jackson School of International Studies at the University of Washington. He has published *Soviet Influence in Eastern Europe* (1981) and co-authored *The Warsaw Pact: The Question of Cohesion* (1984-1986) in four volumes.

BARTLOMIEJ KAMINSKI (Ph.D., Warsaw) served until 1982 as an associate professor of economics at the University of Warsaw. He is currently associate professor of government and director of the Center for the Study of Postcommunist Societies at the University of Maryland, College Park. His latest book is entitled *The Collapse of State Socialism: The Case of Poland* (1990).

ROGER E. KANET (Ph.D., Princeton) is associate vice chancellor for academic affairs and director of international programs and studies at the University of Illinois, Urbana-Champaign, where he is also professor of political science. Among his recent publications are the following edited or co-edited volumes: *The Soviet Union, Eastern Europe and the Third World* (1987); *The Limits of Soviet Power in the Developing World: Thermidor in the Revolutionary Struggle* (1989); and *The Cold War as Cooperation: Superpower Cooperation in Regional Conflict Management* (1991).

ROBERT R. KING (Ph.D., Fletcher School of Law and Diplomacy) earlier served as assistant director of research at Radio Free Europe in Munich, Germany; then as member of the National Security Council staff; and currently is chief of staff to a U.S. congressman. He has written several books, including *The History of the Romanian Communist Party* (1980).

CAROL SKALNIK LEFF (Ph.D., Harvard) is visiting assistant professor of political science at the University of Illinois, Urbana-Champaign, in affiliation with the Russian and East European Center and the Program on Arms Control, Disarmament, and International Security. She is author of *National Conflict in Czechoslovakia, 1918-87* (1988).

3. Opposition political movements would be permitted, only if they supported the basic "socialist" nature of the regime and publicly assumed responsibility to do so.

Moscow decision makers seemed to believe that, under such conditions, their sphere of influence could be maintained. Gorbachev, as later developments showed, modified the above guidelines. His statement at the end of October 1989 in Helsinki seemed to offer the USSR-Finland relationship as a model to be emulated for future Soviet contacts with individual East-Central European governments.[3]

To the surprise of Kremlinologists, both inside and outside the USSR, developments were unfolding at an ever more rapid pace. What took approximately one year and a half for Poland and Hungary could be accomplished in three months by the East Germans. Breaking the total grip on power by the ruling communist parties of Czechoslovakia and Bulgaria was done in weeks. The overthrow and execution of Nicolae Ceauşescu in Romania occurred within less than one week at the end of December. Counting the number of days between the mid-1989 WTO Political Consultative Committee meeting and the overthrow of communist leaders, a Soviet journalist gave 101 for Erich Honecker, 124 for Todor Zhivkov, 131 for Miloš Jakeš.[4]

In order to legitimize the transfer of authority, elections were held in each of the above countries between mid-1989 and mid-1990. Those held in Poland came first and were only semifree by permitting the Solidarity movement to compete for about one-third of the parliamentary seats. However the hitherto subordinate peasant and democratic parties, in the process of forming a coalition government, deserted the communists which development converted the latter into an opposition movement.[5] The elections in East Germany and Hungary came next, during the spring of 1990.

Although the communists had become "socialists" overnight throughout East-Central Europe, and with one exception changed their party designations, in East Germany they won only 16 percent of the vote and in Hungary just half of that. During the summer, however, a National Salvation Front of former communists attained an absolute majority in Romania as did the relabeled "socialist" party in Bulgaria. The Communist Party of Czechoslovakia received support from 16 percent of the voters in Bohemia/Moravia and almost 15 percent in Slovakia.[6]

THE SOVIET ASSESSMENT

In the meanwhile, the Communist Party of the Soviet Union's (CPSU) Commission on International Policies convened at mid-year 1990 under the chairmanship of A. N. Iakovlev to discuss the changes in East-Central Europe. The meeting was opened with comments by the head of the Central Committee's international department, V. M. Falin. He blamed Stalin for enforcing a personal brand of socialism on the region. Hence, the conclusion that only the model and not socialism itself had been defeated. The policies of N. S. Khrushchev and L. I. Brezhnev were also condemned, although Falin recognized that anticommunism had played a role in recent transformations throughout East-Central Europe. The basic question involved whether to maintain a group of neighboring countries that suffer under Soviet "protection" or recognize the results of free choice.[7] Iakovlev summarized the discussion and concluded that developments were continuing in the direction of an all-European system.

Toward the end of 1990, a different meeting convened in Moscow with leaders from the Bulgarian, Czechoslovak, former East German, Hungarian, Polish, and Soviet communist parties. Unification of Germany had already taken place. Those gathered in Moscow attempted to evaluate the radical sociopolitical changes that had occurred in their respective countries. These did not, it was claimed, invalidate the basic concept of socialism. However, the transformations did require leftist forces to address problems of renewing socialist theory and practice. Interviews with four of the party delegation heads were printed by the official CPSU Central Committee journal.[8]

The deputy leader from Bulgaria, Liubomir Kiuchkov, boasted that his "socialist" (formerly communist) movement had won a bare majority of the vote in parliamentary elections. He did not mention that during the second half of 1990, his party had lost three-fourths of its membership.[9] The chairman of the Hungarian "socialists," Gyula Thurmer, complained that privatization would create a strong middle class over the next eight to ten years. He also lamented the fact that leftist forces had been broken up over the preceding two years, without providing any figures. It has been reported that after adoption of a new name, the party actually dropped from 816,622 to between 35,000 and 40,000 members.[10]

The chairman for the Party of Democratic Socialism in what previously had been East Germany, Gregor Gysi, claimed that the Federal Republic of Germany (FRG) became economically strong only because it had exploited the Third World. Without admitting that his movement lost 2 million and was down to 345,000 members, he conceded that it would take a decade before the "workers" could begin to play a significant role in FRG politics. Early in 1991, the East and West German communist party presidia met in Berlin. They decided that differences in structure justified continuing a separate existence.[11]

The last individual to be interviewed, Pavol Kanis, chaired the unrenamed Communist Party of Czechoslovakia. He admitted that his followers had suffered a serious defeat the year before. Leftist forces and the workers' movement were on the defensive. Parliament had just adopted a law depriving the communist party of its property. The chairman did not mention that his organization had gone down from 1.7 million to somewhere between 300,000 and 500,000 members. In Poland, the decline has been even greater, from 2.2 million to about 60,000 names on the rolls. Only the ruling party of the USSR numerically lost more, i.e., some 2.7 million during a 15-month period, which left it with 16.5 million members.[12] In Romania, of course, the 3.8 million communist party members disappeared overnight—only to reemerge as the National Salvation Front (NSF), estimated to total about one million.

At a meeting early in 1991 of the CPSU secretariat, the deputy general-secretary, V. A. Ivashko, led a discussion about the developments in East-Central Europe. He stressed his belief that economic integration of that region with the Soviet Union would prevent any substitute for existing contacts over "the next few years." The above-cited V. M. Falin suggested at this same meeting that one should look at the situation as offering a new beginning for mutually beneficial cooperation, "without allowing any dislocation of our [communist] ideas."[13]

A more comprehensive analysis of the situation came from a deputy chief of the Central Committee's international department. V. L. Musatov admitted that the old system of relations had collapsed, replaced by a vacuum. Formerly a priority, East-Central Europe was being relegated to the background. In this regard, USSR foreign policy was perceived as playing a passive role. The writer warned that these neighboring governments must not allow foreign bases or foreign troops on their territories, now that Soviet armed forces were withdrawing. He also cautioned the northern tier countries (Poland, Czechoslovakia, Hungary) against linking themselves into a *cordon sanitaire* against the Soviet Union. Bilateral relations with Finland were praised, implying that they could serve as a model for those with individual states in East-Central Europe and codified in a series of new treaties with the USSR.[14]

This last suggestion is within the purview of the Soviet government rather than the CPSU. A session of the foreign ministry's collegium dealt with the matter. One of the deputy ministers, Iu. A. Kvitsinskii, listed some of the foreign policy priorities throughout the region. Trade had been adversely affected by the growing balance of payments deficit, caused by the USSR undersupplying energy resources and receiving fewer essential consumer goods in return. New bilateral political treaties were being negotiated, which would guarantee western borders. This meeting was attended by Soviet ambassadors to these six countries (Poland, Czechoslovakia, Hungary, Romania, Bulgaria, and Yugoslavia). Recently appointed, they reportedly have "new views" and are "enthusiasts".[15]

One of the questions asked of the above cited N. V. Shishlin by a Hungarian interviewer dealt with the disparity between change in East-Central Europe and the lack of such in the USSR. It was admitted that this fact "casts a shadow on our relations" and that the changes are not in harmony.[16] A former official in the Central Committee apparatus, Aleksandr Tsipko, gave an interview to a British newspaper and listed several reasons why a revolution along East-Central European lines remained unlikely in the USSR: (1) intellectuals are detached from Soviet society, (2) opposition to the regime is fragmented, (3) Stalinism completely destroyed private property and the middle class, (4) the desire for a strong leader in the USSR, and (5) there remains no other belief system to replace Marxism.[17]

AREA-WIDE DEVELOPMENTS

The transition away from command economies and political power monopolized by local communist parties is well under way throughout most of East-Central Europe. Only Romania and Albania have yet to attain any meaningful political pluralism in their governments. The USSR is no longer in a position to frustrate these developments, however, which suggests that they should continue in the future without Soviet interference.

Each country in the region remains at a different stage of the transition process. Obviously, the former East Germany will make the most rapid progress since becoming an integral part of the Federal Republic. The USSR has agreed to withdraw all of its 380,000 troops plus 120,000 family members from these five eastern provinces by the end of 1994. Moscow already received an advance payment in the form of 5 billion deutsche marks in credits from Bonn, as well as a commitment of another 17 billion through the above period of time, not to mention the 1.2 billion DM currently owed to private West German firms.

Poland, Czechoslovakia, and Hungary belong to the West and should be the first to integrate with the European Community (EC) after a 10-year transition period.[18] All have applied for EC membership or indicated their intent to do so, when conditions are favorable. In the case of Romania, it will take much longer for its application to be considered because of the NSF

official spokesman did not provide any information on how many battle no longer a power to be feared or emulated. Rather, the Soviets themselves are observing developments in Poland's economic "shock therapy," Hungarian agriculture, and what the Federal Republic of Germany is doing throughout its five eastern provinces.

At the same time, a group of scholars in Moscow prepared a programmatic statement on "averting catastrophe and development of society." This document begins by suggesting seven possible scenarios for future events in the USSR:[37]

1. "Global catastrophe" at the end of the twentieth century, because outer space will have been filled with weapons representing a threat to the planet's existence.
2. "Barren land" after famine, epidemics, interethnic conflict, social explosions, revolts, terror exercised by minidictators, etc., would affect only the Soviet Union.
3. "A reservation," where the USSR remains a backward country without any future and the people slowly become extinct, i.e., a Fourth World model.
4. Decline into a source of raw materials, labor, and ecologically harmful industries per the Third World model which presupposes USSR disintegration into a number of independent states.
5. Entry into the Second World of rapidly developing countries and industrial conversion oriented toward mass non-sophisticated yet intensive production.
6. Emergence among developed countries of the First World with access to raw materials, labor, and other global resources.
7. Joining the world leaders (United States, Japan, Western Europe) by means of a Soviet path toward a civilization of a new type.

However, in the new international economic order, a scenario ranking higher than No. 4 above is not envisaged for the USSR according to the study team in Moscow.

Two centuries ago, when moderates could not prevail after the French Revolution, organized extremists launched a "reign of terror and virtue." After only two years, the revolution had turned violent. After seven years, it ended in a military dictatorship. This may indeed be the fate of the Soviet Union. Should such a development occur, let us hope that the pattern does not replicate itself throughout East-Central Europe.

NOTES

1. Ronald Linden, "The End of the Beginning," *Report on Eastern Europe* 2, no. 1 (4 January 1991), pp. 1-4.
2. Interview with Shishlin, "Nous pouvons comprendre la décision hongroise," *Libération* (Paris), 22 September 1989, p. 4.
3. See "Vystuplenie M.S. Gorbacheva," *Pravda*, 27 October 1989, pp. 1-2, for his speech in Finland. Two days earlier, USSR Foreign Minister Eduard A. Shevardnadze told the communist party leader that the Soviets knew what their policy vis-à-vis Poland and Hungary "should not be but did not know what it should be," Mieczysław F. Rakowski, *Jak to się stało* (Warsaw: BGW, 1991), p. 250.
4. Valentin Sharov, "V klubke protivorechii," *Pravda*, 2 January 1991, p. 5.
5. Richard F. Staar, "Transition in Poland," *Current History* 89, no. 551 (December 1990): 401-404, 426-427.
6. Commission on Security and Cooperation in Europe, *Elections in Central and Eastern Europe* (Washington, D.C.: U.S. Government Printing Office, July 1990), pp. 19, 46, 116-17, 132-33, and 156.
7. Mezhdunarodnyi otdel TsK KPSS, "Peremeny v tsentral'noi i vostochnoi Evrope," *Izvestiia TsK KPSS* 1, no. 10 (October 1990): 102-113. On anticommunism throughout East-Central Europe, see Leonid Kuznetsov, "V trevozhnom ozhidanii," *Pravda*, 28 March 1991, p. 5.
8. "Sotsializm: poisk novykh putei," *Izvestiia TsK KPSS* 1, no. 12 (December 1990): 117-120.
9. Sofia Radio (BTA), 14 December 1990; "BSP Membership Drops 75% in Six Months," *Foreign Broadcast Information Service* (FBIS)-EEU-90-242 (17 December 1990), p. 21.
10. Compare figures in Richard F. Staar, ed., *Yearbook on International Communist Affairs* (Stanford, Cal.: Hoover Institution Press), 1989 and 1990 volumes, pp. 329 and 345, respectively. Hungarian figures are from party chairman Gyula Horn in *Magyar Hirlap* (Budapest), 9 March 1991, p. 7.
11. "PDS and DKP Presidiums Meet," *Neues Deutschland* (Berlin), 7 January 1991, p. 3; FBIS-WEU-91-010 (15 January 1991), p. 23.
12. "Oni vstupaiut v KPSS," *Izvestiia TsK KPSS* 2, no. 12 (December 1990): 81; O. Voznesenskii and I. Podsvirov, "U kommunistov net tain ot gosudarstva," *Pravda*, 12 April 1991, p. 2.
13. "S zasedaniia Sekretariata TsK KPSS," *Pravda*, 26 January 1991, pp. 1-2.
14. V. L. Musatov, "Vostochnaia Evropa: 'Taifun' peremen," *Pravda*, 13 March 1991, p. 5.
15. Iu. A. Kvitsinskii, "Vostochnaia Evropa: chto griadet za peremenami," *Pravda*, 18 March 1991, p. 7.
16. Budapest radio, 24 March 1991; "Political Scientist Views East Europe Ties," FBIS-SOV-91-057 (25 March 1991), pp. 22-23.

2

The Future of Soviet-East-Central European Political Relations

Christopher D. Jones

The future of Soviet-East European political relations is only one aspect of a much more complex question: the emergence of postcommunist systems in the national communities that up to 1989 had been bound together in what the ideologists of the Brezhnev era had heralded as the "socialist commonwealth."[1]

By early 1991 the principal international structures of the socialist commonwealth had collapsed. The previous November, Warsaw Pact states agreed to disband their military alliance by 1 July 1991. The beginning of that year, members of the Council for Mutual Economic Assistance (CMEA) agreed to dissolve their organization and replace it with an office for exchange of economic information.[2]

In Moscow, neither the flailing practitioners of *perestroika* nor the neototalitarians from the crumbling bureaucracies of terror could formulate a coherent *Soviet* solution to the interlocking political, ethnic, economic, social, and environmental catastrophes bequeathed to the USSR by Leonid Il'ich Brezhnev.

As the Baltic republics demanded the same right of national self-determination granted to Poland in August of 1989, Gorbachev faced the same murderous dilemma he had been unable to resolve in Afghanistan: the use of a multinational armed force to impose a communist regime despised by the non-Russian local population.[3]

Gorbachev could attempt to preserve the Soviet Union only at the risk of actions likely to set off anti-Soviet rebellions not only in the other non-Russian republics but in the Russian Republic as well. Put another way, the multinational Soviet military could attempt repression of the Baltic states only at the risk of the disintegration of the Soviet military along the ethnic fissures that had rent the enlisted ranks of the Soviet military during the occupation of Afghanistan. Boris Yeltsin, president of the Russian Republic, issued an open appeal to Russian soldiers serving in the Baltic states not to obey any orders from Gorbachev to repress the elected local governments.[4]

In Warsaw, Prague, and Budapest at the end of 1990 new governments led by former electricians, historians, truck drivers, playwrights, and coal stokers were attempting to graft liberal-democratic political systems with market economies onto the precommunist roots of their national communities. If the complex experiments currently under way in East-Central Europe prove successful, these postcommunist models will serve—unintentionally but inevitably—as the relevant models for postcommunist development in the other national communities formerly governed by communist parties, including national communist parties in southeastern Europe as well as ethnic-territorial communist parties in the USSR.

The current postcommunist leaders of East-Central Europe see the solution to their local problems in adopting domestic, foreign, and security policies that will prepare them for eventual membership in the European Community (EC). President Václav Havel of Czechoslovakia argued in his May 1990 address to the Council of Europe in Strasbourg that the region, if supported by the West, could play a catalytic role in the crystallization of a new security structure embracing the entire northern hemisphere and in the creation of European economic space from the Atlantic to the Urals.[5]

The essence of the Havel vision is overlapping accountability: the accountability of national leaders to democratic systems at home and to pan-European agencies linking military, economic, social, human rights, cultural, and environmental issues. During the communist period dissidents like Havel and his counterparts throughout the socialist commonwealth had concluded that they could place effective restraints on even the most unscrupulous political leaders of both Eastern Europe and the USSR by mobilizing constituencies in democratic countries and by appealing to the all-European institutions chartered by the Helsinki Agreement of 1975. They had every reason to believe that these techniques could be used even more effectively in the postcommunist period. In power, the former dissidents offered open support to anti-Soviet democratic movements in the Baltic and other republics of the USSR.[6]

Put another way, the dissidents-turned-presidents of East-Central Europe are accustomed to seeking imported solutions to the problems facing their societies. The most dramatic example is that of East Germany, which voted for complete incorporation into the existing institutions of the Federal Republic. During the presidential campaign in Poland, the surprising electoral appeal of Stanisław Tymiński, a Polish Canadian, might be best understood as an expression of the desire for an imported solution to Poland's problems.

Another demonstration of the Polish desire for imported solutions was President Lech Wałęsa's decision to retain Leszek Balcerowicz as finance minister, even after Wałęsa's campaign had denounced the hardships resulting from the Balcerowicz Plan. The "shock therapy" of exposing Polish enterprises to market mechanisms was openly based on recommendations by Western consultants. The patron saint of Poland's return to Europe remains John Paul II, perhaps Europe's most eloquent critic of purely local solutions to national problems.

Should successful postcommunist models fail to emerge in East-Central Europe, then the nations of the late L. I. Brezhnev's socialist commonwealth are likely to enter a prolonged "time of troubles" during which neototalitarian leaders will try one bankrupt policy after another. The emerging sovereign republics of the present USSR, beset by profound political, ethnic, economic, and environmental crises, will be much less likely to develop successful postcommunist models, if they cannot import postcommunist policies worked out in East-Central European societies with similar but generally less severe problems—not to mention much easier access to Western aid.

In the USSR the previous political and economic structures of the union republics are disappearing into the ideological black hole resulting from the collapse after 73 years of "communist construction." As Evgenii Evtushenko sadly observed in mid-January 1991, if there are to be any solutions to the present crises of the USSR, they will probably be "European" solutions which absorb the USSR's separate republics into a larger European system.[7]

The future of what used to be called Soviet-East European political relations will thus be determined by whether Warsaw, Prague, and Budapest can build bridges linking Moscow with Brussels. The Conference on Security and Cooperation in Europe (CSCE), meeting in Paris during November of 1990, laid the foundations for such bridges by establishing three new organizations based in East-Central Europe: a CSCE Secretariat in Prague to serve a newly created permanent Council of the CSCE; an Office for Free Elections based in Warsaw; and a Conflict Prevention Center to deal with issues of military security in Vienna. (After considerable debate, a Western-backed European Bank for Reconstruction and Development to aid Eastern Europe was located in London.)[8]

The precondition for the development of successful postcommunist models in East-Central Europe and the export of these models eastward is the development of a cooperative European mutual security system, including both the United States and what is presently the USSR. Such a system can also make possible the peaceful disintegration of the USSR and the eventual integration into a new Europe of the present Soviet republics, above all, the Russian Republic.

Two of the three pillars for a cooperative European security system are already in place: the agreement on Conventional Forces in Europe and the Charter of Paris, both signed in November 1990 under CSCE auspices. The third pillar, a Soviet-American agreement on major cuts in strategic weapons had been scheduled for signing in February of 1991 at a summit meeting that was postponed.

As Gorbachev moved closer to outright military occupation of the Baltic states, he ran the risk of sabotaging both sets of arms control agreements and the construction of a cooperative European security system.

This essay will present several sets of arguments in support of the conclusions presented above.

THE DILEMMAS OF THE SOCIALIST COMMONWEALTH

The ideological myth of Brezhnev's socialist commonwealth was derived from the constitutional myth of Stalin's state: the components of communist polities were "national in form, socialist in content." As Teresa Rakowska-Harmstone has noted, the Bolsheviks risked this potentially explosive concession to separate national political cultures on the basis of their expectation that the communist experiment would eventually give rise to a new Soviet political culture that would prove genuinely socialist and internationalist.[9] The "new Soviet man" would be the common descendant of the Russians, Ukrainians, Belorussians, and the Caucasus/Central Asian nationalities of the USSR.

The communist party that had emerged victorious from the civil wars of 1918-1922 was for all practical purposes a Russian communist party camouflaged by the internationalist rhetoric that its founders had believed in, as did many members of the subsequent generations of the CPSU. But after the horrors of Stalinism had alienated virtually all of the non-Russian populations and much of the Russian population as well, the survival of the USSR came to depend on the loyalty of the Russian people to the Soviet Army at the disposal of the CPSU. During the Nazi occupation, large segments of the non-Russian communities, and some Russians, had initially welcomed the German armies as liberators from Soviet rule.[10]

But, as was the case with the White generals of 1918-1922, large numbers of non-Russians in the former Romanov empire came to see the Red Army as the lesser of evils. During both these conflicts (1918-1922 and 1941-1944) and during the Soviet march into Eastern Europe (1944-1945), the Red Army could plausibly claim to be the army of "national liberation" from foreign occupiers, with the qualification that the liberated territories were to be governed by ethnic-territorial and national communist parties closely linked to Moscow.

After 1945, the Communist Party of the Soviet Union (CPSU) expanded to include satellite parties in the Baltic states, in Moldavia, and new *oblast'* and *raion* parties in territories annexed to the USSR from Finland, Poland, Germany, Czechoslovakia, and Romania. For all practical purposes, the CPSU during the late Stalin era also incorporated the national communist parties placed in power in separate East European states by the Red Army. Expansion of the empire had the demographic and cultural effect of reducing the Russians from a majority of the USSR population in 1939 (58.4 percent)[11] to a mere plurality in a highly diverse multinational system held together by the multinational Soviet army and ethnic-territorial communist parties in the USSR and national communist parties in Eastern Europe.

Unlike the other nationalities of the socialist commonwealth, the Russians alone lacked a separate national communist party equivalent to the communist parties of Uzbekistan, Georgia, Lithuania, or Czechoslovakia. Russian communists were organized on the district and municipal levels but were forbidden to meet on the republic level except as members of non-Russian ethnic-territorial parties. They could meet as a community only at the all-union level of a congress of the CPSU. These sessions were attended by ruling fraternal parties that as a rule dutifully convened their own congresses shortly afterward (sometimes shortly before) to bring their national policies in line with Soviet policies.[12]

The absence of a separate Russian party was the manifestation of the submerged political reality that after 1945 held together both the USSR and the socialist commonwealth: the reliance of the CPSU on the cohesion of its ethnic Russian community around the intertwined values of Marxism-Leninism, Russian military patriotism, and Russian bureaucratic culture.[13]

By the early Brezhnev era, the CPSU, in collaboration with the fraternal parties of Eastern Europe, had elaborated an extended myth that offered

Russians and non-Russians alike a justification for the central political and cultural role of Russians in the expanded empire: just as the Russians were the "elder brothers" of the union republics in the USSR, so the Soviets were the "elder brothers" of the socialist commonwealth.[14]

The extended myth took the form of an even more complex pseudostructure. This structure was formally organized in a series of overlapping multinational agencies: the Council for Mutual Economic Assistance (CMEA, formed in 1949); the Warsaw Treaty Organization (WTO, formed in 1955); the multilateral agencies of the bloc academies of science, formally codified in 1971; and the multilateral programs of the regime ministries of culture, loosely codified during the 1969-1971 period.[15]

In addition, the fraternal ruling parties developed during the Brezhnev era an elaborate system of mutual consultation based on party congresses, meetings of equivalent party agencies, and annual summer summit meetings at Brezhnev's Crimean resort. Gorbachev continued the tradition of regular meetings with party leaders, but used the Kremlin as the point of rendezvous.[16]

In the USSR, sovietized Russians and russified Soviets upheld the power of the center under the cover of ethnic-territorial branches of the party in the union republics of the USSR. In the Soviet Union, the CPSU also promoted common "Soviet" political and aesthetic cultures through intensified russification of the political, economic, cultural, and scientific bureaucracies of the non-Russian union republics.

In Eastern Europe, Russians and Soviets upheld the power of the center through "Soviet" domination of the overlapping networks of the WTO, CMEA, the party-to-party ties, and the interlocking scientific and cultural bureaucracies. Ivan Volgyes described these policies as a Soviet attempt at the "folklorization" of indigenous political and cultural traditions in Eastern Europe.[17]

In Eastern Europe, national intelligentsia waged rearguard battles in defense of their distinct political and aesthetic cultures. Most of their national traditions could plausibly be considered more complex and diverse than the russified Soviet political and aesthetic cultures imposed on the nations of the USSR. Even if this were not the case, the distinct national traditions of Eastern Europe were at least in closer connection with the pluralist political and aesthetic traditions of Western Europe. As the Czech writer Milan Kundera observed in exile, the cultural essence of "Central Europe" was maximum diversity in the smallest possible space; the essence of russified Soviet culture was minimum variety in the greatest possible space.[18]

The intensity of the East European cultural resistance in part reflected the region's trauma at undergoing in less than seven years the same kind of drastic sociopolitical changes that had taken place in the USSR over the period from 1917 to 1953. The effect of this East European resistance was to lay the basis for a potential coalition of the non-Russian communities in the socialist commonwealth.

The formation of such a coalition became possible, as Rakowska-Harmstone has argued, because the federal structure of the USSR had given rise to a post-Stalin national intelligentsia capable of resisting the "Soviet" political and aesthetic cultures forged by Stalin, Beria, Zhdanov, Lysenko, and the other partisans of "socialist realism."

The crystallization of an anti-Russian/anti-Soviet coalition of national cultures evoked a certain Russian nationalist backlash. But under the influence of Russian Orthodox religious dissidents and prominent intellectuals such as Solzhenitsyn, Tvardovsky, Sakharov, and other self-appointed spokesmen for the Russian values trampled by Stalin, key members of the Russian intelligentsia attempted to redirect this backlash against the Soviet regime, which they accused of having pirated Russian political and aesthetic cultures for their own "internationalist" purposes.[19]

The domestic political and cultural resistance to the ethnic communist parties of the socialist commonwealth interacted with the dynamics of conflict among ruling parties. The installation of ruling communist parties in Eastern Europe had presented Stalin and his successors with a new imperative for claiming leadership over the international communist movement (and for implicitly insisting on the central role of ethnic Russians in the international communist system).[20]

This imperative arose out of the conflict inherent between the multinational CPSU and each of the victorious communist parties that had come to power largely on its own in a war of national liberation against foreign invaders: the Yugoslav, Albanian, and Chinese movements. Each of these independent parties stood, consciously or not, for the principle of national roads to communism under the guidance of "ethnic" communist parties with national control over their national movements, their national militaries, and their national governments.[21]

At a minimum, this principle threatened Soviet hegemony over the ruling East European parties outfitted by Stalin with all the accoutrements of national sovereignty. At worst, the principle of the full independence of "ethnic" communist parties was a potential program for the fragmentation of the CPSU into national components and for the disintegration of the USSR into separate national states.

The dynamics of this inherent conflict between independent national communist parties and the multinational CPSU played themselves out not only during Stalin's conflict with the Yugoslav party, but during Khrushchev's conflicts with the Chinese, Albanian, and Romanian parties; Brezhnev's conflicts with the Chinese, Czechoslovak, Romanian, and Albanian parties; and even during Gorbachev's disputes with the anti-*perestroika* leaderships of the East European and overseas ruling parties.

In Eastern Europe, neither Albania nor Yugoslavia had become members of the formal structures and formal programs of the multinational pseudocommonwealth nor, for all practical purposes, had Romania. In each of these states, anti-Soviet nationalism provided the ultimate basis for legitimacy of domestic regimes peculiar to each of these countries.

The political conflicts inherent between the multinational CPSU and independent ethnic communist parties were the primary Soviet motivation for Moscow's attempts to integrate the pseudostructures of the socialist commonwealth during the regimes of Khrushchev, Brezhnev, Andropov, Chernenko, and Gorbachev. The basic rationale for the pseudointegration of the Soviet bloc was that this policy was the only alternative to disintegration.

Before 1989, the higher structures of the CPSU had linked the fate of the regional party organizations of the Russian republic with the survival of the ethnic-territorial communist parties within the USSR and national communist parties within the extended socialist commonwealth. In other words, the collapse of any of the ruling ethnic communist parties threatened the survival of the entire pseudostructure of the WTO/CMEA/USSR system. Such a collapse also threatened the outbreak of the repressed conflict between the minority of Russians at the core of the system and the majority of non-Russians on the periphery. At the same time, such a collapse also threatened a conflict between the Russian leaders of the "Soviet" center and nationalist spokesmen for the revival of a non-communist Russian society in a Russian republic.[22]

In reality, the pro-Moscow national communist parties of Eastern Europe had been brought to power and sustained in power by the multinational Soviet armed forces, of which the Russians remained the indispensable core. The Main Political Administration (MPA) of the USSR military openly identified this dynamic in its political indoctrination programs. In the Soviet armed forces, the official MPA line was that the Russians were the "elder brothers" of the non-Russian soldiers. In the WTO, the allied MPAs took the line that the Soviets were the "elder brothers" of the non-Soviet Warsaw Pact forces.

The political officers of the WTO drilled captive audiences on their collective obligation of "joint defense of the gains of socialism against internal and external enemies."[23] Translated into military commands, this meant a Warsaw Pact security guarantee to the ruling ethnic parties of Eastern Europe. In the greater socialist army built around the multinational forces of the USSR, the key to allied cohesion was preservation of the legitimizing myth that in the socialist commonwealth Russian and Soviet soldiers had historically carried the banners of "national liberation" in wars waged in defense of "the socialist fatherland." Too much evidence to the contrary, as in Afghanistan, threatened the Soviet Army and the Warsaw Pact with disintegration.[24]

Paradoxically, the USSR military guarantee had the long-term effect of undermining these parties. The Warsaw Pact security guarantee undercut the legitimacy of the pro-Moscow parties by emphasizing their roles as Soviet viceroys. The USSR security guarantee also diminished the incentive for the ruling parties to manage their societies and economies efficiently.

These two counterproductive results of the security guarantee combined to exacerbate the crises endemic to the centrally planned economies of Eastern Europe. Furthermore, as Valerie Bunce noted in her aptly titled article, "The Empire Strikes Back," the greater the domestic political crises in Eastern Europe, the greater the economic subsidies the beleaguered Soviet economy had to provide to the CPSU's clients. And these subsidies in turn further undercut the incentives for domestic economic reform.[25]

Finally, the logic of a military security guarantee to the East German regime, where the preponderance of Soviet expeditionary forces were stationed, locked the USSR into a permanent military confrontation with West Germany and its NATO allies. In this military confrontation the historic pattern was for the United States and its allies to shift the terms of the competition into high-tech weaponry, a field in which the Soviets were at a disadvantage.

The enormous costs of the conventional and nuclear arms race with the NATO states thus had had the effect of further exacerbating the strains on the Soviet economy and on the economies of its East European client regimes. Economic difficulties in turn intensified the sociopolitical crises of the East European systems. The resulting political instability then required revalidation of the USSR military guarantee to the ruling parties. But reaffirmation of Soviet military capabilities in Eastern Europe inevitably set off alarms in Brussels and initiated another round in the East-West arms race.[26]

GORBACHEV'S SOLUTION TO THE DILEMMAS OF THE SOCIALIST CONFEDERATION: A COMMON EUROPEAN HOME

Gorbachev's foreign minister, Eduard Shevardnadze, took the lead during the 1986-1988 period in articulating "new thinking" in foreign policy, an approach which sought to shift the focus of East-West interaction from confrontation over military issues to cooperation on an interdependent set of economic, environmental, and social issues. Gorbachev's ideologists identified these objectives as "universal human values," of which the highest was peace in the nuclear age.

The practical focus of the new military and foreign policies was the attempt to build what Gorbachev called as early as 1986 "a common European home." In this conception, the Warsaw Pact states were to cut back drastically the military threat they posed to the West, which in turn was to call a halt to the deployment of exotic and expensive new military technologies.[27] Gorbachev and Shevardnadze argued that greatly reduced military expenditures in both NATO and the WTO would provide financial resources for revitalization of CMEA bloc economies. Shevardnadze specifically called upon the West to respond to military detente by expanding trade and technology transfer with the East.[28]

In Eastern Europe, Gorbachev wanted to prod the ruling parties to more efficient management of their economies and societies. As an incentive, he promised in the Belgrade Declaration of March 1988 not to intervene with armed force against ruling communist parties,[29] as Brezhnev had done to Czechoslovakia in 1968. This did not mean revocation of the Soviet security guarantee against anticommunist threats. Gorbachev made clear that the Warsaw Pact would retain a "counteroffensive" capability, intended to defend "the gains of socialism."

As an additional prod to domestic reforms, Gorbachev announced his intention to cut back Soviet economic subsidies to Eastern Europe. At the same time he sought a vast expansion of regional scientific, technical, investment, and production ties in an integrated CMEA market. Contrary to the opinions of Western arms control specialists, Gorbachev did not intend to let communist regimes fall in Eastern Europe. Rather, he sought to integrate the political, economic, military, scientific, and cultural bureaucracies of the bloc into a larger socialist commonwealth characterized by decentralized decision-making through quasimarket mechanisms.[30] The intensified integration of the CMEA states would be accompanied by expansion of East-West economic links in a common European home.

Gorbachev presented the most detailed explanation of his vision of the common European home on 6 July 1989 in a speech to the Council of Europe at Strasbourg. In this speech he said that the common European home was to contain two separate socioeconomic blocs, living peacefully together in the space from the Atlantic to the Urals.

But he specifically warned the parliamentarians of Western Europe that he would not accept a Europe "from Brest to Brest" [Brest on the tip of the Brittany Peninsula to Brest on the Polish-Soviet border]. He declared that the "Brest-to-Brest" formula was not a program for overcoming the division of Europe but a program for "overcoming socialism" and for expelling the USSR from Europe. Such attempts, he warned, would lead "to confrontation or worse." He added that both the USSR and the United States rightfully belonged in the common European home. The key to the construction of the common European home, he explained, was the renunciation of the use of armed force.

In exchange for reduction of the security risks and economic costs of the East-West arms race, Gorbachev hoped to obtain from Brussels the right to confer on the subjects of the WTO/CMEA bloc a kind of honorary citizenship in a common European home from the Atlantic to the Urals. In exchange for their honorary citizenship in Europe, the populations of the WTO/CMEA states were expected to move toward EC standards of productivity and, thus, to revive the faltering economies of the Soviet bloc.

On the eve of Gorbachev's reforms, Milan Kundera had complained that Western Europe, by using the term "Eastern Europe," had accepted the permanent sovietization of what Kundera saw as the distinct political and aesthetic cultures of "Central Europe." The Polish (Lithuanian-born) Nobel laureate in poetry, Czesław Miłosz, replied that the proper term for the territories transformed by sovietization was neither Eastern Europe nor Central Europe but "Western Asia." What both writers were trying to convey was that the political culture of the socialist commonwealth had sought to cut off national communities, including the Russian community, from their roots in the political and aesthetic cultures of the larger European community.

Kundera summed up this dynamic by claiming that the ultimate objective of all political dissidence in Central Europe was to bring nations back into the community of European political and aesthetic culture. What the West saw as anticommunism was, argued Kundera, an attempt "to return to Europe."[31]

Gorbachev's policy of building a common European home required a partial dismantling of the military barriers that had previously separated

Western Europe from Western Asia. In promising to lower these barriers, he unintentionally revoked the Soviet military guarantee to the ruling ethnic communist parties of the socialist commonwealth. In gratitude, the Norwegian parliament awarded him the Nobel Peace Prize for 1990. For Gorbachev, the price of peace with Western Europe proved to be surrender to the national communities of Eastern Europe.

THE COLLAPSE OF COMMUNISM

The immediate precipitant to the collapse of communist systems in Eastern Europe were a series of events from August to October 1989 which collectively signaled that the CPSU would no longer use Soviet military power to maintain communist parties in power in Poland, Hungary, East Germany, Czechoslovakia, and Bulgaria, the five "loyal" members of the Warsaw Pact.

These events began with the formation of the Solidarity-dominated coalition government in Poland on 19 August 1989 under Tadeusz Mazowiecki. Gorbachev's decision not to use armed force to prevent Solidarity from forming a coalition government was not the result of any failure on the part of the command structure of the Warsaw Pact or the Soviet military. The decision came as the unanticipated result of the interaction of the peculiar political crisis in Poland and the fact that domestic politics of *perestroika* in the Soviet bloc had become hostage to the requirements of building the common European home. The most important of these requirements was not using armed force in Europe.

In Poland the imposition of martial law in 1981 had revealed the total collapse of the capacity of the Polish United Workers' (communist) Party to govern without debilitating daily socioeconomic crises.[32] By the Roundtable Agreement of April 1989, the military government established by General Wojciech Jaruzelski had come to a similar point of near total collapse. The Roundtable Agreement secured Solidarity's acquiescence to participate in rigged elections (the communists and their allies were guaranteed two-thirds of the seats in the lower house). But Jaruzelski's government managed to lose the elections anyway, as Polish voters refused to elect communists to the seats reserved for them in the lower house and gave noncommunists all 100 seats in the largely ceremonial Senate.

Though Gorbachev could have suppressed Solidarity by force when it formed a government in August, there was no Polish regime he could have left in place. Neither the local communist party nor the indigenous military could have governed in the face of the overwhelming electoral repudiation of the old regime. But for Gorbachev to have imposed Soviet military rule on Poland would then have destroyed the East-West accord necessary for construction of a common European home.

Instead, Gorbachev gambled that Solidarity's power could be limited by reserving for the communists the state presidency and the ministries of defense, interior, transportation, and foreign trade. He also gambled that a successful power-sharing arrangement in Poland would prompt the other ruling parties to seek working compromises with their own alienated societies.

But the essence of the new policy was that Gorbachev had revoked the Soviet military guarantee to ruling East European parties. On 23 October 1989 Foreign Minister Shevardnadze delivered a speech to the USSR Supreme Soviet in which he stressed the ruinous long-term political, economic, and social results of the previous uses of Soviet armed force in Afghanistan. He argued that Soviet foreign policy could serve the interests of the USSR only if the policy was based on the moral principles accepted by the larger international community. Shevardnadze told the Supreme Soviet, "As a minister, I will carry out any lawful decision, reserving the right to resign, however, when I cannot agree with a decision for political or moral considerations."[33]

On 26 October in Helsinki, Mikhail Gorbachev and Mauno Koivisto, the president of Finland, jointly proclaimed a policy of absolute respect for the right of national self-determination in Eastern Europe, including the right of national choice of socioeconomic systems. On that day and in subsequent statements, Gorbachev emphatically declared that the right of national self-determination in Europe did not include the right of the two Germanys to unite.

In Helsinki, Gorbachev specifically called for a new Helsinki session of the Conference on Security and Cooperation in Europe (CSCE). He evidently wanted this conference to affirm two conditions he insisted on throughout 1989: the permanence of the two Germanys and the indivisibility of the Union of Soviet Socialist Republics.[34]

On 27 October 1989, Shevardnadze signed in Warsaw a statement by the WTO Committee of Foreign Ministers that renounced the right of military intervention in the internal affairs of its members. The Warsaw declaration also affirmed the right to national self-determination of sociopolitical systems in Europe but also insisted on the preservation of the German Democratic Republic.[35]

Deprived of the Soviet military guarantee, the ruling fraternal parties crumbled quickly before whatever groups had the temerity to take Gorbachev at his word that the Soviet military would no longer intervene in Eastern Europe.

Solidarity, already in power in Poland, proceeded to rule as if communists no longer held the crucial portfolios given to them in August. In Hungary, the communist party attempted to save itself from popular rejection by metamorphosing into a "socialist party" that in turn faded into oblivion in the free elections held during early 1990. These elections scuttled the communist hope that Imre Pozsgay, a reform communist, would win a special election to the powerful office of the Hungarian presidency.

In East Germany, church groups and an ad hoc collection of intellectuals led mass demonstrations in late October of 1989. These boisterous protests, in a Joshua-like chorus, brought down the Honecker government, the Berlin Wall, the Krenz government, and the Gysi remnant of the Socialist Unity Party. In Czechoslovakia, student demonstrations that began in late November had by late December brought a dissident playwright, Václav Havel, to the presidency of the country. In Bulgaria, an environmental protest group began demonstrations that multiplied into mass protests. These eventually toppled the Zhivkov regime, though the Bulgarian Communist Party remained in nominal control of the government.

In Romania, the removal of the former threat of Soviet military intervention undercut the military's traditional support for Ceauşescu as the champion of national sovereignty against Soviet claims. The eruption, another in a recurrent string of popular demonstrations against Ceauşescu, enabled the military to turn against the Ceauşescu family dynasty. The Romanian Communist Party, however, remained in control of the country, renamed as the National Salvation Front.

The triumph of the principle of national self-determination in Eastern Europe prompted existing nationalist organizations in the Baltic states to demand the same rights of national self-determination claimed by the other East European states created at the Versailles Conference of 1918-1919. "National Fronts" in Lithuania, Latvia, and Estonia made successful challenges to the local ethnic communist parties and then demanded complete secession from the USSR. In Moldavia, Georgia, Armenia, Azerbaidjan, in the Ukraine and finally in ethnic Russia itself, similar movements voiced demands for national sovereignty.

After having promised in December 1989 that the CPSU would not—for the foreseeable future—renounce its leading role in the USSR, Gorbachev agreed in February of 1990 to the removal of Article 6 from the Soviet constitution, which had guaranteed this role to the CPSU at both the all-union and republic levels. Whether he understood the consequences or not, this act removed whatever legitimacy there may have remained for the use of the Soviet military to preserve rule by ethnic communist parties in each of the union republics of the USSR, including the Russian Republic.

Just prior to the CPSU Congress in July 1990, ethnic Russian members of the conservative communist party apparatus, at the core of the former socialist commonwealth, assumed the leadership of a spontaneous movement to create for the first time a separate communist party of the Russian republic. Despite the "conservative" and "imperial" character of the fledgling leadership of the Russian Communist Party, the formation of a separate Russian communist party constituted (against the wishes of the party's founders) both a renunciation of ethnic Russia's identification with the cause of communism in the non-Russian republics and an implicit renunciation of Russia's messianic tradition of rule over non-Russians.

In turn, the revocation of Article 6 placed an unprecedented question before the predominantly ethnic Russian cadres of the Soviet officer corps: to what entity did they owe their primary loyalty: the CPSU, the federal government of the USSR, the Russian Republic, or the Communist Party of the Russian Republic? The symbol of this confusion was the eruption of an intramilitary debate over the role of the Main Political Administration which, since the founding of the Workers' and Peasants' Red Army, had been the institutional representative of the communist party in the Soviet military. The substance of the confusion was massive evasion by non-Russian soldiers of conscription.[36]

This dilemma could be expressed in different terms: if the Soviet military were no longer to defend the power of the ethnic detachments of the CPSU in the non-Russian republics, then it had to witness the disintegration of the CPSU as the only political organization which could hold together the Union of Soviet Socialist Republics. If the USSR in turn disintegrated, the Soviet army could survive only by transforming itself into the Russian army of a Russian state, or perhaps the military force of a federal Slavic state.

At the CPSU congress, the party proceeded to complicate the impossible questions placed before the Soviet officers' corps. The 28th Congress agreed to transfer day-to-day political decision-making from the party politburo to the newly created state bodies of the USSR. The July 1990 congress then witnessed crucial defections from both the new party and state bodies.

By the end of the congress, Boris Yeltsin, president of the Russian Republic, plus Gavril Popov, mayor of Moscow, and Anatolii Sobchak, mayor of Leningrad, led a wave of resignations from the party (both the all-union CPSU and the Russian Communist Party). In their recently won elected offices Yeltsin and his counterparts not only dismissed contemptuously the claims of the newly formed Russian Communist Party but proceeded to challenge the new all-union bodies of the USSR and to develop regular relations with the insurgent non-Russian republics and with the independent postcommunist republics of East-Central Europe.

The collapse of the effective power of the CPSU meant the disappearance of all the socioeconomic networks previously managed by the party. The disintegration of these networks in turn meant that the previous flow of goods and services among the country's regions, circuitous to begin with, was blocked by new obstacles. This blockage transformed even favored cities like Moscow into isolated outposts short of basic commodities. The blockage also imperiled the continuation of economic ties with the states of East-Central Europe.

By the end of 1990 Gorbachev was frantically reorganizing the crumbling structures of the Soviet government, whose principal function was coming to be that of negotiating with Western governments for aid to compensate for the collapse of the inefficient production and distribution networks previously managed by the CPSU.

The significance of Western assistance was largely symbolic: the aid demonstrated that the only available solutions to the most basic problems of daily life were imported solutions. Reactionary *apparatchiki* and security policemen ludicrously protested the Western assistance as attempts to subvert a system already in ruins. In dramatically resigning his post as foreign minister on 20 December 1990, Eduard Shevardnadze warned the functionaries of the old structures of terror that if they tried to hold the nations of the USSR together by armed force, they would bear the responsibility for the additional hardships caused by the cessation of cooperation with the West in the rebuilding of the Soviet portions of Eurasia.

In early 1991, Gorbachev raised the prospect of using the Soviet military to prevent the secession of the Baltic states from the USSR. Prominent political and cultural figures of Russian heritage joined Shevardnadze, a Georgian, in denouncing Gorbachev's threat of armed action against Baltic nationalists. In threatening armed repression of the Balts, Gorbachev confronted the same dilemma he had confronted in Poland during August of 1989. There was no possibility of restoring an ethnic communist party acceptable to the local population. The imposition of direct Soviet military rule would mean the renunciation of *perestroika* and an end to East-West cooperation on security and economic matters. New military barriers would rise to separate Western Asia from a Western Europe, now redrawn from Brest to Brest.

To use Soviet military power to suppress noncommunist governments in the Baltic will almost certainly ignite anticommunist/anti-Soviet uprisings in the other non-Russian republics and provoke the Yeltsin government of the Russian Republic to attempt the overthrow of Gorbachev's Soviet government.[37] The multinational USSR military could not possibly preserve its cohesion if such events took place. The Russian officer corps of the Soviet military would find the only means of institutional survival in defecting to the Yeltsin government of the Russian Republic, which has already recognized the right of the Baltic countries to full sovereignty as independent republics.

The events of 1989-1990 suggest that the entire Soviet period should be reconsidered as a sociohistorical winter,[38] imposed by the capacity and willingness of the CPSU to use armed force against all its opponents in the national communities of "Western Asia." During the prolonged winter, the party built an elaborate compound of ice palaces, crudely modeled on the structures of prewar Russia and postwar Western societies. The history of the Soviet-East European bloc is the history of change and evolution in the fashioning of these structures, but the variations among the ice sculptures of the Stalin, Khrushchev, Brezhnev, Andropov, or Chernenko periods were less significant than the differences between the permanent winter in the East and the ever-changing and sometimes stormy seasons of the West.

Gorbachev's 1985-1990 domestic policies of *uskorenie* (speed-up), *glasnost'* (feedback), and *demokratizatsiia* encountered the frustration of trying to build flexibility into structures that had to remain frozen if they were to endure.

When Gorbachev withheld the use of armed force in Poland during August 1989, he abruptly put an end to the prolonged winter of the socialist commonwealth. As the ice palaces of communist rule melted, the prospects for *perestroika* evaporated. The remaining question was whether the CPSU and the Red Army still had the capability to restore winter to the Baltic states and the other national communities of the USSR. The answer to this question will determine the future of the relations between the East-Central European and Soviet members of the former socialist commonwealth.

NOTES

1. This term was used widely in the bloc literature on Soviet-East European relations before and after Gorbachev. At the first party congress of the Gorbachev era, the program section entitled "Cooperation with the Socialist Countries" frequently refers in special type to the "socialist commonwealth." See *Materialy XXVIII S"ezda Kommunisticheskoi Partii Sovetskogo Soiuza* (Moscow: Politizdat, 1986), pp. 170-174.
2. The WTO decision to disband was reported by Prague Domestic Radio Service in Czech, 14 November 1990; *Foreign Broadcast Information Service* (FBIS)-EEU-90-222 (16 November 1990), p. 1. For coverage of news reports on the CMEA decision to disband see FBIS-SOV-91-005 (8 January 1991), pp. 1 and ff.
3. Yeltsin's speech broadcast by Moscow Radio, 13 January 1991; "Yeltsin Says Lithuania 'Next Afghanistan,'" FBIS-SOV-91-009 (14 January 1991), pp. 92-93. The Russian president stated, "We consider this to be unacceptable and that this is the next Afghanistan."
4. He asked them instead to transfer their allegiance to the Russian republic. See ibid., p. 94.
5. See speech by President Václav Havel to the Council of Europe, "The European Dream is Coming True," *Lidové noviny*, 11 May 1990, pp. 3-4; FBIS-EEU-90-061 (17 May 1990), pp. 8-13, esp. p. 11. Compare the ten-point program that emerged from the November 1990 CSCE conference as "The Charter of Paris," a document containing concepts similar to those in Havel's address to the Council of Europe.
6. Report of the joint Havel-Wałęsa communique by PAP in English, 17 March 1990; "Wałęsa Meets CSSR's Havel; FBIS-EEU-90-053 (19 March 1990), pp. 65-66. See also "Conference of Soviet Dissidents Opens," FBIS-EEU-90-129 (5 July 1990), pp. 35-36.
7. Evgenyi Evtushenko, "Mud and Blood Are Sisters," *The New York Times*, 19 January 1991, p. 19. The author is a prominent poet and also member of the Soviet legislature.
8. "The Charter of Paris for a New Europe," 21 November 1990 (unpublished version), section entitled "New Structures and Institutions of the CSCE Process;" See also "New European Bank to be Based at Broadgate," *The Financial Times* (London), 17 July 1990, p. 8.
9. Lecture by Teresa Rakowska-Harmstone, University of Washington, 25 May 1990.
10. See Alexander Dallin, *German Rule in Russia, 1941-1945* (Boulder: Westview Press, 1981).
11. A. P. Artem'ev, *Bratskii boevoi soiuz narodov SSSR v Velikoi Otechestvennoi voine* (Moscow: Mysl', 1975), pp. 57-58.

12. See Ch. 5 in B. S. Popov, ed., *Internatsionalizatsiia opyta stran sotsialiticheskogo sodruzhestva: politika, ekonomika, ideologiia* (Moscow: Nauka, 1987), prepared under the auspices of the CPSU Central Committee.
13. This assessment can be read in Alexander Prokhanov's essay, "The Tragedy of Centralism," *Literaturnaia Rossiia,* 5 January 1990; *Current Digest of the Soviet Press* (CDSP) 42:4 (28 February 1990), esp. pp. 1-2.
14. This argument is most fully documented in Hélène Carrère d'Encause, *Big Brother: The Soviet Union and the Soviet Empire* (New York: Holmes and Meier, 1987).
15. Three Soviet surveys written during the Gorbachev period on the past, present, and future of the overlapping programs for integrating the socialist commonwealth are B. S. Popov, ed., *op. cit.*; O. T. Bogomolov, ed., *Sotsialisticheskoe sodruzhestvo i problemy otnoshenii vostok-zapad v 80e gody* (Moscow: Politizdat, 1987); and A. V. Antosiak, et al., *Voenno-politicheskoe sotrudnichestvo sotsialisticheskikh stran* (Moscow: Nauka, 1988).
16. B. S. Popov, *Internatsionalizatsiia,* Ch. 5.
17. Ivan Volgyes, "Traitors or Revolutionaries? An Examination of the Role of Culture and Intellectuals in Communist East Europe" in Trond Gilberg and Jeffrey Simon, eds., *Security Implications of Nationalism in Eastern Europe* (Boulder: Westview, 1986).
18. Milan Kundera, "The Tragedy of Central Europe," *The New York Review of Books*, 26 April 1984, p. 33.
19. See John B. Dunlop, *The New Russian Revolutionaries* (Belmont, Mass.: Nordland Publishing, 1976) and *The Faces of Contemporary Russian Nationalism* (Princeton: Princeton University Press, 1983), esp. Ch. 6.
20. See Ch. 2, "The International Influence of Revolutionary Russia on the World Revolutionary Process" in V. P. Sherstobitov, ed., *Internatsionalizm sovetskogo naroda* (Moscow: Nauka, 1982).
21. Christopher Jones, *Soviet Hegemony in Eastern Europe* (New York: Praeger, 1981).
22. Alexander Solzhenitsyn had raised all these issues in his *Letter to the Soviet Leaders* (New York: Harper & Row, 1974). He raised them again in "Kak nam obustroit' Rossiiu," *Komsomol'skaia pravda*, 18 September 1990, 16-page supplement.
23. Teresa Rakowska-Harmstone, Christopher Jones, et al., *The Warsaw Pact: The Question of Cohesion; The Greater Socialist Army* (Ottawa: Department of National Defence, 1984), vol. I, Ch. 9.
24. See Christopher Jones, "Just Wars and Limited Wars: Restraints on the Use of the Soviet Armed Forces," *World Politics* 28:1 (October 1975), pp. 44-68.
25. Valerie Bunce, "The Empire Strikes Back," *International Organization* 39:1 (Winter 1985), pp. 1-46.
26. See Christopher Jones, "The Origins and Outcomes of Unreasonable Sufficiency" in Derek Leebaert, ed., *New Soviet Military Thinking* (New York: Cambridge University Press, forthcoming).

27. See Vitaly Zhurkin (director of the USSR's Institute on European Affairs), "A Common Home for Europe—Reflections on How to Build It," *Pravda*, 17 May 1989; CDSP 41:22 (28 June 1989), pp. 15-17.
28. See his speech to the special UN session on disarmament, "Towards a Safe World," *International Affairs* (Moscow), September 1988, pp. 3-15.
29. "Sovetsko-Iugoslavskaia deklaratsiia," *Pravda*, 19 March 1988, p. 1.
30. Jozef M. van Brabant, *Economic Integration in Eastern Europe: A Handbook* (New York: Routledge, 1989).
31. See M. S. Gorbachev, "The All-European Process Moves Ahead," *Pravda*, 7 July 1989; CDSP 41:27 (2 August 1989), pp. 5-6. Kundera, "The Tragedy of Central Europe," op. cit., p. 35.
32. Andrew Michta, *Red Eagle: The Army in Polish Politics, 1944-1988* (Stanford: Hoover Institution Press, 1990), Chs. 5 and 6.
33. "Speech by E. A. Shevardnadze," *Pravda*, 24 October 1989; CDSP 41:43 (22 November 1989), p. 3.
34. "Sovetsko-finliandskaia deklaratsiia," *Izvestiia*, 27 October 1989, p. 1.
35. "Communiqué of the Warsaw Pact Foreign Ministers Committee," *Pravda*, 28 October 1989, p. 4; FBIS-SOV-89-208 (30 October 1989), p. 5.
36. Marshal Viktor Kulikov (retired WTO commander), "Komy zhe vygodno possorit' armiiu s narodom?" *Partiinaia zhizn'*, no. 13 (July 1990), passim.
37. See the appeal to ethnic Russian soldiers by Yeltsin's government not to carry out repression in the Baltic states from Riga Domestic Radio Service, in Russian, 13 January 1991; FBIS-SOV-91-009 (14 January 1991), p. 94.
38. The image of the Soviet epoch as a sociohistorical winter comes from Shevardnadze's speech of 23 October 1989 to the USSR Supreme Soviet in which he refers to two previous "thaws" of Soviet history during the post-Stalin period. See speech by E. A. Shevardnadze, "Foreign Policy and Restructuring," *Pravda*, 24 October 1989, pp. 2-4; CDSP 41, no. 43 (22 November 1989): 2.

3

The Framework of Soviet-East-Central European Economic Relations in the 1990s

Bartlomiej Kaminski

INTRODUCTION

The institutional underpinnings of the framework of Soviet-East European economic interaction were enshrined in the statutes and practice of CMEA (Council for Mutual Economic Assistance).[1] CMEA traditionally had been a vehicle organizing economic relations between Moscow and its former satellite regimes in this region. It underlined the radial pattern of interaction centered on the USSR. Hence, the question of Soviet-East-Central European relations is twofold; it concerns the future of the institutional framework, i.e., CMEA, underpinning these relations; and the impact of the domestic institutional change in response to new expectations and political demands of its participants on economic relations between Moscow and its former dependancies.

The economic interaction between the USSR and these junior partners is undergoing a transition in a potentially unstable international and domestic environment. Because of a simultaneous collapse of the communist political order in East-Central Europe, the disappearance of the German Democratic Republic from Europe's political map, and the economic crisis throughout the former Soviet bloc, economic relations are under stress. The raison d'être of CMEA has disappeared in consequence of political developments throughout East-Central Europe and a dramatic change in the Soviet approach to relations with that geographic area.

The framework of Soviet-East-Central European relations has not proven immune to the reformist sway of Gorbachev which brought unexpected changes to the USSR and East-Central Europe. Its foundations have been under tremendous pressures because of dismal economic performance by members and their search to dismantle the institutional framework of central planning. Although, as in the past, the framework embodied in CMEA had, until recently, adjusted to the prevailing program coming from Moscow, its leverage will continue to decline. The USSR domestic economic crisis, combined with recently gained political sovereignty of East-Central European states, proved deadly for the traditional framework of their relations with Moscow and for the organization. Soviet-East-Central European economic relations either will evolve toward rules characteristic of monetary, investment, and trade regimes of the "free" world or become marginalized.

With the shift of Soviet-East-Central European trade to world prices and convertible currencies, the transition from an administrative economic system has been extended to "intra-CMEA" relations. The cost of the transition will be enormous for all concerned. For the newly established fledgling democracies in East-Central Europe, the worsened terms of trade with the USSR are an unwelcome addition to a highly unfavorable external economic environment, defined by the loss of the GDR and Iraq as trading partners, the increased oil price triggered by the Persian Gulf crisis, the simultaneous economic crisis among all CMEA members, and a rapidly expanding foreign debt. The timing of the transition could not have been worse from the point of view of external conditions. Its effect on the stability of the transition and Soviet-East-Central European relations remains to be seen.

INSTITUTIONAL UNDERPINNINGS OF SOVIET-EAST-CENTRAL EUROPEAN RELATIONS AND DOMESTIC TRANSITION

CMEA celebrated its forty-first anniversary in 1990. The question of bureaucratic inertia natural to communist systems, aside from this longevity, is somewhat surprising. CMEA was not founded out of pressing economic necessity, and does not seem to have gained in productive economic value through the years. The source of its survival, it would seem, is largely a matter of CMEA evolving in response to the changing requirements of Soviet policy. It may indeed have been the case that the past demands placed upon it as a socialist international economic organization have not been onerous.

In the climate of collapse of the Soviet grip over East-Central European countries, it is a pressing question as to how it will stand up to the much more rigorous demands of moving away from the communist economic system.

In many interviews, various economic officials and observers, especially from Czechoslovakia and Hungary, gave the assessment that CMEA was a dead letter and an empty shell.[2] When viewed against the rhetoric of radical transformation of economic systems based on command planning, the organization is indeed a dead letter, because its organizing principle of state controls and central planning is not compatible with the reform measures that are either contemplated or being implemented in East-Central Europe and the USSR.

Yet, the organization is neither a dead letter nor an empty shell—it still sanctions primacy of politics over economics in member countries and provides an outlet for Soviet intervention in domestic economic decisions. It comprises a gigantic bureaucracy organized around principles incompatible with a market economy. As long as its bureaucracy remains intact, CMEA will not become an empty shell and will remain a stumbling bloc to the transition from administrative economic systems. The organizational framework of CMEA itself has many of the same traits of command planning hierarchies, characteristic of the Soviet Union and other CMEA members. In the absence of markets and autonomous activity to establish links across borders, interdependence can only be promoted and coordinated by explicit action of the states involved through the intermediate role of a vast bureaucracy.

The quintessential nature of CMEA has never been "fraternal solidarity, great commitment to one another's success, complete equality, and comradely mutual assistance," as Soviet permanent representative to that organization N. V. Talyzin once noted.[3] CMEA's problems derive from several of its unique features. Formally, it is not a supranational organization, since the CMEA charter explicitly points out that decisions are not binding on members and hence membership involves no transfer of sovereignty. This is a reflection of a basic organizing principle underlying membership, that of the "interested party," according to which members retain full discretion over their participation in CMEA programs. As will be shown, however, this principle could not be taken at its face value.

On the other hand, given the fundamental place that the administrative mechanism has in the allocation of resources, it cannot function as a common market. It was not a customs union either, since tariffs had little impact on members' trade. Vladimir Sobell describes it as an international trade protection system.[4] Although there clearly had been a low level of trade, this was more due to domestic shortcomings of command economies than to the structure of the organization per se.

Most simply CMEA functioned as a framework for the economic interaction of its member countries but in a way defined by several important and unique characteristics.[5] In the first place, there was an extremely high degree of inequality between the USSR and other members in terms of size and economic and technical levels of development.[6] Not only did this create potential for conflict among member countries but it engendered a particular set of political problems as well, which had always complicated consensus building on questions of specialization and direction of development.

Secondly, CMEA was more than a trading bloc. It also comprised an enormous bureaucracy, impeding on sovereignty of economic decision-making in such areas as development programs, investment, transportation, energy, and research and development—extending beyond pure trade among member countries. Despite considerable resistance, members were forced to divert resources to the uses not necessarily serving their individual interests. To cope with integrative efforts, there emerged a myriad of functional and branch organs within a centrally administered framework.

Because of secrecy surrounding the operations of various organs of CMEA, it remains unclear which of them were empowered to make decisions binding on all CMEA members. Despite a principle that a country could participate in whatever ventures it wished, sectoral permanent commissions and some international associations had supranational authority, although this principle was vehemently rejected by CMEA *nomenklatura* officials. For instance, the chairman of the executive committee, Andrei Lukanov, declared:

> As distinct from, say, the West European Economic Community, our organization does not incorporate supra-national elements. Each of the countries retains full sovereignty in the field of its economic policy and in its economic decisions and the ways and means of managing economic life.[7]

In fact, CMEA bureaucracy had directly intervened with the domestic economic policy-making process and imposed "mandatory state-level decisions."[8]

The four-point Hungarian program submitted by then Prime Minister Miklós Németh to the 45th CMEA session in Sofia included a recommendation that sectoral commissions and committees be suspended. There would be no need for this recommendation, if actions could be unilaterally vetoed by a member government. In a similar vein, Czechoslovak Prime Minister Marian Čalfa said that CMEA "—now an inter-governmental organization competent to make its acts binding for the member states—should turn into a platform for consultations and for the creation of a contractual system suiting our requirements."[9] Finally, senior Polish official Waldemar Kuczyński observed that CMEA "must in no way restrict the economic freedom of its member states nor hinder their contacts with the EC."[10]

CMEA had also created large groups with a vested interest in petrifying existing administrative structures. Since the CMEA institutional arrangements cut across member governments' ministries and lower layers of economic bureaucracy, these are beyond direct control of their respective governments. Although their influence on economic decision-making has been weakened by Moscow's policy of disengagement from East-Central Europe, as well as the emergence of governments reliant on public rather than Soviet support, these groups remain an impediment to radical institutional restructuring of domestic economic systems.

There exist other obstacles that appear to be of more immediate concern to most European postcommunist governments. Leaving aside domestic political and economic constraints, the transition to a market economy cannot succeed unless CMEA is restructured by applying similar principles to those employed by its members in national reforms. These new principles advocated by recently established governments include competition, monetization, internal and external convertibility of domestic currencies, and autonomy of economic actors.

Last but not least CMEA's rules of the game represented a formidable obstacle to meaningful change in the economic system also because of the "weight" of CMEA (Soviet) trade. Hungarian Deputy Finance Minister Zsigmond Járai noted that CMEA is "the main reason for the rigidity of Hungary's economy, since 45 percent of Hungarian foreign trade must be conducted by cutting out the role of money."[11]

Instead of "money," Soviet-East-Central European relations were based on state trade and obligatory quotas which offer little room for flexibility and the development of ties at the level of firms. Attempts to remedy the situation through promoting the use of domestic currencies (instead of the transferable ruble) and establishing direct ties among firms, which, having been a backbone of Soviet policy toward CMEA under Mikhail S. Gorbachev, could not have worked although a number of direct ties among enterprises have been established.[12] While recently several CMEA countries (Bulgaria, Czechoslovakia, Hungary, Poland, Mongolia, and the Soviet Union) signed bilateral agreements to settle accounts in their respective domestic currencies, the problem is that domestic currencies are domestically nonconvertible, i.e., an enterprise having a surplus cannot directly purchase goods on a domestic market of its partner.

Thus, the organizational structure of CMEA is not compatible with the institutional underpinnings of market economies. Governments of the countries that do not have command planning are not in a position to conclude foreign trade agreements on behalf of private corporations. Once the state gives up direct control over enterprise activities, then it will no longer have the authority to make delivery commitments to other CMEA partners. When planning is abolished, as is currently the case in Poland and Hungary, there remains no room for the coordination of plans, the hallmark of CMEA integration. If what to produce is decided by enterprises and not directly by central authorities, then the existing CMEA mechanism becomes incompatible with the domestic economic system and an impediment to change.

What still kept CMEA alive in 1990, aside from bureaucratic inertia, was the fear of unknown economic and political consequences from termination. East-Central European countries have had an interest in importing fuel and raw materials from the Soviet Union and "exporting . . . not-too-modern manufactured goods, in the environment of extremely limited development of cooperation in production."[13] From the point of view of East-Central European members, their major concern has been gradually to phase out administrative rules governing their trade relations with the Soviet Union in favor of market rules in order to avoid the shock of adjustment to new, sharply deteriorated terms of trade. Although Soviet proposals presented at the Sofia CMEA summit suggested that this also was a road that the USSR had wanted to follow, the subsequent decision to use hard currency and world prices in intra-CMEA transactions amounted to a rejection of the gradualist approach. In addition, Soviet supplies of oil and gas to CMEA partners fell by about 20 percent in 1990.[14]

As a result, the CMEA contract is on the brink of collapse and there seems to be little value for both East-Central Europeans and Soviets in prolonging the existence of this organization. The changes implemented in the early 1990s have effectively redesigned the institutional framework of economic interaction between the USSR and East-Central Europe. The traditional primacy of politics over economics is being replaced by subordinating those relations to the imperative of economic efficiency. While the links that have emerged as a result of the integrationist effort of the last 40 years will remain binding, they will become weaker at a considerable short-term cost to Eastern Europe.

UNRAVELING OF THE CMEA CONTRACT

The contract underlying Soviet-East-Central European relations, i.e., the cohesiveness of CMEA, is beyond repair. Calling for relative insulation from the noncommunist world economy, it rested on two interdependent pillars: political and economic. The political pillar was based on the dependence of East-Central European regimes on Moscow to stay in power. Against the backdrop of the threat of force and dominance within the Warsaw Pact, the political pillar was based on the imposition on East-Central Europe of three key principles as defined by Moscow: socialist internationalism (the Brezhnev doctrine), democratic centralism (full political control by the Soviet communist party), and the leading role of the indigenous communist party.[15] The 1989 revolution witnessed the final breakdown of all three principles.

In the course of the evolution of Soviet-East-Central European relations, these two pillars, political and economic, had become intertwined and complemented one another. Although a network of ideological, intraparty, and security links had been central to assuring Moscow's grip over East-Central Europe, the combination of the autarchic communist economic system and Soviet resource endowment added an economic link that bound the region to the USSR.

The economic pillar, which relied on a special code—distinct from the one observed in the noncommunist world—of organizing economic relations between Moscow and its junior partners, and which has resulted in a structural dependence of their economies on the USSR, received a devastating blow from the Soviet economic crisis. The structural dependence of East-Central Europe on the USSR stemmed from the asymmetry in natural-resource endowment in favor of the latter, the rules of price setting, and below world standard (domestic) quality requirements in their trade relations. These conditions were responsible for the asymmetry in the proportion of goods that could be sold on world markets between CMEA exports by the USSR and by East-Central European countries.

With the erosion of ideology and improvement in East-West relations, cohesion of the "bloc" was maintained by an implicit contract according to which the Soviet Union supplied oil, gas, and other raw materials in exchange for East-Central European manufactured goods. The increasingly limited Soviet capacity to provide its CMEA partners with cheap energy frustrated this arrangement and exacerbated economic difficulties of the East-Central European countries during the 1980s. The systemic aspect of the contract was that raw materials cannot be "spoiled" by the inefficient economic arrangements in a marked contrast to manufactures that are vulnerable to organization of the economy. The huge demand generated by the Soviet economy offered considerable space which East-Central European exporters could fill without undercutting one another: no other country in CMEA could serve as such an easy outlet, simply because of demand constraints. But it had been more than merely a question of the relative sizes of the economies: there existed an important *structural factor* which underlies this bilateralism.

This Soviet predominance and East-Central European dependence created a radial pattern of economic relations within the bloc. There was an ongoing intensification of integration for individual CMEA states' ties to the Soviet Union and the relative atrophy of multilateral relations. Shifts in trading patterns within the bloc generally were at the expense of trade between smaller (i.e., the Soviet Union excluded) member states. In the 1970s, when the East-Central European states sought to increase trade with the West, the share of trade among non-Soviet CMEA members dropped in total CMEA trade from 48 percent during 1971-1975 to 38 percent during 1981-1985.[16] When these economic ties to the West later declined, due to import cutbacks in response to the debt crisis, the weight of trade with the Soviet Union increased (in part due to increased world oil prices). It is interesting to note that during the same period, the Soviet share in East-Central European trade had also increased, as it continued to do during the 1980s and in 1990.

Thus, a pattern emerged in which the Soviet Union dominated East-Central European trade, while an important amount of trade has remained with the West, providing East-Central Europeans with technological know-how and capital goods. The region has been torn between the USSR and the West; denial of access to Soviet natural resources would bring their economies to an immediate halt, while the loss of access to Western markets would undercut their development capacities. The inability of CMEA countries to sustain economic growth, without relying on the West, was bound to produce disintegrating tendencies within the organization. And the Soviet inability to meet energy export requirements also inevitably was bound to undercut special arrangements underlying Soviet-East-Central European economic relations.

Because of growing indebtedness of the East-Central European economies and the contraction in Soviet raw materials and energy supply, this structural arrangement could not go on indefinitely. In fact, it began to unravel in the early 1980s, as Eastern Europe was hit simultaneously by steeply increasing costs of Soviet oil and the external debt crisis. The congruence of these two developments revealed the weaknesses of the intra-CMEA framework. During the 1982-1984 credit squeeze that followed the imposition of martial law in Poland, CMEA—defying its official name of Council for Mutual Economic Assistance—offered no "mutual assistance." To the contrary, CMEA members sought to outbid one another as they scrambled for the same markets because of the previous absence of coordination in the purchases of capital equipment and technology from the West during the 1970s—a phenomenon which Soviet economist Iurii Shiriaev dubbed a "secondary ["imported"] parallelism." In contrast to the period following the first oil shock, CMEA did not provide a shield against external economic disturbances. If anything, CMEA proved to be inconsequential. And last but not least, to the chagrin of bankers, the Soviet Union did not extend its "financial umbrella" and take care of East-Central Europe's hard currency indebtedness.

The stagnation in USSR oil supplies, combined with soaring prices of oil precipitated by the 1979 second oil shock, contributed to a fall in Soviet-East European trade. While between 1960 and the late 1970s the volume of Soviet oil deliveries to the region increased by 50 percent,[17] it stagnated during the 1980s because of a significant increase in production and transportation costs combined more recently with the fall of oil output.[18]

Therefore, the decline in oil prices, a burden for Moscow, did not particularly benefit other CMEA countries. Because of depressed oil prices, the energy bill of the Soviet CMEA partners significantly fell and their terms of trade vis-à-vis the Soviet Union considerably improved. As a result, the growth of Soviet-East European trade lagged behind the growth of trade of CMEA countries with other partners. Until 1988, the stagnation stemmed in part from the improved terms of trade vis-à-vis the USSR, whose exports in value terms fell by 4 percent in 1988.[19]

The situation deteriorated during 1989-1990, producing another shock in Soviet-East European economic relations, much more devastating than the previous oil shocks because of the USSR unwillingness to maintain supplies of energy and other raw materials.[20] While exports of crude oil to the developed West increased by 16.3 percent during the first nine months of 1990, they fell by 19.4 percent to East-Central European CMEA members.[21] Moscow unilaterally cut supplies of fuel to Czechoslovakia by 20 percent in January 1990, and by 30 percent to Poland during January-March of 1990.[22] Exports were later stepped up, but still remained significantly lower than in 1989. During the first nine months of 1990, Soviet deliveries of crude oil fell by 45 percent to Romania, by 20 percent to Bulgaria and Hungary, by 18 percent to Czechoslovakia, and 16 percent to Poland.[23] Only exports of natural gas continued to grow in 1990.

East-Central European governments remain uninformed about the amount of oil and gas they will be able to buy from the Soviet Union, and at what prices, after 1990, despite their considerable investment in the development of the USSR gas and oil pipeline networks. It is also unclear what portion of their financial claims on the Soviets, accumulated thanks to trade surpluses, and what ruble/dollar exchange rate they will be able to use to pay for the USSR deliveries of oil.

As a result of the Soviet crisis, trade with East-Central Europe has been crumbling. Moscow's inability to maintain exports has already depressed the level of bilateral trade. Because of the plunge in Soviet exports, East-Central European CMEA members ran record trade surpluses in their trade with the USSR during both 1989 and 1990 despite deliberately imposed cuts on their exports. During the first three quarters of 1990, Soviet exports fell by 17.3 percent. According to a PlanEcon estimate, this contraction was the result of several developments: the decline in the value of fuel exports (10 to 12 percent in the average Soviet ruble export price), the decline in their volume (by 8 to 10 percent), and a 20 percent cutback in arms exports to the region. East-Central European imports fell by 2.7 percent during this period, and their aggregate trade surplus with the USSR increased from 2.8 billion in 1989 (first nine months) to 6.1 billion rubles during the same period in 1990.

These surpluses contribute—because of the inconvertibility of the ruble—to inflationary pressures in East-Central European economies and to the diversion of exports to other markets. While surpluses for Bulgaria and Poland reduced their debts—whose actual size and "sign" is challenged by Poles—to the Soviet Union, Czechoslovakia and Hungary had to credit Soviet purchases. These considerations prompted the International Monetary Fund (IMF) to make its assistance to Hungary conditional upon bringing the surplus with the Soviet Union down to zero. The Hungarian government temporarily suspended exports to the USSR in early 1990. Other countries also have imposed limits on their exports. Bulgaria reduced them by 20 percent, whereas Poland introduced a system of licensing designed to keep its exports within the amounts stipulated in trade agreements. Yet the surpluses soared, with Poland accounting for roughly two-thirds of the East-Central European CMEA surplus with the USSR.[24]

However, as we shall see later, East-Central Europe's surpluses in trade with the USSR result to a large extent from the artificial system of pricing in intra-CMEA transactions. Under these circumstances, another component of the economic pillar which has come under scrutiny is the price-setting code, dating back to the 1958 Bucharest agreement. According to this document, the prices used in intra-CMEA dealings were based on five-year average world prices and revised every five years in order to stay in line with five-year economic plans. After the first oil shock, triggered by OPEC's fivefold increase of oil prices, one provision of the 1958 Bucharest arrangement was amended at Soviet insistence; beginning in 1975, prices were to be revised every year instead of every five years.[25] Facing extremely adverse economic conditions, the Soviet Union began in the late 1980s unilaterally to modify the rules of intra-CMEA trade, such as the use of convertible currencies in mutual payments. These hard currency transactions accounted for a small fraction of the turnover, although they significantly expanded in 1990, especially in the trade of Hungary and Poland with the Soviet Union.

The decision to adopt freely convertible currencies and world prices in Soviet-East European trade, effective 1 January 1991, put an end to the "insulating" price system based on the transferable ruble for intra-CMEA settlements and payments. On 31 July 1990, the Soviet Union had withdrawn from the system of agreements on nontrade payments with other CMEA countries dating back to the 1960s and 1970s.[26]

While the switch to the use of Western currencies and world prices may be judged as favorable in the long run to the integration of the region with international markets, it does not augur well for the future of CMEA. Because of bureaucratic inertia and despite CMEA's growing irrelevance for Soviet-East-Central European relations, it may still exist for some time. However, the organizational framework of these relations will continue rapidly evolving beyond the boundaries set by CMEA. The elimination of "funny money" in intra-CMEA trade and the use of world prices is likely to be the final nail in the coffin of the original contract underlying the organization, since trade interaction based on rules, distinctive from those used in the world economy, was what had been left from the original CMEA "bargain."

Contrary to the expectations of some Soviet officials, the introduction of a new pricing system will not infuse CMEA with vitality. The statement by the chairman of the USSR State Bank's Foreign Currency Economics Administration, O. Mozhaiskov, that "hard currency settlements are capable of reviving it," is wishful thinking.[27] Full convertibility of domestic currencies may eventually boost trade but simultaneously will remove any interest in maintaining the CMEA bureaucracy.

Moscow clearly hopes the new mechanism of international settlements will redress the imbalance so that the shares of respective "hard currency sellable" goods are more or less equal. As recipients of Soviet raw materials, especially oil, the former communist governments had an implicit subsidy for their economies. CMEA members were able to produce goods of a high enough quality for the Soviet market, but not for the world market. For instance, it was estimated that only about 30 percent of Hungarian goods exported to the USSR could have been hard currency earners as compared with 70 percent of Soviet exports to Hungary.[28]

In effect, East Europeans were able to obtain raw materials sellable on the world market for some noncompetitive goods, representing a net opportunity cost to the Soviet Union. This was a situation about which Moscow became critical; as Gorbachev remarked, the Soviet Union does not want to be the "garbage can" for East-Central Europe.[29] In other words, quality requirements should be set at the level of world standards.

For the time being, without diverting exports from the West and increasing the share of consumer goods, the equalization of respective shares may be difficult to achieve although East-Central Europeans already have been compelled to increase deliveries of food and other consumer products to Moscow. These items have significant convertible currency content and can be easily sold in international markets. While this change in the composition of Soviet import demand could not produce a full symmetry in the proportion of hard goods (i.e., goods easily sold in Western markets) that are mutually traded, it promises to further erode the foundations of trade relations within the region.

To sum up, the contract underlying cohesiveness of CMEA is on the verge of collapsing, and Soviet-East European trade is crumbling. The two pillars have been either destroyed or seriously weakened by Mikhail Gorbachev's policies, designed to cope with an all-encompassing USSR crisis and political developments in East-Central Europe. The political one disappeared, because the newly established postcommunist regimes no longer depend on Moscow to remain in power. The economic one, or protective shield, also has been definitely removed thanks to the establishment of a mechanism for price-setting similar to the one organizing commercial interaction in the "noncommunist" world economy. What is left of the institutional arrangements underpinning Soviet-East European trade relations is the legacy of parallel economic strategies which will continue to bind them together, low competitiveness of their manufactured goods in international markets, and a potential for conflict that may result from disputes over their accumulated liabilities vis-à-vis one another.

CONSEQUENCES OF THE NEW ACCOUNTING AND PRICING SYSTEM

While there are many uncertainties concerning Soviet-East European economic relations in the 1990s, it can be taken for granted that they will represent a significant departure from the past. Introduction of the new pricing and accounting system will generate at least a temporary break in economic ties. Because of the complexity of problems involved in shifting those relations to a new framework of accounting and pricing, based on Western principles and world prices, the transition will not occur immediately.

The problems to be solved are multifold. First, while it is relatively easy to determine prices for raw materials and energy, i.e., those items which can successfully be marketed in the West, it is difficult to set prices for manufactured goods which have not been sold in Western markets. Thus, one may witness a continuation of the relatively unconstrained bargaining which has been a trademark of CMEA. Then the only tangible difference with the past will consist in higher prices for raw materials and energy.

Second, it is also unclear who will set prices—enterprises or governments. Should governmental agencies participate in the process? In the countries that have made considerable progress in dismantling the administrative economic system, foreign transactions are made at the discretion of enterprises. However, in those countries that have not adopted radical reform measures, they are set by state agencies. Will, then, a monopolistic state agency of one country be in a position to play one potential exporter against the other from the same country, while depriving its importers of the advantages flowing from competition? Poles and Hungarians argue in favor of prices negotiated by enterprises, with no interference by indigenous economic bureaucracies. While this goal is within reach in their respective relations, Soviet enterprises still operate in a bureaucratic environment. If the prices of other products are determined by enterprises without the participation of the state—the issue still discussed among CMEA members—then the procedure will be markedly different from the one used in the past.

Finally, the system that emerged after 1 January 1990 is initially more complex than the previous system of settlements in transferable rubles.[30] Because of the inconvertibility of most currencies in East-Central Europe and in the Soviet Union, provisional arrangements will include clearing as well as settlements in part with hard currencies and in part through clearing. For instance, a Bulgarian-Soviet agreement provides for the use of both rubles and hard currencies between 1991 and 1994.[31]

Under these circumstances, the switch of Soviet-East European trade to world prices and convertible currencies will not, at least initially, result in the emergence of a new institutional framework or more precisely in the use of mechanisms characteristic of market economies. It is expected, for instance, that about 20 to 25 percent of trade will be conducted at the central government level with the remaining portion carried out at the republic and enterprise levels. The hybrid of arrangements will exist until a limited convertibility of domestic currencies obtains. As long as the Soviet ruble is neither internationally nor domestically convertible, a delegation of the right to conduct foreign trade to enterprise management will have little impact on its real capability to trade with enterprises from those CMEA countries (Hungary and Poland) that have limited convertible currencies. There will be little room for the expansion in trade, simply because the exchange will remain based on barter arrangements. Thus, without a total dismantling of central planning in the USSR and ruble convertibility, its trade will remain subject to similar administrative constraints as in the past. However, because of higher prices and the Soviet economic crisis, trade will become even more suppressed than in the past. According to many estimates, intraregional trade will fall by 30 percent in 1991.[32]

The distribution of benefits will drastically change in favor of the Soviet Union at the expense of East-Central Europe in the short run. In the longer perspective, however, East-Central European economies may benefit from eliminating the protective shield of their trade arrangements with the USSR. They will be compelled to restructure their economies, so as to make them competitive in international markets; Soviet trade will no longer provide them with a tempting alternative of adapting to less demanding conditions. They will no longer be forced to adjust their economies to USSR requirements which, as a rule, have been much less demanding than those of world markets. Whether they can tap benefits from reintegration with the world economy will depend on the capacity of their emerging political systems to mobilize resources and to redesign their economic systems to attract foreign investment and Western assistance.

The Soviet Union will be an immediate winner, because the shift of USSR-East-Central European trade to a new accounting system will result in improved terms of trade, higher oil revenues, and the substitution of CMEA manufactured goods for higher quality Western capital goods. According to an estimate by the World Bank, the total Soviet annual gains will amount to between $10 and $13 billion.[33] This extra revenue consists of gains accrued thanks to improved terms of trade ($5 to $7 billion) and additional oil revenues (about $5 billion).

The Soviet gains are East-Central Europe's losses in revenues from trade with the USSR. The $13 billion surplus projected by the World Bank amounts to about 5 percent of total East-Central European domestic product and will "wipe out 2 to 3 years of economic growth."[34] The Vienna Institute for Comparative Economic Studies estimates that a shift to world prices and hard currencies in 1989 would have generated a Soviet trade surplus of $4.6 billion, instead of a deficit of $3.9 billion. Assuming that the USSR met its contractual obligations for 1990, East-Central Europe's deficit would have amounted to $3.3 billion, had the settlements been conducted in hard currencies.[35] If the price of oil stabilizes at $30 per barrel, its deficit vis-à-vis the Soviet Union will amount to $20 billion in 1991.

The losses are mainly due to the lower price of USSR oil than that on the international market and East-Central Europe's dependence on its oil supplies. Except for Romania, USSR supplies account for 80 to 90 percent of individual country import demand. This high level of dependence, combined with the special code of CMEA pricing, has become perceived by the Soviets as detrimental to their economic interests. According to the USSR trade representative to Hungary, Vladimir Usanov, "the Soviet Union was actually losing about 8 billion rubles in trade with East-Central European countries, owing to a sharp decline in world prices of raw materials and energy carriers."[36] Indeed should the official transferable ruble-to-dollar exchange rate ($1.52 per transferable ruble) be applied to oil, the Soviet price for a ton of oil charged in 1990 would have been 152 instead of 130 rubles (the world price was $100 per ton). But the official exchange rate was artificially high, and the actual cross rates used in trade among East-Central European countries were significantly lower, ranging between $.625 per ruble (Romania) to $.278 per ruble (Poland).[37] Taking the average of these extreme rates, the 130 ruble price would equal $58.6 paid for a ton of oil at a Soviet net loss of $41.3 per ton. While this is a result of the USSR-imposed pricing code, the loss nevertheless represents a subsidy to East-Central Europe which will disappear in 1991.[38]

The degree to which individual countries will be affected by the new pricing system depends on the composition of their trade with the USSR and their dependency on its supplies of energy. The countries whose main exports comprise manufactured goods, which were overpriced, will suffer the largest losses in their terms of trade with the Soviet Union. Bulgaria and Czechoslovakia, with estimated trade deficits in 1991 of $1.8 to 2.0 and $2.0 to 2.5 billion respectively, will be probably hit the hardest. Poland and Czechoslovakia will be most affected by the extra oil bill, according to the World Bank estimate.[39] The estimates of deficits by the Vienna Institute for Comparative

Economic Studies for other countries are as follows: Hungary—$1.1 to 1.5 billion; Poland—$2.0 to 2.4 billion; and Romania—$0.6 to 1.0 billion.[40] (These figures may be at the higher end, because the compression of Soviet import demand for manufactures may also reduce energy and raw materials consumption; many production lines servicing the USSR have been characterized by high energy- and raw materials-intensity.)

The switch to world prices for oil will exacerbate inflationary pressures in East-Central European economies and erode, at least initially, the competitiveness of their products that had been profitable thanks to cheaper energy and raw materials imported from the USSR as well as undermine their standard of living. For instance, a Polish commentator estimates that the price of $30 per barrel would raise the price of gasoline by at least 56 percent, and the oil bill for the last quarter of 1990 would increase by $432 million.[41] The inevitable increase in production costs could be only offset by either conservation and energy-saving measures or cuts in other cost components. Since the fall in energy consumption is not likely to compensate for the oil price increase, declining exports and increased prices will bring down real incomes. The truck and taxi driver blockade of Budapest, triggered by the 60 percent increase of gasoline prices in October 1990, reminded one that a sudden drop in real incomes may become politically destabilizing.

Another source of additional economic difficulties that the region will face relates to the already observed fall in the Soviet import demand for East-Central European manufactured goods, caused by the declining purchasing power of the USSR and the contraction in its investment programs. Finding new markets may be difficult, because firms exporting to the Soviet Union have been under no pressure, stemming from competition in a market economy, to produce more efficiently and originate technologically sophisticated goods. In the past, East-Central European planners responded to the necessity of boosting exports to the Soviet Union by increased investment in products and sectors which were not at the forefront of modern research and development. As they sought to adjust their development plans to meet USSR requirements, their capacity to compete in the noncommunist world weakened.[42] Given the inevitable cuts in their investment programs during the transition away from the administrative economic system, they may find it time-consuming to adjust to new demands by their former metropole.

The loss of Soviet markets already has compelled some Polish and Hungarian enterprises to reduce employment. For instance, the Budapest firm producing buses that had relied previously on secure contracts with the Soviet Union and GDR,[43] has been struggling desperately to survive. With the elimination of subsidies, many enterprises or even whole industrial sectors may disappear. On the other hand, many East-Central European firms may not lose Soviet markets to Western newcomers, because their products may be in line with comparative advantages and the long trading relations may offer them a competitive edge. Thus, the greatest danger stems from the possibility of a prolonged economic and political crisis in the USSR.

Although in the nearest future a decline in terms of trade, possibly a shrinking Soviet market for East-Central European manufactured goods, and higher oil bills will significantly increase the social cost of dismantling the administrative economic system, these adverse developments may yet turn out to be beneficial. They may find closing technologically outdated plants easier, when the blame can be placed on exogenous developments. Accusing the Soviet Union and a legacy of communist development strategies offers more room for making hard and politically risky decisions. Nevertheless, the economic and social costs will be extremely high, and they are likely to generate political tensions.

CONCLUSION

The future of Soviet-East-Central European economic interaction will be determined by three processes: the disintegration of the USSR's economic and political system; economic crisis and adjustment with liberalizing institutional changes in East-Central Europe; and the new dynamic momentum of German unification and integration in the West. All of those processes will contribute to the demise of CMEA—which according to some observers already "lies in ruins"[44]—as a framework for Soviet-East European relations.

While it is impossible to predict the future of the Soviet Union, the reemergence of the former communist bloc in East-Central Europe is rather unlikely. By the same token, the old trade regime will converge with the General Agreement on Tariffs and Trade (GATT) regime. Disintegration of the USSR economy will certainly depress the level of Soviet-East European trade, unless future sovereign republics dismantle the USSR foreign trade monopoly, introduce limited convertibility, and market clearing prices. Clearly, the faster the Soviet-East European regime becomes liberalized, the greater the prospects for trade.

Soviet-East European economic relations will be to a large extent determined by their respective domestic developments. In the latter, the ability of postcommunist governments to manage the politically precarious transition from communism is yet to be tested. Poland and Hungary have made substantial strides in dismantling the bureaucratic economic system. In the USSR, its future in present form remains highly uncertain, as many of the

15 republics have already declared "independence." In addition, it is impossible to predict either the length and depth of the current economic crisis or the pace of the transformation of the economic system in the Soviet Union. If there is little progress toward marketization and the crisis persists, like in Poland since 1978, there will be a forced diversion of trade away from the USSR. Assuming that Moscow somehow withholds centripetal pressures of the republics, the question is whether it will be able to introduce changes in the economic system conducive to economic growth and trade.

CMEA's chances of survival are rather low. The agreement reached at Moscow in January 1991 to replace CMEA with a new body, to be called the Organization for International Economic Cooperation, seems to have only token political value and mainly for Moscow. The reformed organization will not become a "Council for Mutual Economic Development." Instead, it "will perform primarily the task of undertaker." Its rather limited budget of 6.8 million rubles (about $11 million at the official exchange rate) will not allow for any extended intraregional activities as in the past. Czechoslovak economics minister, Vladimír Dlouhý, probably expressed the opinion of Central European delegates, when he noted: "We do need it very much. Trade links can be handled on a bilateral basis. I would give it five or seven years maximum lifetime."[45]

In fact, the sooner member states liberate themselves from economically damaging arrangements, embodied in CMEA, the better the chances for their rapid reintegration with the world economy. In the meantime, they will have to display considerable institutional innovativeness to keep alive their mutual trade links. Their artificial suppression would produce losses to all concerned.

Even assuming that the organization is redesigned so as to support the transition to a market economy and not to impinge upon the autonomy of domestic economic actors, East-Central European economies will gravitate (and so will the USSR) to the sources of modern technology and capital, i.e., Western Europe. Yet the Soviet Union will remain an important trading partner, comparable to the Middle East for Western Europe, and a major supplier of energy and other raw materials as well as a market for East-Central European manufactured goods. Because of already established commercial links and the existing infrastructure, East-Central Europeans will have considerable comparative advantage in dealing with Soviet firms.

NOTES

1. As of January 1990, there were 11 full members of CMEA: Albania, Bulgaria, Czechoslovakia, Cuba, the German Democratic Republic, Hungary, Mongolia, Poland, Romania, Vietnam, and the USSR. Albania joined CMEA in 1949 but, since 1961, has not participated in any CMEA activities nor has it paid its dues (Richard F. Staar, *Communist Regimes in Eastern Europe,* 5th rev. ed. [Stanford: Hoover Institution Press, 1988], p. 292). Yugoslavia had limited participant status. Three countries—Finland (1973), Mexico (1975), and Iraq (1976)—ratified cooperative status agreements with CMEA. Since 1978, the observer status group included the following nine countries: Afghanistan, Angola, Kampuchea, Ethiopia, Laos, Mozambique, Nicaragua, North Korea, and South Yemen. Apparently, not all of them retained this status.
2. Czechoslovakia's finance minister, Václav Klaus, declared at a press conference: "Czechoslovakia will suggest the abrogation of all binding agreements and will propose annulment to the other countries." Quoted by Craig R. Whitney, "Prague is Seeking New Trade System for the East Bloc," *The New York Times,* 5 January 1990, p. 4.
3. Interview in *Pravda,* 9 January 1989, p. 7.
4. Vladimir Sobell, "Introduction," *The Red Market* (Aldershot, Hant: Gower Publishing Co., 1984).
5. See Jozef M. van Brabant, *Socialist Economic Integration* (Cambridge, Engl.: Cambridge University Press, 1980).
6. For more, see Bartlomiej Kaminski, "Council for Mutual Economic Assistance: Division and Conflict on Its 40th Anniversary," in Richard F. Staar, ed., *1989 Yearbook on International Communist Affairs* (Stanford, Calif.: Hoover Institution Press, 1989), pp. 413-430.
7. Interview over Moscow Television Service, 25 January 1989; FBIS-SOV-89-016 (26 January 1989), p. 4.
8. Unidentified member of the Romanian delegation at the CMEA meeting, carried by Sofia Radio (BTA); FBIS-EEU-90-007 (10 January 1990), p. 2.
9. Prague Radio (ČTK), 9 January 1990; FBIS-EEU-90-007 (10 January 1990), p. 5.
10. See Warsaw Radio (PAP), 30 July 1990; FBIS-SOV-90-147 (31 July 1990), p. 18.
11. Budapest Radio (MTI), 21 July 1989; FBIS-EEU-89-140 (24 July 1989), p. 18.
12. During 1986-1989, direct ties were established mainly between Soviet enterprises and those from other member countries. In 1987, for instance, some 116 Hungarian and Soviet enterprises established direct ties, and 19 joint enterprises as well as two associations were set up (*Ekonomicheskaia gazeta,* no.6, 1988). According to a former Polish prime minister, Zbigniew

Messner, "more than 200 production enterprises, 190 trade organizations, and 100 R&D organizations established direct links with Soviet partners" (*Rzeczpospolita*, 6 July 1988, p. 1). Coal and energy enterprises from the GDR concluded agreements with Soviet enterprises during 1987-1988.
13. Paweł Bożyk, "Operacja w trójkątach," *Przegląd tygodniowy*, no. 46, 13 November 1988, p.3.
14. *PlanEcon Report* (Washington, D.C.): 6, no. 48-49, January 1991, p. 10.
15. Karen Dawisha, *Eastern Europe: Gorbachev and Reform, The Great Challenge* (Cambridge, Engl.: Cambridge University Press, 1988), pp. 73-86.
16. Author's calculations from data compiled by the German Institute of Economic Research, published in European Parliament Working Documents, No. A 2-187/186.
17. Paul Marer, "Foreign Trade Strategies in Eastern Europe: Determinants, Outcomes, Prospects"; paper presented at the 12th International Workshop on East-West Economic Interaction, 1-5 April 1989, Athens, Georgia.
18. The cost of extraction increased from 50 rubles to recover one additional ton of oil in the early 1970s to 88 rubles in 1985 and 219 rubles in 1990. See "Interview with S. Iakovlev," *Trud*, 12 March 90, p. 3. The increase occurred despite significant investment effort; fuel accounted for 40 percent of Soviet capital investments in the industrial sector during 1987. This situation did not prevent a fall in output. According to a Polish source (*Życie gospodarcze, 14 January 1990, p. 6), Soviet export of oil was about 50 percent below 1989 plan targets.*
19. *Gospodarka światowa i gospodarka polska w 1988 roku* (Warsaw: Szkoła Główna Planowania i Statystyki, 1989), p. 42.
20. Soviet deliveries of timber to East-Central Europe fell short of the contracted by 267,000 cubic meters, of coal by 100,000 tons, and of fuel by 46,000 tons in 1989. See *Izvestiia*, 8 May 1990, p. 5.
21. *PlanEcon Report:* 6, no. 48-49 (January 1991).
22. *The Financial Times* (London), 14 February 1990, p. 2.
23. *PlanEcon Report*, op. cit.
24. During the first three quarters of 1990, Poland accumulated a 4 billion ruble trade surplus. For the entire year, Poland's surplus reached a record level of 4.6 billion rubles, principally due to Soviet export cuts. Paweł Tarnowski, "To był piękny rok," *Polityka-Eksport-Import*, no. 1 (January 1991), p. 1.
25. This protective shield was crucial to the survival of CMEA. As Soviet economist S. Iakovlev recently observed,
    We have essentially used our national resources, so that our CMEA partners could build socialism Stalinist style. The principle of proletarian internationalism was for us not a simple slogan but a guide for action [*Trud*, 12 March 1990, p. 3].
    One should bear in mind, however, that "socialism Stalinist style" as well as CMEA were imposed on East-Central Europe by the Red Army. And proletarian internationalism was a not too well disguised ideology of Soviet

imperialism. Without the protective shield of distinct intra-CMEA trade arrangements, Moscow would have had to use brute force to make sure that East-Central Europeans continue building "socialism Stalinist style," which would not have been necessarily a cost-effective solution.

26. Moscow Television Service, 30 July 1990; "Katushev Reviews Changes in CEMA," FBIS-SOV-90-148 (1 August 1990), p. 1.
27. Quoted in V. Mikhailov, "Farewell, National Ruble," *Izvestiia,* 2 July 1990; FBIS-SOV-90-129 (5 July 1990), p. 1.
28. Moscow radio, 30 May 1990; "Trade Ties with Hungary reviewed," FBIS-SOV-90-105 (31 May 1990), p. 26.
29. *The New York Times*, 4 January 1988, p. 8.
30. See Stanisław Długosz, "W obliczu trudnego wyzwania," *Rynki zagraniczne*, 26 July 1990, p. 3.
31. See Kjell Engelbrekt, "Agreement with the USSR on Step-by-Step Transition to Hard Currency Trade," *Report on Eastern Europe*, 13 April 1990, pp. 1-4.
32. "Deterioration in Intra-Regional Trade of the Central European Countries," *Meeting Report* (New York: Institute for East-West Security Studies, 1991), p. 1.
33. The World Bank, *Socialist Economies in Transition:* 1, no. 6 (September 1990), p. 4. Other estimates are in a similar range; Soviet experts, for instance, predict a surplus of $10 to 12 billion.
34. Ibid.
35. Quoted from "Krociowe zyski ZSRR," *Życie gospodarcze, no. 39 (30 September 1990), p. 12.*
36. "Trade Ties with Hungary Reviewed," Moscow radio; FBIS-SOV-90-105 (31 May 1990), p. 26.
37. For the cross exchange rates, see Marie Lavigne, "The CMEA Transition from the Transferable Ruble," *Report on Eastern Europe* (2 November 1990), p. 36.
38. The term "subsidy" should be qualified. Because of the insulation imposed by Moscow through CMEA on the East European countries, they were subject to a different regime than the one prevailing in the rest of the world. As a result, relative scarcities and prices of goods and commodities differed from those in the world economy. Because of the lower level of CMEA industrialization, industrial products were relatively more expensive than raw materials. Therefore, had there been no contacts with the outside economic environment, there would have been no grounds to mention subsidies. For an excellent discussion of this point, see Marian Guzek, "Sytuacja Europy Wschodniej a Hipoteza Marrese-Vanousa," *Gospodarka świata i Polski w 1989 i 1990* (Warsaw: Instytut Koniunktur i Cen Handlu Zagranicznego, 1990), pp. 64-70.
39. *Socialist Economies in Transition*, op. cit.
40. See *Życie gospodarcze,* 30 September 1990, p. 5.
41. Paweł Tarnowski, "Ile będziemy płacić za benzynę ?" *Polityka*, 10 November 1990, p. 4.

42. For a seminal study on the dramatic decline of East-Central Europe's competitiveness during the 1970s, see Kazimierz Poznanski, "Competition between Eastern Europe and the Developing Countries in the Western Markets for Manufactured Goods," in U.S. Congress, Joint Economic Committee, *East European Economies: Slow Growth in the 1980s, Selected Papers* (Washington, D.C.: U.S. Government Printing Office, 1986), vol. 2, pp. 62-90.
43. For instance, the GDR had a CMEA-sanctioned agreement to purchase buses exclusively from Hungary (*The Economist*, 31 March 1990, p. 49). Similar "monopoly-type" arrangements existed for other products. They provided suppliers with no incentive to improve quality or technologically to update their products.
44. Katalin Antalóczy, "Mi lesz a KGST után?" *Magyar Hirlap*, 8 August 1990, p. 9.
45. Quentin Peel, "Members agree to bury Comecon," *The Financial Times*, 7 January 1991, p. 2.

4

Security in Europe's Eastern Half

Daniel N. Nelson

Soviet hegemony in East-Central Europe belongs to history, and Moscow's fragile control over the USSR is clear. From the Baltic to Bosporus to Urals, Europe confronts a postcommunist and posthegemonic environment. The effort to create democratic systems and the effort to construct new foundations for national security are, thus, inextricably intertwined.

The Warsaw Treaty Organization (WTO or Warsaw Pact) represented Soviet hegemony. That it no longer functioned and would soon cease to exist became common observation by late 1989.[1] What was once an instrument by which the USSR's High Command would have absorbed non-Soviet Warsaw Pact forces into the Red Army's theaters of military operations (TVDs)[2] became, probably by late 1989 and certainly by early 1990, a fiction maintained both to mollify the Russians and to simplify the Conventional Forces in Europe (CFE) talks at Vienna.

For all of this, NATO members can breathe a sigh of relief since the type of threat against which the United States and its allies created a common defense has evaporated. No one sees the remaining Soviet troops in the five eastern provinces of Germany, notwithstanding their number, as an imminent threat; their pay, after all, is coming from the German treasury and their morale and readiness are highly questionable. The Red Army withdrawals from Czechoslovakia and Hungary were completed in mid-1991, although the ecological devastation left behind will be a reminder of their presence for decades to come.[3] In 1990, Hungary joined the GDR to become the second state to withdraw from the Warsaw Pact,⁴ and the time line of the WTO expired on 1 July 1991.⁵

The collapse of the Warsaw Pact, and the larger political-military condominium of communist party regimes, was not as sudden as it appeared. There had been ample evidence during the prior ten years of divergent "alliance behavior" in the Warsaw Pact that accelerated and deepened toward the end of that decade.⁶

Yet, when it finally came, the USSR's strategic retreat and abdication by communist parties in other pact states rapidly denuded the alliance of any military significance—with the Soviets doing their utmost simply to insist that the edifice had some residual consultative role in the political realm.⁷

Even such a minimal role seems unlikely to have much of a future. During the CFE negotiations, members of both NATO and the WTO had to determine the proportion of total weapons in their alliance that could be held by one member. Of agreed-upon alliance ceilings—e.g., 20,000 tanks each for NATO and the WTO in the Atlantic to the Urals (ATTU) region—the next question became an intraalliance issue: What is the maximum number of weapons in each category that one country can possess? On this issue, the USSR argued initially that its level of sufficiency ought to be 40 percent of the entire ATTU total (or 16,000), which would constitute 70 percent of the WTO's total after CFE. The Poles and others objected to this limit on their own military equipment, because it would have allowed only 4,000 tanks for all non-Soviet Warsaw Pact (NSWP) countries, and aimed for a lower Soviet allocation—about 65 percent of the intraalliance total.

This dispute, which flared up in September 1990, at the pact's "Special Commission on Disarmament" meeting, threatened to delay a WTO agreement critical to CFE. Another problem, *among* the non-Soviet pact members, involved misgivings about being allotted smaller shares of WTO equipment than neighbors. Soviet flexibility was demonstrated when Moscow accepted lower levels (13,150 tanks) than those to which James Baker and Eduard Shevardnadze had agreed, enabling various NSWP countries to retain slightly larger inventories. The Czechoslovaks also gave ground, accepting smaller tank totals and proportionately larger cuts from existing stocks of other weapons so that the remaining East-Central Europeans could retain somewhat higher levels.⁸ Only through these Soviet and Czechoslovak efforts were pact negotiators able, on 3 November 1990 in Budapest, to sign an accord setting limits for such conventional weapons in the WTO area.

This episode is illustrative, for it points unerringly to the national focus for security that has replaced anything resembling a consortium of like-minded governments seeking to defend their political systems. Now that the façade of Warsaw Pact unanimity has been destroyed, one finds national security decision-making consummated in the environments of reemergent, sovereign states with uncertain protodemocracies and/or postcommunist turmoil. Writing in the *Stuttgarter Zeitung*, Andreas Braun spoke of the countries between Germany and the USSR as facing "nationalism, countless minority problems and a temptation to resort back to totalitarianism" while "in the Balkans, there has even been the horr[ible] vision of general civil war."[9]

Under these new conditions, how will the states between the Baltic and Bosporus seek their security? And, as new national security policies take shape, what effects can be expected on the USSR's deepening socioeconomic and political turmoil?

DESPERATELY SEEKING SECURITY

Security is a dynamic ratio between threats and capacities. To be threatened is to be placed in peril; threat is not the act of harming, but the imminent danger of being harmed. This environment or condition is not amenable to simple quantification, since inherent to threat assessment are judgments of the intent, skill, or sophistication (among many other intangibles) of an adversary.

For states as much as for individuals, security is an ongoing effort to sense and assess threats, to diminish or limit them if possible, and always to retain capacities equal to or greater than the threats perceived in one's environment. "Capacities," in this context, are the raw material of power—human and material resources—that have been fashioned into social, economic, political, or military strengths.

Security's dynamic character is evident whenever efforts to heighten capacities exacerbate threats, and a perilous reciprocity is begun. This is the conceptual anatomy of an arms race or of economic competition and trade wars.

Raising these preliminary conceptual points is critical for the following discussion. Contrary to early and more hopeful judgments about Europe's future, politico-military transformations have meant that the security needs of the continent's states and political systems have *grown* and not diminished. However, achieving a dynamic equilibrium between threats and capacities is no longer the unambiguous military-focused effort it had been during the more than four decades of post-World War II superpower bipolarity.

Instead, as unilateral reductions of force levels have outpaced CFE-imposed limitations on conventional arms, security will be sought less and less from capacities created in the military realm. Military effort, gauged both in *extractive* and *performance* components,[10] is being diminished significantly within Europe. Expensive standing armed forces will remain, although they will confront budgetary stringencies that limit research, development, and deployment of new weapons. Further, defense establishments will be limited by public opposition to conscription, to defense burdens that absorb vast resources without adding to socioeconomic well-being, and to weapons production, deployment, and testing that raise environmental concerns.

An important part of the pressure for demilitarizing security comes from the recognition, argued by Mikhail Gorbachev already in 1986 as he sought to articulate his view of the "new thinking," that "no country [has] any hope of safeguarding itself solely with military and technical means, for example by building up a defense, even the most powerful."[11] The broadening of security to mean the absence of peril to economic, social, or environmental well-being is entirely appropriate and overdue. Yet, this adds urgency to the issue of ensuring an equilibrium between threats and capacities; popular expectations see new dangers that have little to do with adversaries against whom heavily armored divisions and supersonic combat aircraft have been arrayed.

If one were to presume a stable threat scenario, the replacement of military capacities with diplomatic skills, economic strengths, and social cohesion would be a plausible route to security in Europe of the 1990s and beyond.

Unfortunately for Europe, and sadly for the peoples now rid of communist party rule, the entire east-central half of Europe is a "threat-rich" environment, composed of weak (low-capacity) political units. Some are stronger than others, and some face fewer or less ominous threats. But the overall characterization is appropriate; in posthegemonic, and largely postcommunist Europe, there are few capacities with which to deter or defeat emerging threats.

The entire region, notwithstanding the end of Soviet and communist party dominance *and* an arms control accord that lowers superpower (especially Soviet) conventional armaments, has minimal economic efficiency, doubtful viability in the world market, endangered social cohesion, and still-dubious political legitimacy. Institutions are transitional, leaders inexperienced, and policies tentative. There are weak governments and postcommunist systems that, in several cases (the USSR, Yugoslavia, and perhaps elsewhere in the Balkans), cannot easily protect the state.

threats and different ways in which to protect governments, systems, and, ultimately, the state.

When Poles, Hungarians, Bulgarians, and so on, now ask "Who is our enemy?" or "From where are we threatened?", their assessments in the 1990s clash with those of the previous regimes. There remains no longer even a minimal deference to Moscow, except in the case of Bulgaria and even this is waning. Rather, there is a forceful resurgence of historical animosities and fears evident, for example, when Polish parliamentary leader and long-time Solidarity strategist Bronisław Geremek said that any German attempt to alter the Oder-Neisse line would precipitate war.[24] That the "Two plus Four" Accord spoke to these concerns of Poland, and that a bilateral Polish-German agreement in late 1990 may have mitigated this sensitivity, do not obviate the reorientation of Warsaw's security. Poles and others who had been subservient allies to the USSR are now redefining what their security means. As noted earlier, security is a function of the dynamic balance between threats and capacities. How capacities may be enhanced, and the degree to which one is the target of immediate and significant threats, are thus two sides of the same security calculus.

Internal threats, as enumerated above, are no less "real" to the new systems of postcommunist Europe or the USSR's central and republican governments. Indigenous communists and recalcitrant secret police, neofascists, and mass unrest among minorities, workers, and students are the subjects of widespread fears. Imminent armed conflict across state borders is not the daily concern of new governments and leaders, whereas internal threats are palpable. Nevertheless, interstate disputes are real, and political actors utilize these conflicts to enhance their rhetorical appeal, thereby heightening extant tensions.

For each state's new postcommunist government, different conditions have already led to divergent national security policies. Nevertheless, there are some uniformities. Although bilateral security ties with Moscow are not rejected by Bulgaria or even Poland, there is a keen desire to avoid alignment with the USSR or any successor Russian-focused union. Moreover, no country between the Baltic and Bosporus would willingly accept any continuation of a Soviet/Russian military presence on its territory in the form of combat units. All—particularly Czechoslovakia, Hungary, and Poland—see themselves as "Western" and want to pursue their security by looking away from, not toward, Moscow.

Beyond these broad elements, however, there is little consistency among the five remaining former non-Soviet Warsaw Pact states. Were one to add other Balkan states (Yugoslavia, Albania, Greece, and Turkey) to this mix, the security "disorder" in Europe's eastern half begins to appear fraught with dangerous uncertainty.

At one end of the spectrum, so to speak, are Hungary and Czechoslovakia. By late 1989 and early 1990, restructuring of the Hungarian military and plans for cuts in Czechoslovak forces made it clear that both countries have adopted a war-fighting strategy akin to territorial defense.[25]

Neither country's ground forces by 1992 will possess heavily armored tank divisions, and both will field only a few mechanized rifle divisions that will be insufficient to provide a credible conventional force. Instead, both states will rely on lightly armored, mobile infantry, plus quick mobilization of reserves to provide an "all-around" defense. Rather than deploying heavily armored forces in one operational direction, both countries have elected to redeploy troops away from western borders and toward the center and eastern borders. Were either state attacked by larger well-equipped forces, without sufficient time to mobilize reserves, it will be prepared only to mount a conventional defense for a few days, after which its fate will depend on outside help.

Czechoslovak force levels will fall to about 130,000 (plus or minus 10,000) from approximately 200,000. The Hungarian armed forces will diminish from just above 100,000 to as few as 70,000 active-duty personnel.[26] Much lower troop strength in the active forces, the deactivation of units, and the destruction of principal weapons have all been undertaken unilaterally, distinct from the CFE process (which, by itself, has very little impact on most former non-Soviet WTO states' military establishments).

Total reductions to be made and the rapidity with which they will be undertaken have both been heightened in the period since Mikhail Gorbachev's 7 December 1988 speech at the United Nations, where he announced a 10 percent cut in the Red Army's manpower and partial pullbacks from East-Central Europe. For example, the former Hungarian defense minister, Ferenc Kárpáti, at first announced an 11,400-man cut from his armed forces (about 12 percent) as well as elimination of 251 tanks and 430 artillery pieces. By December 1989, then Prime Minister Miklós Németh was speaking of a 24 percent reduction of active-duty forces to be implemented by the end of 1991.[27] In the summer of 1990, military officials in Hungary were themselves acknowledging that a "considerably smaller army" in the range of 70,000 to 75,000 would be adequate (i.e., more than a 30 percent drop in manpower).[28]

Poland also had reduced the number of personnel on active duty from over 320,000 in late 1988 to about 302,000 in early 1990. The Jaruzelski-Rakowski government announced, in early 1989, that "tens of thousands" of troops were to be released and two motorized rifle divisions eliminated that year. These rather vague goals were later clarified to mean a cut of 40,000 troops over two years, plus the withdrawal from service of 850 tanks and 80 fighter planes. The Poles also indicated that they had already placed two mechanized divisions into Category III status (cadres only) and had downsized two airborne divisions into brigades.[29] Further according to General Zbigniew Blechman, who commanded the important Pomeranian military district until late 1989, the army's three mechanized infantry and two armored divisions would be restructured into three mechanized divisions, with corresponding changes in armaments (fewer tanks, more antitank weapons).[30] *Żołnierz wolności* provided additional information on the reorganization of Polish ground forces and the restructuring of two tank divisions into less heavily armored mechanized-rifle divisions.[31]

Ultimately, Polish force levels will probably fall to 250,000 men. Although the Poles may have ample reason to maintain a relatively large and well-equipped military, the general staff has begun to speak out about the costs of independence (from the Soviets). The new chief of the Polish general staff, Lieutenant General Zdzisław Stelmaszuk (appointed to that post on 1 October 1990), is known to advocate a smaller, more modern force. Defense Minister Piotr Kołodziejczyk, for example, has noted that even a smaller force calls for "significantly increased" funding if the country is to modernize its inventories at a time when buying the same tanks or aircraft at world-market prices will cost many times the "old" intra-WTO cost.[32]

The significant difference between Polish and Czechoslovak or Hungarian high commands, however, is that the Poles continue to insist that higher spending *is* needed and that further cuts are unwise. Some Hungarian defense officials have, it should be noted, argued that "conflicts of interest" could increase between Hungary and other countries, and defended military expenditures as a contribution to the country's technological development.[33] Poland's national security, however, cannot be based on territorial defense and will certainly continue to imply a robust conventional force sufficient to give pause to any adversary who might attack the country's national territory. Defense Minister Kołodziejczyk, during a radio broadcast in October 1990, made this *caveat* clear:

> Despite the great optimism that we attach to the Helsinki process, to the Vienna negotiations, the easing of tensions in Europe, we are not free from certain fears, for we, as military people, must always accept as the foundation of activity the least favorable, the most difficult, situation. And it is in such a context that we are planning our activity for the coming year. . . . We are . . . conscious that the

armed forces, as long as they are indispensable to the state, must be efficient, and must give full guarantees for the security of our borders....[34]

The Balkan WTO members, Romania and Bulgaria, have not taken proportionate steps. In early 1989, the Zhivkov regime agreed to a 10 percent reduction in Bulgarian People's Army (BPA) personnel, and by early 1990 the armed forces were down to 107,000 men.[35] The BPA, particularly while Dobri Dzhurov remained defense minister (he was replaced in late summer 1990), was adamantly opposed to further reductions and its spokesmen often compared the sizable Turkish forces deployed in Eastern Thrace and just east of Istanbul to the Bulgarian armed forces.[36] The BPA is likely to retain over 100,000 on active duty, but only parts of its three army commands should be considered effective, and all will experience increasing difficulties with equipment maintenance and readiness because of severe budgetary shortfalls. Manpower constraints will also impinge on BPA vitality, since ethnic Turks constitute a disproportionate part of the conscript pool.

The Romanian army is uniquely insulated, for the moment, from restrictions. Although its budget will be constrained by the country's severe economic problems, the government is both dependent on the army and fearful of Defense Minister Victor Stănculescu's ability to control his own officers and troops. About 180,000 personnel are in the Romanian armed forces, although only a small proportion might be considered even close to "combat ready." The military's principal role in Romania has become, since it fought Nicolae Ceauşescu's *Securitate* in Bucharest and elsewhere, primarily political. General Stănculescu, of course, vigorously denies that the army would ever serve the interests of any party or consider the possibility of a military dictatorship.[37] Although army public relations efforts stress its role as a defender of the country's frontiers, most of its best-trained and well-equipped forces are now deployed in and around the capital as well as in regions of the country where ethnic unrest is most likely. However, because internal discipline is so uncertain[38] and the precise direction of its activities questionable, most Romanian political figures hope to let the army rest undisturbed.

Security based solely on military capacities has been abandoned by the new leaders in Prague and Budapest, and the defense establishments lack the political strength or will to offer much resistance. Poland, with its own economic limitations and the enormity of once again awakening to find ominous instability to the east and a reunified Germany, must still maintain credible ground and air defenses. Yet, Poles also are looking elsewhere for security reinforcements. Armed forces in Romania and Bulgaria are worried less today about securing frontiers than their role in domestic political turmoil, although the number and volatility of interstate disputes might propel the militaries back into the security business.

ALTERNATIVES FOR EAST-CENTRAL EUROPEAN SECURITY

In late September 1990, the ministers of defense and foreign affairs of Poland, Czechoslovakia, and Hungary attended a meeting at Zakopane, Poland, to consider "the role of these states' armed forces under the new conditions."[39] All were WTO members at the time of this meeting. The event remains significant because it was the first time a public session among that alliance's East-Central European members had taken place at which Soviet representation was specifically not invited. As explained by Polish Deputy Defense Minister Bronisław Komorowski to *Gazeta wyborcza,* and quoted by *Izvestiia,* the exclusion of the USSR had been purposeful: "The USSR has not been able to make sufficient progress on the path of democratization. Moreover, its army has always played a preeminent role among the allies, and that is exactly why we are not inviting its representatives."[40]

Detaching themselves from any security linkage with the USSR is the *first* step in developing truly national capacities vis-à-vis threats. That requires, of course, a multifaceted approach. Most obviously, Red Army combat units, technicians, and/or advisors must leave. Officers within East-Central European armies, who have been most closely associated with the Soviets and subservient within the Warsaw Pact, need to be retired or moved aside. Further, residual obligations and ties through the Warsaw Pact have to be terminated. In addition, however, arms purchases must be diversified, and officer training and education must be indigenous or broadened.

Withdrawals from Czechoslovakia and Hungary were completed in mid-1991.[41] Hungary has already enacted the necessary legislation to end its membership in the pact. Czechoslovak President Václav Havel stated in October 1990 that the pact should cease by summer 1991, because it had "outlived its day."[42] Former Polish Prime Minister Tadeusz Mazowiecki, despite an early reluctance to counsel the departure of Soviet troops or a quick abandonment of the Warsaw Pact, urged the Red Army to depart from Poland by the end of 1991. Further, he suggested in November 1990 that the pact should end and be replaced with "bilateral agreements between sovereign nations."[43]

Gradually, the older officers' corp that held command during the decades of Soviet hegemony is being retired. Occasionally, the ouster of such officers—even defense ministers—has been precipitated by revelations about their actions in the waning year or months of communist rule. Such was the case with General Miroslav Vacek, who, prior to being appointed by Havel as defense minister, had been chief of the general staff of the Czechoslovak army. In the latter capacity he had, it was revealed in October 1990, "complied with orders aimed at the use of the army against the population" in the November 1989 period. Havel replaced Vacek with a civilian—Luboš Dobrovský, who had served as deputy foreign minister, but had no prior military experience. His credentials for the post were primarily the long-time association with Charter 77 and Civic Forum.[44]

The five former non-Soviet WTO countries, independently, have requested training for their military officers in the United States as part of the International Military Education and Training Program.[45] Were the Pentagon to approve such requests, Polish, Hungarian, et cetera, higher-ranking officers would begin courses at institutions such as U.S. command and staff colleges. Romania's defense minister acknowledged a desire to see his officers receive "further studies" in England, France, Italy, and Germany (in addition to the USSR).[46] Czechoslovak officers have already begun to attend the *Bundeswehr Akademie* near Munich.[47]

Thoroughly rejecting Soviet or Russian security guarantees does not mean that these states anxiously await a protective presence from other powers. Instead, as a foreign policy counselor to Bulgarian President Zhelyu Zhelev noted upon returning from a trip to Turkey, "guarantees should be sought *not* from this or that great power, but should be secured by joining the all-European security system and by settling openly and honestly our relations with our neighbors."[48]

Bilateral, regional, and multilateral security arrangements are thus being sought as a means by which to enhance capacities and limit threats.

At the multilateral level, East-Central European views extend well beyond the tentative steps toward institutionalizing CSCE, taken at the Paris summit in November 1990. Czechoslovak and Polish ideas for a Pan-European security structure emerging out of CSCE, but far different from the consensual and limited Helsinki process, were floated in spring 1990 and continue to be advocated by foreign ministers and presidents of those countries.[49] Czechoslovak efforts to have Prague named as the site for the small permanent CSCE Secretariat were successful.

Involvement is eagerly sought with institutions that had their origins in post-World War II Western Europe. Hungary and Czechoslovakia have been at the forefront of this effort, in part because they are (correctly or not) viewed as having the best chance for a smooth transition to a stable democracy.

Budapest's entry into the Council of Europe (the parliament at Strasbourg) in November 1990 will almost certainly be followed by Czechoslovak and Polish admissions in 1991. The council may become, in the early 1990s, the basis for a Pan-European assembly that operates as a representative organ of CSCE. Whether or not the council's secretary general, Catherine Lalumière, is too hopeful when she suggests that it may be the basis for a future "European confederation," it *is* clear that the former communist-ruled states of East-Central Europe want to be included wherever the "action" is.[50]

Regional groupings also have been vigorously pursued. Yet, such security arrangements have obvious pitfalls; they usually consist of countries most likely to be antagonistic toward one another, and often include only states that are weak individually, and together are weaker yet. Their proximity is, then, no guarantee of security.

Nevertheless, the *Pentagonale* is one example of the experimentation with alternative groupings that might enhance governmental, systemic, or state security. An inaugural Venice meeting in early August 1990 implied strongly overlapping economic, environmental, and human rights interests, with evident concern for stability in the region.[51] Géza Jeszenszky, Hungarian foreign minister, spoke of his hopes for the Venice meeting by emphasizing the possible future role of the *Pentagonale* in dispute mediation.[52]

How the *Pentagonale* might underpin the capacities of a particular state when confronting internal or external threats is not clear. Yet in autumn 1990, as Hungary was being rocked by debilitating strikes and some signs of violence, the Italian foreign ministry issued a note concerning these events. In part, it read that "Italy is prepared, ... in the framework of ... *Pentagonale* cooperation, to take all measures, giving concrete support and assistance to Hungary."[53]

In the Balkans, a continuation of foreign ministers' conferences, begun in 1988, led to an important meeting on 24-25 October 1990 in Tirana. Balkan cooperation has a long, and inglorious, history.[54] But the efforts now are toward expanding intra-Balkan activities in many domains, some of which affect security although not incorporating military ties per se. Broadly speaking, there is no question that regional stability and a greater Balkan "voice" in European political structures represent goals of these meetings.[55] Romania seems particularly eager to institutionalize the Balkan conferences into, according to Foreign Minister Adrian Năstase, a "forum" with both a structure and dedicated tasks in human rights, economic cooperation, and security.[56] There is no shortage of interstate complaints and criticisms, yet the larger aims have thus far continued to drive each country toward continued participation.

Bilateral contacts and de facto security guarantees multiplied enormously during 1989 and especially 1990. Romania has renewed pre-World War II ties with the French army and has been discussing possible ship-building and training cooperation with the Spanish navy. The defense ministers of Hungary and Romania met in October 1990 as well to begin a program, according to the Romanian side, "designed to increase trust between our armies, including mutual checks to ensure that neither side has intentions that are belligerent."[57] The Hungarian view mirrored that intention; Defense Minister Lajos Für noted that, in the condition of a "superpower vacuum . . . it is vital for us to fill this vacuum in some way." And, Für continued, "Bilateral military relations are inevitable in this transitional period, if security is to be guaranteed. These bilateral relations could eliminate a situation of threat or endangerment."[58]

Perhaps the most well-developed bilateral security arrangement emerging in the posthegemonic period has been the Bulgarian-Greek linkage. Sofia and Athens, even before the ouster of Zhivkov or the defeat of Papandreou, were providing assurances to each other about peaceful intentions and a cooperative spirit.[59] The countries signed a September 1986 protocol, for example, that was viewed as threatening by Turkey, against which the rapprochement was clearly directed. By 1990, even while Bulgarian-Turkish relations had improved somewhat, the assiduous efforts of both Greek and Bulgarian leaders to speak of warm ties and special relationships suggest an attempt to enhance capacities vis-à-vis shared threats—Macedonian nationalism and possible Serbian involvement, plus the Turk and Muslim populations.[60] This effort by both sides to enhance the bilateral relationship, one should underscore, spanned parts of the political spectrum in Greece and Bulgaria. PASOK and New Democracy parties (socialist and conservative) in Greece were equally eager to see improved ties with Sofia, and both the Bulgarian Socialist (communist) Party prime minister, Andrei Lukanov, as well as the Union of Democratic Forces (opposition) leader Zhelyu Zhelev, who later became Bulgaria's president, traveled to Athens prior to their country's June 1990 elections.[61]

A widening net is being cast, then, to rebuild a new basis for security in the eastern half of Europe. With much less devotion to military efforts, these systems must now reinforce their sometimes negligible capacities. Although only illustrative examples have been offered here, there is no question that new governments in states over which the USSR long held decisive control are exploring many routes simultaneously—bilateral, regional, and multilateral. For none of these countries is the question of national security yet resolved. Policies are formative, and initiatives are tentative. But the old dilemmas of finding strengths with which to deflect present or future peril to nation and state in a "threat-rich" environment are once again omnipresent.

EFFECTS ON SOVIET SECURITY

Disintegrative trends are widespread within the USSR and need no encouragement from East-Central Europe. By late 1990, few positive assessments could be heard from within Soviet academic or political circles concerning the country's prognosis.[62] Pockets of entrepreneurial activity will not alone lead to economic recovery, and the absence of central political authority has reverberated throughout the "union."

But the dangers to USSR security, and specific threats emanating from within and between the union republics and all-union government, *have* been affected considerably by changes in the Baltic-to-Bosporus corridor and current efforts by each new system to resecure itself. The disjunctive effects on USSR and/or republic security are of several varieties.

First, *direct* ties between countries of East-Central Europe and the unrest within Soviet borders exist in several cases. The violence in the Moldavian SSR in late 1990 cannot be disassociated from the overthrow and execution of Nicolae Ceauşescu in neighboring Romania. Encouraged by the end to Ceauşescu's tyranny, and their long-standing ethnic/linguistic identity with the Romanian state, Moldavians sought explicit linkage to Romania—a step that is entirely unacceptable to the sizable Russian, Turkic, and other minorities in Moldavia. Schisms among these communities exploded not only because Kishinev had wider latitude from Moscow in the Gorbachev era, but also because Ceauşescu's ouster provided hope, opportunity, and a sense of historic destiny to "reunite" into a "greater Romania" that had existed from 1918 until the Red Army occupation in 1944. Other minorities, with either a national state across the border or additional population with the same ethnic identity (e.g., Poles in Ukraine and Belorussia), were similarly emboldened by East-Central European transformations.[63]

There are, moreover, disruptive consequences *in* Soviet political life from the "loss" of East-Central Europe. Before, during, and after the 28th CPSU Congress, the "who lost East-Central Europe" debate was raised in earnest by an amalgam of antireformists to discredit the Gorbachev leadership.[64] Each demand for accelerated Soviet withdrawal or compensation, and every assertion of political or military ties to the West, added to the sense in Moscow that historic interests in a *cordon sanitaire* had been sacrificed and that a strategic retreat had become destabilizing. For Russians, it now seems that they are alone, without any long-coveted buffer zone.

And, there is also the for now remote but still plausible emergence of an anti-Russian coalition from East-Central Europe that would pose a real and imminent *military* threat against Moscow's heartland. As much as Germany of the early 1990s is democratic, with a *Bundeswehr* limited to 370,000 personnel, and otherwise occupied by rebuilding its eastern provinces, no security planner in Moscow can presume that German interests and those of countries between the Baltic and Bosporus may not someday coalesce again in an anti-Russian coalition. One does not have to look too deeply to recall substantial Ukrainian, Slovak, Romanian, and other nationalities' cooperation with the Germans in their attacks on the Russian-dominated Soviet Union during World War II. As these new political systems and governments launch their own autonomous foreign and defense policies, one can be assured that the Red Army's general staff will watch carefully for any signs that such a remote contingency is becoming less remote.

CONCLUSION

Security from the Baltic to Bosporus to Urals, once "provided" to communist regimes via the Red Army and the bonds of the Warsaw Pact, was ultimately not much security at all. As in so many other cases, wherein massive military expenditures were thought to buttress illegitimate rulers, the failure of systemic performance and public antipathy formed the nucleus of a "popular *coup*."

Once the old regimes were ousted and the Red Army began its withdrawals, every internal and external threat that had been in Europe's eastern half since World War II has recurred. Some are now muted because of Germany's democracy. But many others are as much, if not more, disruptive to postcommunist governments, political systems, and even states themselves than disputes in the first years of this century.

The national security policies of new leaderships reflect the perils within and around their states; there is evident uncertainty about how to proceed, and only one conclusion self-evident to all—try everything that might limit threats and/or enhance capacities vis-à-vis perceived threats. As East-Central Europeans undertake these multifaceted steps, the ripples will be felt in Moscow. As old *Russian* fears about potential alliances against them are exacerbated, and intra-Soviet ethnic schisms are made even more volatile by association with, or in reaction to, neighboring states, Moscow's security planners will look nervously beyond the Bug and Prut rivers. In these respects, security after hegemony will provide rest for no one.

NOTES

1. One of the more evocative ways of stating this was provided by George C. Wilson, "An Age of Lower Limits," *The Washington Post National Weekly Edition*, 4-10 December 1989, p. 6, when he wrote that "[the] Warsaw Pact [is] breaking up like an ice pack under a hot sun."
2. Polish defector Colonel Ryszard Kukliński's widely cited revelations, first published in the Polish-language journal *Kultura* (Paris), were summarized in "The Crushing of Solidarity," *Orbis* 32:1 (Winter 1988) by Richard Pipes.
3. A good example of the devastation in Hungary is reported in "A kártérités variációi," *Magyar Hirlap*, 5 September 1990, p. 9. Rather bitterly, the editorial notes that the Soviets ask for 30 to 35 billion forint to finance their withdrawal while, in fact, the Red Army is leaving behind many illegally constructed buildings that are now in terrible disrepair. Further, the report notes that Hungary is seeking compensation for environmental damage that will total "billions of forints."
4. The Soviets carried a brief announcement of the definitive Hungarian announcement in *Pravda*, 4 October 1990, p. 5.
5. When the WTO military structure was abolished on 25 February 1991, it was agreed that the last Political Consultative Committee session would be held in Prague on 1 July 1991 to dissolve also that organ. Tibor Ferkó (from Budapest), "Full Stop Behind Military Organization," *Národná obroda* (Bratislava), 26 February 1991, pp. 1 and 4; FBIS-EEU-91-040 (28 February 1991), p. 1.
6. For the background of varied behavior among the seven WTO members, see Daniel N. Nelson, *Alliance Behavior in the Warsaw Pact* (Boulder: Westview Press, 1986). An assessment of the politico-military implications of communist regimes' demise in 1989-1990 appears in Daniel N. Nelson, *Watching the Pact Unravel* (Cologne: Bundesinstitut für ostwissenschaftliche und internationale Studien, 1990), no. 32.
7. See, for example, a 24 October 1990 Moscow World Service statement by Iurii Solton regarding the postponement of the WTO Political Consultative Committee meeting that was to have been held in Budapest on 3-4 November, as translated in *Daily Report: Soviet Union*; FBIS-SOV-90-207 (25 October 1990). See also the TASS commentary of 27 October 1990, entitled "Future of Warsaw Pact," FBIS-SOV-90-209 (29 October 1990), p. 1.
8. The final numbers for tanks, combat aircraft, attack helicopters, armored combat vehicles, and artillery were published in a number of sources. See *Reports from Vienna*, no. 11 (8 November 1990), p. 3.
9. *Stuttgarter Zeitung*, 17 October 1990.

10. This distinction and the measurement of both dimensions of military effort have been discussed in a number of articles. For example, see Daniel N. Nelson, "The Distribution of Military Effort in the Warsaw Pact", in U.S. Congress, Joint Economic Committee, *Pressures for Reform in East European Economies* (Washington, D.C.: Government Printing Office, October 1989), pp. 187-207.
11. This statement was contained in Gorbachev's report to the 27th CPSU Congress in "Politicheskii doklad tsentral'nogo komiteta KPSS XXVII s'ezdu," *Kommunist,* No. 4 (1986), p. 54.
12. The security implications of social heterogeneity have been explored in Daniel N. Nelson, "Security and Society in Eastern Europe" (Washington, D.C.: Carnegie Endowment, 1990), unpublished manuscript.
13. A case study of uncertain civil-military relations in south-eastern Europe are discussed in Daniel N. Nelson, *Political Dynamics and the Bulgarian Military* (Cologne: Bundesinstitut für ostwissenschaftliche und internationale Studien, 1990).
14. Two argumentative essays about the case of Poland and its effort to make a radical economic transformation beginning in January 1990 are Jon Wiener, "Capitalist Shock Therapy," *The Nation,* 25 June 1990; Jeffrey Sachs and David Lipton, "Poland's Economic Reform," *Foreign Affairs* 69:3 (Summer 1990), pp. 47-66. Both articles, and many others, acknowledge the social consequences of marketization, although there is wide disagreement about the political consequences and the potential for unrest.
15. A comprehensive look at the anatomy of Polish political apathy—its sources and consequences for democratization—are in David Mason, Daniel N. Nelson, and Bohdan Szklarski, "Apathy and the Birth of Democracy: The Polish Struggle," *East European Politics and Societies* 4:1 (forthcoming, 1991).
16. This list is taken from Daniel N. Nelson, "Not All Quiet on the Eastern Front," *Bulletin of the Atomic Scientists* (November 1990), pp. 35-38.
17. This was the view of Bronisław Geremek, Solidarity parliamentary leader, while in the United States during October 1990. See also John Tagliabue, "Germans and Poles Agree to Pact on Oder Border," *The New York Times,* 9 November 1990.
18. One such commentary was by Tibor Bogdán in *Magyar Hirlap,* 27 September 1990, p. 5; translated in FBIS-EEU-90-192 (3 October 1990), pp. 24-25.
19. "Greek Official Makes 'Anti-Albanian Statements,'" Tirana Domestic Service, 3 September 1990; FBIS-EEU-90-171 (4 September 1990), p. 1. Also, "Greece is Warning Albania on Killing of 2 Ethnic Greeks," *The New York Times,* 9 October 1990.
20. Francis X. Clines, "6 Killed in Ethnic Violence in Moldavia," *The New York Times,* 5 November 1990; also Leyla Boulton, "Soviet Troops Sent to Moldavia," *The Financial Times* (London), 29 October 1990.
21. For a consideration of how large this problem might become and its dangerous implications, see Daniele Joly and Clive Nettleton, *Refugees in Europe* (London: Minority Rights Group, 1990).

22. Nelson, "Not All Quiet...", op. cit.
23. This section draws on material first presented in Daniel N. Nelson, *Watching the Pact Unravel*, op. cit, pp. 26-35.
24. Geremek's statement was quoted in "Poles Would Fight to Keep Border," *International Herald Tribune* (Paris), 1 February 1990.
25. These plans were made clear by General László Borsits, then Hungarian chief of staff, and by his Czechoslovak counterpart, Major General Anton Slimák, at the 35-nation Confidence and Security Building Measures (CSBM) conference in Vienna during January 1990. Borsits stated directly that his country's armed forces were moving toward territorial defense, while Slimák pointed out adaptations to domestic and international changes which include cuts in the armed forces, budgets, and length of military service. See Andrew Slade's account in "WP Command Changes Ahead," *Jane's Defence Weekly*, 27 January 1990, p. 136.
26. The figures for prior force levels are taken from *The Military Balance* (London: IISS, 1986 through 1989). Projected force levels for the 1992-1993 period are drawn from the author's interviews with CFE/CSCE delegations from these countries in Vienna during late April and early May 1990. One should note that these numbers are lower than, for example, Hungarian Defense Minister General Lajos Für was acknowledging at the end of September 1990. In an interview with Budapest Television on 30 September 1990, Für spoke of a 90,000-man Hungarian military force at the end of 1992. See FBIS-EEU-90-191 (2 October 1990), p. 21. This was, however, an estimate based upon earlier 1990 plans. The 70,000 figure reflects cuts projected, apparently, into 1993-1994.
27. A report on Németh's announcement appeared in *The Washington Post*, 2 December 1989.
28. Colonel György Szentesi, head of the Defense Ministry's main department of security policy, as interviewed on Budapest Domestic Service, 8 August 1990; FBIS-EEU-90-154 (9 August 1990), p. 26.
29. Defense Minister Florian Siwicki, as quoted in *Trybuna ludu*, 4 January 1989.
30. "General Details Polish Force Cuts," *Jane's Defence Weekly* (17 June 1989).
31. See *Żołnierz wolności*, 7 September 1989.
32. Interview with Vice Admiral Piotr Kołodziejczyk, Polish defense minister, in *Rzeczpospolita*, 8 August 1990.
33. These views were expressed by Ernö Raffray, political secretary in the ministry of defense over Budapest Domestic Service, 6 October 1990; FBIS-EEU-90-195 (9 October 1990).
34. Defense Minister Vice Admiral Piotr Kołodziejczyk, speaking over Warsaw Domestic Service "Radio Military Magazine" program on 28 October 1990; FBIS-EEU-90-210 (30 October 1990), p. 36.
35. BTA Dispatch of 8 August 1990; FBIS-EEU-90-154 (9 August 1990), p. 15.

36. See, for example, Colonel General Vasil Zikulov's commentary in *Narodna armiia*, 29 May 1990, pp. 1-2.
37. Bogdan Ficeac, "Vrem Armată Modernăși Unitate", *România Liberă*, 17 October 1990, p. 7. See also an interview with Defense Minister General Victor Stănculescu in *Adevărul*, 13 October 1990, p. 1, in which he explicitly denies political concerns of the army.
38. That the defense minister himself is concerned about his hold on the army was suggested at a 16 October 1990 press conference, the text of which was released by Rompres that day and translated in FBIS-EEU-90-202 (18 October 1990), p. 39.
39. Plans for this meeting were first reported in *Gazeta wyborcza*, 20 September 1990, and announced by a Reuters dispatch of the same day. This quote is from coverage by *Izvestiia*, 21 September 1990, p. 3.
40. Ibid.
41. The agreement between Czechoslovakia and the USSR for troop withdrawal was signed in Moscow on 27 February 1990. By the end of October 1990, according to the Czechoslovak Embassy in Washington, D.C., "78 percent of Soviet tanks, 66 percent of armored vehicles, 79 percent of artillery, 81 percent of planes, [and] 58 percent of soldiers" in the Red Army had departed from Czechoslovakia.
42. Reuters dispatch (21 October 1990), as carried in *Current News Early Bird*, 22 October 1990.
43. UPI dispatch (5 November 1990), as cited in *Current News Early Bird*, 5 November 1990, p. 16.
44. Accounts of this episode were, for example, contained in broadcasts and dispatches by Prague Domestic Service and ČTK. See their accounts of 18 October 1990; cited in FBIS-EEU-90-203 (19 October 1990), p. 12.
45. "U.S. May Train Warsaw Pact Officers," *The Baltimore Sun*, 5 November 1990, p. 5.
46. Stănculescu interview, op cit.
47. As reported in *Lidové noviny*, 19 October 1990, p. 4.
48. Interview with Dimitŭr Ludzhev in *Otechestven vestnik*, 24 October 1990.
49. The Czechoslovak notion of Pan-European security was presented in an April 1990 memorandum issued by the Ministry of Foreign Affairs of the Czech and Slovak Federal Republic, entitled "Memorandum on the European Security Commission" (Prague, 6 April 1990). Foreign Minister Jiří Dienstbier had developed this theme in an address at the Royal Institute of International Affairs in early April 1990. See Edward Mortimer, "Prague Suggests New European Security Set-up," *The Financial Times* (London), 4 April 1990, p. 3.

The Polish views were articulated on several different occasions. See, for example, "The Proposal of Polish Premier Tadeusz Mazowiecki to Create the Council for European Cooperation, CEC" (Washington, D.C.: Embassy of Poland, 1 May 1990). Also the Polish Foreign Minister Krzysztof Skubiszewski expanded these views in "Discours à la session

extraordinaire du Comité des Ministres du Conseil de l'Europe" (Lisbon, 24 March 1990); mimeographed.
50. The Italian news agency ANSA carried an account of Hungary's Council of Europe membership on 26 October 1990; reprinted in FBIS-EEU-90-210 (30 October 1990), p. 29.
51. Several accounts of *Pentagonale* meetings are worth consulting. For example, the Czechoslovak reaction can be found in *Hospodarské noviny*, 2 August 1990, pp. 1 and 8.
52. Géza Jeszenszky was interviewed over Budapest Domestic Service on 31 July 1990, before the Venice meeting. See FBIS-EEU-90-148 (1 August 1990), p. 34.
53. The Italian note was quoted in an MTI (Hungarian news agency) dispatch from Rome on 28 October 1990; FBIS-EEU-90-210 (30 October 1990), p. 29.
54. For a brief account, see Daniel N. Nelson, "The Warsaw Treaty Organization and Southeast European Political-Military Security," in Paul S. Shoup, ed., *Problems of Balkan Security* (Washington, D.C.: Wilson Center Press, 1990), pp. 123-150.
55. See, for example, the statement of Albanian Foreign Minister Reiz Malile in *Zëri i popullit*, 21 October 1990; FBIS-EEU-90-205 (23 October 1990), p. 5.
56. Năstase's proposal was contained in an interview published by *Libertatea*, 17 October 1990.
57. Stănculescu interview, op. cit.
58. Interview with Defense Minister Für, conducted by Péter Vajda and published in *Népszabadság*, 20 October 1990, p. 1; FBIS-EEU-90-205 (23 October 1990), p. 31.
59. The 1986 document is discussed by Stephen Ashley, "Greek-Bulgarian Friendship Treaty," in Vojtech Mastny, ed., *Soviet-East European Survey, 1986-1987* (Boulder: Westview Press, 1987), pp. 318-325.
60. Bulgarian Prime Minister Andrei Lukanov stressed that "a new state in our relations" had blossomed because of his meeting with the new and conservative Greek prime minister, Constantin Mitsotakis, in Athens during mid-May 1990. Mitsotakis had earlier spoken of Bulgarian-Greek relations as being "essential as an important stabilizing factor in the Balkans and in Europe." See the BTA dispatch of 17 May 1990; FBIS-EEU-90-097 (18 May 1990), p. 6.
61. For a somewhat more thorough account of these visits and their political rationale, see Daniel N. Nelson, "Political Dynamics and the Bulgarian Military," op. cit., pp. 40-42.
62. Innumerable articles and commentaries, of course, have appeared on this topic, i.e., Soviet disintegration and the ethnic, economic, or other propellants of such a catastrophe for a unitary communist-ruled state. Here, however, the comment is based principally on personal observations and discussions, especially in September and November 1990 when traveling to Moscow, Leningrad, and Central Asia.

63. A review of these ethnically embedded problems of interwoven peoples and borders is far too complex a task for a brief paper. For a broad treatment, and useful comparative discussion, see George Schöpflin's "National Minorities in Eastern Europe," in G. Schöpflin, ed., *The Soviet Union and Eastern Europe,* rev. ed. (New York: Facts on File, 1986), pp. 302-312.
64. A flavor of these criticisms can be found in the interviews with the chief of the Soviet general staff, General of the Army Mikhail A. Moiseev, *Krasnaia zvezda,* 10 February 1990, p. 2, and of USSR defense minister, Marshal Dimitrii T. Iazov, also in *Krasnaia zvezda,* 5 June 1990, p. 2.

5

Relinquishment of East Germany

Robert Gerald Livingston

As for Germany, Mikhail Gorbachev wrote in his book *Perestroika* (1987), "What has formed historically here is best left to history. This also holds true for the issue of the German nation and for forms of German statehood... There are two German states with different social and political systems... And what there will be in a hundred years is for history to decide. For the time being, one should proceed from the existing realities and not engage in incendiary speculations."[1]

It took not a hundred but only a single year, 1989-1990, for German realities to change more rapidly and completely than during the entire 45 years since the end of World War II. By the close of 1990, one of Gorbachev's two German states, the German Democratic Republic (GDR), had disappeared, absorbed by the other, the Federal Republic of Germany (FRG). German unification occurred so quickly—and so smoothly and peacefully—largely because Gorbachev and his foreign minister, Eduard Shevardnadze, had the sense to see that outsiders could not halt it, the audacity to change Soviet policies totally, and the skill to gain substantial concessions for what by any measure is the greatest setback for the Soviet Union since Hitler's invasion a half century ago.

Gorbachev paid little attention to German issues for the first four years after his assumption of power in 1985,[2] giving top priority instead to his domestic reform agenda and, in foreign affairs, to relations with the United States. His readiness in 1988 to allow the communist regimes of Eastern Europe a "freedom of choice" in setting their policies, his encouragement of reforms in those countries, and his renunciation of military means to enforce Soviet discipline upon them did, however, set the stage for the subsequent dramatic shift in Moscow's policy on German unity.

Until June 1989 there were few signs that such a shift was coming. Gorbachev rebuffed several West German overtures;[3] and the East German communist party (the SED or Socialist Unity Party) continued spurning his reformist ideas, even going so far as to censor out from the East German press passages in his speeches which it adjudged too liberal.

When, in mid-1989, Gorbachev decided to operationalize his policy toward Germany, he moved with the calculation, decisiveness, and flair which had become his hallmark. Visiting West Germany in June, where he was welcomed by rapturous crowds in the streets, the Soviet president signed a declaration that underscored "the right of all peoples and states freely to determine their destiny . . . [and also] respect for the right of peoples to self-determination." Such wording signaled Soviet willingness to give the German people, although divided in two states, freedom to choose their "form of German statehood."[4]

Hitherto Gorbachev had displayed little new thinking about the Soviet policy position on Germany, which had remained virtually unchanged since at least 1953. Since World War II, the supreme Soviet objective in Europe had been to prevent Germany's again becoming a threat to Soviet security, as it had twice been since the Bolsheviks seized power in Russia. The best way to accomplish this, as Stalin and all his successors until Gorbachev had concluded, was to keep the Germans divided in two states.

With time the Soviet-dominated one, the GDR, assumed great importance in and of itself for Moscow. It became the keystone in the Soviet Union's protective security structure in Eastern and Central Europe. Some 380,000 Soviet troops (with 120,000 dependents) were stationed there permanently, five times more than in Czechoslovakia and seven times more than in Poland. The GDR became the glacis of Soviet power in Central Europe. It was the richest fruit of the great victory over the Germans in World War II, a victory purchased at the cost of more than twenty million Soviet dead.

With time too the GDR became a great economic asset.[5] It was Moscow's largest foreign trade partner, delivering quality manufactures on the one hand and depending almost 100 percent on Soviet gas, oil, and other raw materials on the other. With occasional mild deviations, its leadership, until Gorbachev came along, distinguished itself by a fealty to the Kremlin that bordered on obsequiousness.

It is hardly surprising, then, that even the best foreign analysis right down to 1989 held that the Soviet Union would not relinquish its grasp of the GDR.[6]

The "key to German unity," it was held by Chancellor Kohl of West Germany no less than by all other western leaders, lay in Moscow, as it had since the 1950s. That phrase implied both that without the Kremlin's support the GDR might cease to exist—a view which the events of 1989-1990 proved correct—and also that Moscow would not abandon it—one which they proved wrong.

Let us not forget that while the West German government had not abandoned its constitutional and political commitment to unification Bonn, since the early 1970s had been treating the GDR much like any other state. Its devotion to unity had assumed the form of ritualistic incantation. In 1987 Kohl received Honecker with full honors on a state visit in Bonn. Kohl and other West German leaders regarded unification as, at best, a goal for the next century. As late as September 1989, the West German chancellor stated his belief that it was not an issue currently on the international political agenda.

Evidently by late 1987 some Soviet academic advisors were arguing that the division of Germany no longer lay in the Soviet interest.[7] Their chief contention was that with the growing autonomy of Poland, Czechoslovakia, and Hungary, the keystone function of the GDR in the Soviet security system had become superfluous. What, if any, influence such think-tank analyses may have had on Gorbachev is hard to say. Even after his affirmation during his West German visit of the Germans' right to self-determination, he remained during the summer of 1989 with the position which he had presented to the readers of *Perestroika* two years earlier—that the division of Germany resulted from history, that German unification was "unrealistic," and it was not on the international agenda.[8]

GERMAN UNIFICATION ACCEPTED: OCTOBER 1989-JANUARY 1990

Within less than a year, the Soviet Union accepted not only German unification but membership of a united Germany in the adversarial alliance, NATO. In so doing Gorbachev completely overturned the Soviet Union's postwar German policy, relinquished its control over the GDR, and abandoned its advanced strategic position in the center of Europe.

This stunning reversal occurred in three distinct stages: during the first, from early October 1989 until late January 1990, Gorbachev continued to resist the idea of German unification in the short run while gradually coming to accept it in principle; during the second, the decisive stage, from early February until June 1990, he came to accept it in fact as well as in principle, while insisting that a united Germany must be embedded in international security structures and then, with great reluctance, conceding that NATO membership for the new Germany could serve that purpose; and finally, during the third stage, from July until September 1990, the Soviet Union conducted intensive bilateral negotiations with West Germany on compensation in economic and security terms for its agreement to unification.

Let us briefly examine the events that defined each of these three stages and brought about this dramatic alteration of long-standing Soviet policy. Scholars dispute the degree to which the Soviets were surprised by and were mainly reactive to these events and the degree to which they anticipated them, acted according to plans, and tried to control them.[9]

The upheaval that speeded the downfall of Erich Honecker, the communist party chief who had ruled since 1971, began the first Monday of October 1989 on the streets of Leipzig, spreading later to Berlin, Dresden, and other East German cities. The first wave of demonstrations roughly coincided with Gorbachev's 7-8 October visit to Berlin for the GDR's fortieth-anniversary celebrations. Without doubt he privately urged reforms upon Honecker and his politburo as a way to preempt the forces building against them. Publicly he threw out broad hints, observing within earshot of Western reporters that "life punishes whoever comes too late."[10] But Honecker and his colleagues turned a deaf ear. As Gorbachev later recounted to friendly West German social democrats, he realized then and there that communist rule was doomed and the GDR itself was probably no longer salvageable.[11]

It is likely also that Gorbachev made it clear to Honecker that Soviet army units in the GDR would not intervene to put down the demonstrations. Whether orders to that effect came from him, from the Defense Ministry in Moscow, or from the commander of the Western Group of Forces, the GDR-based units themselves, is in question. In any case, the Soviet army remained in its barracks and showed unexpected tolerance as the demonstrations, always peaceful and nonviolent, gathered momentum during October and November. Without assurances of Soviet military support, Honecker and those who succeeded him in October and November at the head of the SED, first Egon Krenz and then Hans Modrow, lacked the cold-blooded will to order East German army and police units alone to suppress the upheaval.

By November it seemed clear that the Soviets were being driven by the revolutionary process. Neither they nor the new communist leadership in East Germany were controlling it. The East Berliners breached the Wall on 9 November. They and their countrymen throughout the GDR began to move west in ever-growing numbers, with emigration to the Federal Republic

(FRG) from East Germany reaching 2,000 to 3,000 each day by early January 1990.

Even though the SED's authority was slipping away and the GDR starting to disintegrate, the Soviet leadership for several months clung to hopes that a "reformist" communist party might yet save the day. The SED rebaptized itself in December, first into the SED-PDS and later into the PDS (*Partei des Demokratischen Sozialismus* or Party of Democratic Socialism), but its mass membership was deserting. Of 2.3 million SED members in the early autumn of 1989, only 700,000 remained in the PDS as 1990 began.

The Soviet Union also clung to its traditional policy position on Germany, even as the foundations for that policy crumbled away. Its spokesmen kept reiterating during November, December, and on into January that the two German states were "realities" which were necessary to secure peace in Europe, that a unified Germany would be a threat to stability, that unification was not a matter for "current politics," and that the GDR was a Soviet ally to whom no harm would come.[12]

The Soviet president could hardly fail to see that the interactive pressures between the two Germanys, whose borders were now open to each other, and the gathering pace of revolutionary upheaval inside East Germany threatened to deprive the Soviet Union of control and even of influence over developments in Germany. And not only the Soviet Union.

Britain, France, and even the United States—the other three of the four victorious powers of World War II with special responsibilities laid down by the Potsdam Agreement of 1945 and subsequent accords—were all growing uneasy at the tumult and trends. Chancellor Kohl and his center-right administration in Bonn had been worried since September that the upheaval in Leipzig, Dresden, and East Berlin would end bloodily, with perhaps a Soviet military intervention. On 28 November, Kohl announced in the Bundestag a ten-point program which envisaged first a package of treaties (*Vertragsgemeinschaft*) between the two German states, leading in four or five years to "confederal structures," then eventually to a confederation (*Staatenbund*) and finally to a federation (*Bundesstaat*) between them. This was the first West German effort to seize the initiative and apply controls to the German-German unification process—an effort which was to expand rapidly and eventually come to dominate the process in the ensuing eight months. Bonn did not yet dare to come out foursquare for unity soon, and Kohl shrank from doing that during an emotion-laden visit to Leipzig where he met Modrow on 19 December 1989.

It would appear that Gorbachev came to see during January that since, as the veteran social democratic leader Willy Brandt had expressed it just before

Christmas, "what belongs together is growing together," the better part of wisdom was for the Soviet Union to accept what it could not prevent. The East German party and state were rapidly withering away. The moment for Moscow itself to act had come, if it were to remain a party to the unification process, to help influence its outcome, and to gain at least some benefits and concessions from it.

On 30 January then Gorbachev gave the first public sign that Moscow was changing course. During a visit to the Kremlin by the new East German leader, Hans Modrow, the Soviet president observed that "in principle" German unification was not in doubt. Of course, he added, a unified Germany must be neutral between the alliances, NATO and the Warsaw Treaty Organization.[13]

UNITY ENDORSED AND NATO MEMBERSHIP ACCEPTED: JANUARY-JUNE 1990

Gorbachev's 30 January announcement opened the second stage of Soviet policy on German unity, during which Moscow joined with Washington, Paris, London, and even more intensely with Bonn, to bring the unification process under international control, develop a framework for managing it, and then identify an international structure into which the unified German state would be integrated so that it would pose no threat to Soviet security. The USSR now became a partner in the unification process, an often uncertain, decidedly reluctant, and quite unhappy partner to be sure, but a partner nonetheless.

The next breakthrough came right on the heels of Modrow's visit: during a meeting with Kohl at the Kremlin on 10 February, Gorbachev agreed publicly that the Germans had the "right" to live in a single state. To Kohl's assertion that a united state would want to belong to NATO, the Soviet president made no rejoinder—but also no public objection. With Gorbachev's agreement now pocketed, Kohl's satisfied national security advisor Horst Teltschik observed on the trip home to Bonn that the "key to German unity" had at long last passed from Moscow to Bonn.

The Soviet Union had finally accepted German unity in the near future as being inevitable, but it now also started to explain that German unification must be "synchronized" with the broader process of East-West European unification. This contention, of course, relegated German unity to a distant day, for nobody could imagine East-West European unification (whatever it might mean) coming soon. Moreover, the Kremlin had already begun asserting that "Four Power Rights and Responsibilities" must be brought into play. At its initiative, a meeting of ambassadors representing the Four had been called in Berlin on 11 December—the first time they had met for 18 years. Bonn, correctly, interpreted this as a warning flag from the Soviets (and also from the British and French) that they planned to play a role in the management of German unification.

Seeking a framework that would accommodate the Four and the Federal Republic as well, the U.S. secretary of state hit upon the negotiating formula "Two plus Four", the order of precedence being designed to acknowledge demonstrably that the "two" German states should lead. James Baker first won the West German foreign minister, Hans-Dietrich Genscher, for this scheme, then his British and French counterparts, and finally Shevardnadze.[14] Announced at a foreign ministers conference in Ottawa during mid-February, "Two plus Four" served thereafter as the framework for negotiating the international aspects of unification. In the event, the talks quickly took on the character of "One plus Four," as the East German representative played only a bit part compared with the role of his experienced, energetic, and ever resourceful West German colleague.

Pressures within East Germany for quick union mounted as the winter wore on. The outflow into the promised land of West Germany surged. On Leipzig's streets the cry now was, "If the deutsche mark does not come to us, we will go to it." Responding to the pressures, Kohl overrode the arguments of his central bank and announced in mid-winter that a German-German currency union would take effect on 1 July 1990. To guarantee democratic legitimacy of East German assent to decisions that were ending the communist system and preparing union with the Federal Republic, elections to the GDR's parliament, the Volkskammer (the first free balloting in the eastern part of Germany since before Hitler) were moved up to 18 March.

Faced with such inexorable domestic German pressures, the "Two plus Four" negotiators, when they finally got together for their first plenary session in May, discovered that the issues had reduced themselves to only two real ones: the settlement of a united Germany's eastern frontier, the so-called Oder-Neisse question (after the rivers which the Potsdam Agreement had decided upon as the provisional frontier with Poland), and the question of a united Germany's alliance membership.

Even when urged by President Bush at their Camp David meeting at the end of February, Kohl was not quite ready yet to alter the long-standing West German legal position that only the government of a united Germany would be empowered to settle the frontier issue definitively. His calculation was mainly of a domestic political nature, a wary unwillingness to expose himself to attacks and a possible loss of votes in the forthcoming national elections in December 1990 to the extreme right, now represented by the *Republikaner* who were showing some solid strength in Bavaria, Berlin, and a few other areas. Nevertheless the Oder-Neisse issue seemed by May to be resolvable soon, since many other leading West German politicians, including some important ones within Kohl's own Christian Democratic Union, were prepared to make the concessions needed to satisfy the Poles. A way was soon found—in the form of resolutions sanctifying the existing frontier that were to be passed before unity by both the West and East German parliaments. The Oder-Neisse was never the problem it initially appeared to be, especially to the anxious Poles.

But the second "Two plus Four" issue threatened to imperil the negotiations and, briefly, even German unification itself. Washington insisted that a united Germany must belong completely to NATO, that is, also to its integrated military command and not merely, as France since 1966, to the alliance alone. After some slight initial hesitation, Kohl too agreed with this and said so publicly at the Camp David meeting.

Equally adamant and insistent from the moment they accepted unity in principle, on 30 January, Gorbachev and Shevardnadze rejected NATO membership for the united Germany. During his meeting with Modrow on 6 March, the Soviet president emphasized "with all resolve" that it was "unacceptable" and "absolutely excluded."[15] At the first "Two plus Four" meeting in early May, Shevardnadze used tough language when he ruled the idea out.

Between January and July, Soviet representatives from Gorbachev on down floated a variety of often irrelevant and sometimes contradictory proposals relating to unification and the alliance membership of a united Germany. Puzzling, backtracking and self-deflating trial balloons during these months made it unusually difficult to understand the Soviet policy objectives, other than slowing the pace of German unification.

The plethora of Soviet proposals during these months included calls for a "peace treaty"; an international referendum on unity; neutrality for a unified Germany; membership in both alliances, NATO and the Warsaw Pact; a "French solution" of membership in NATO but not its military command; and—as late as the end of June—continuance of Four Power rights in the unified Germany for three to five years. Soviet officials and commentators also kept making a variety of random proposals during the period on conventional and nuclear force dispositions in Central and Eastern Europe after German unification.[16]

Leading voices in this scattershot campaign were the usual Soviet academic experts on Germany such as Viacheslav Dashichev of Moscow's Institute of East European and Foreign Policy Studies and Yurii Davydov of the Institute of U.S. and Canada Studies, as well as Nikolai Portugalov, a member of the party's Central Committee staff, and Valentin Falin, head of the Central Committee's international department and former Soviet ambassador to Bonn. A half-dozen lesser experts and military officers kept busily offering their opinions on Germany's unification and its inclusion in NATO to eager West German newspaper, television, and radio interviewers, most of whom identified their interlocutors as Gorbachev advisors.

Behind the cacophony, contradictions, and changeableness of these official, quasiofficial, and unofficial Soviet views on Germany doubtlessly lay an effort to deal with internal opposition to Gorbachev's growing willingness to accede to German unification by a heterogeneous group of conservative party *apparatchiki*, Russian nationalists, and hard-line military men. Venting this group's anxieties, resentments, and anger, Egor Ligachev, a conservative politburo member, vehemently assailed Gorbachev's policy in early January. He warned against the "imminent danger" and the "unpardonable shortsightedness . . . not to see that now on the international horizon there is arising a Germany with gigantic economic and military potential," against a repetition of the "prewar Munich," and a "swallowing up of the GDR."[17]

Gorbachev continued to have to contend with such resurgent conservatives until German unification was complete—and afterward during the "Two plus Four"" treaty ratification debate in the Supreme Soviet in early 1991. They charged him with selling out the legacy of the Soviet Union's historical World War II victory and permitting Germany for the third time within a century to arise as a threat. Had they been consulted, they would no doubt have wanted Soviet tanks to move into Leipzig in 1989 as they had into Prague in 1968 and Budapest in 1956. Convincing them and perhaps skeptical Foreign Ministry veterans like Falin or the Berlin expert A. P. Bondarenko that there would be gains and benefits too from consenting to German unification must have been one of Gorbachev's most pressing domestic political tasks during the second stage of Soviet policy developments that are being reviewed here.

Developing positions which would help Gorbachev in his struggle with such adversaries became a central feature of western, particularly American and West German, diplomacy during this stage and the last. The aim was to construct a package which Gorbachev and Shevardnadze could "sell" to these men. USSR diplomacy and communist party politics became tightly interwoven as seldom before.

By May the Soviet foreign minister was ready to give up his previous insistence that German and European unification be synchronized.[18] And the crucial concession came at the 1-2 June Washington summit between Bush and Gorbachev, where the USSR leader finally consented to full NATO membership for the united Germany.

What factors precipitated this decisive concession? They included a lack of plausible alternatives combined with Western efforts to limit NATO in new ways and to transform it so as to make the alliance more acceptable to the Soviet Union.

Whatever forlorn hopes the USSR may still have cherished about the viability of a reformed East Germany were dealt a death blow in the GDR's 18 March parliamentary elections. The Soviet Union was shocked when the communists' successors, the PDS, fell to a mere 16 percent of the vote and the social democrats, Moscow's next best hope, won only 22 percent while the East German versions of Bonn's liberals (FDP) and Christian Democrats together scored a smashing 53 percent.[19] Any conceivable thought of maintaining an autonomous East German state now vanished entirely.

For all the spate of proposals put out by Soviet officials and commentators during the spring, moreover, Moscow was unable to come up with a credible politically viable international security structure other than NATO to contain the united Germany, which everyone agreed, the Germans themselves above all, must be integrated into such an organization. What in fact was there besides NATO to bond the new Germany to its neighbors and friends? There remained only NATO. At a Warsaw Pact meeting on 17 March, the Soviet Union discovered that its own allies, the Czechoslovaks, Poles, and Hungarians favored NATO membership for a united Germany.[20] East German voters a day later in effect chose NATO too by electing the pro-NATO CDU and FDP. The Soviet Union now found itself completely isolated in its opposition to the NATO option for the united Germany.

The framework of the Four Powers responsible for Germany had outlived its day, for the united Germany would in many ways outshadow all of them. The Conference on Security and Cooperation in Europe (CSCE), a loose set of continuous meetings among East and West European countries with the United States and Canada, had not yet evolved sufficiently. The U.S. and Britain in any case remained doubtful that the CSCE could serve as much more than a collective security system somewhat like the interwar League of Nations, an organization which had tragically demonstrated its inadequacy.

As part of their effort to convince Gorbachev that Germany's NATO membership would be more to the advantage the Soviet Union more than would its neutrality, the United States and West Germany decided to limit and modify the alliance in ways which would make it look less threatening to Moscow and which would, as the Kremlin liked to put it, "take account of legitimate Soviet security interests."

The first step to that end, in the early spring of 1990, was the Genscher Plan.[21] The German foreign minister proposed that after unity NATO would not move either non-German NATO troops nor any nuclear weapons into the territory of the former GDR, that for several years to come only German territorials not NATO-assigned units would be stationed there, and that Soviet troops could remain until 1994.

The second step was taken at the Bush-Gorbachev summit in early June 1990, where the American president offered to advocate at the next NATO meeting (in early July), the diminishing of reliance on nuclear weapons and to make other changes in strategy which would underscore the defensive character of the alliance. (The ensuing NATO communiqué even went so far as to proclaim "friendship" for the Warsaw Pact countries.) At the same time, the West German government conveyed to Moscow its readiness to reduce the army of a united Germany well below the combined levels of the West German *Bundeswehr* and the GDR's *Nationale Volksarmee*.

The West German-American concessionary strategy toward Gorbachev at this point was twofold. On the one hand Bonn and Washington offered concessions to the Soviet leader which would make it easier for him to swallow the bitter pill of German unification and to present it to his adversaries in Moscow as beneficial to the USSR. On the other hand they tried to maximize Gorbachev's stake in preserving future relationships with Washington and Bonn, an element of the strategy that became pronounced after June in the third stage of Soviet policy development.

The question of German membership in NATO, which was the principal issue during this second stage, placed Gorbachev before a terrible dilemma. To try to block German unification over this issue was to risk a crisis in Europe which would most surely set back his efforts to open up his country to the modernizing impulses of a European connection. To accept unification in NATO, however, was to acknowledge a strategic defeat of historic dimensions. Even the American and German strategy of concessions could not obviate this dilemma.

COMPENSATION FROM THE GERMANS: JULY-SEPTEMBER 1990

In this final stage, the concessionary strategy took the form of West German compensation to Moscow for its agreement to unification within NATO.

Events moved quickly. At the 28th congress of the communist party in early July, orthodox ideologists had upbraided Gorbachev over his German policy. Shevardnadze offered the same argument in defense of that policy at the congress which Dashichev had made more than two years earlier in his memoranda—that a security guarantee for the Soviet Union based on the "...artificial and unnatural division..." of the Germans could not be reliable.[22] Once Gorbachev and Shevardnadze had emerged from the congress victorious, the duo hastened to conclude an agreement with Kohl and Genscher. Like all the decisive turns in Soviet policy toward Germany during the past year, these final steps bore the clear personal imprint of the Soviet leader. West German diplomats were convinced that the conclusive agreements with the USSR at this stage were the product of Gorbachev's and Shevardnadze's decisions alone, taken by them without the knowledge of and likely against the advice of Falin and the German experts of the foreign ministry.[23]

On the Western side, initiative now rested wholly with Kohl and Genscher. With the "key" completely in their grasp, they turned it quickly to open the door to German unity.

The two traveled to the Caucasian resort of Zheleznovodsk for a 16-17 July meeting with Gorbachev and Shevardnadze at which the deal was struck. It not only opened that door but also initiated what may become a new era of German-Soviet bilateralism.

To seal the Soviet Union's agreement to Germany's unification and its integration in NATO and to assure the final withdrawal of the Soviet army from the territory of the former GDR by 1994, the two negotiators from Bonn offered significant compensation, both in security and economic terms.[24] Besides the Genscher Plan's provisos, which excluded NATO-assigned troops from East German territory and created a zone free of nuclear weapons there, Kohl and Genscher agreed that the *Bundeswehr* of a united Germany would not exceed 370,000 men. That was a level which was, as Shevardnadze had pointed out to the communist party congress, smaller by far than the West German army alone (494,000 men). As importantly, the West Germans agreed to make major contributions toward easing the financial burdens of the Soviet military withdrawal and toward helping Gorbachev to modernize the USSR economy.

At the end of June, the German federal government had already announced that it would guarantee the entire amount of a DM 15 billion, 15-year commercial credit from German banks, the largest guarantee ever given by the government.[25] Now Bonn agreed to cover the stationing costs for the Soviet troops remaining in East Germany (estimated later at DM 6 billion over four years) and for their relocation and housing back in the Soviet Union (estimated later at DM 12 billion over the same period). It also promised to implement selected commercial commitments previously made by the GDR to Soviet enterprises (estimated at DM 3 billion for 1990 and 3.4 billion for 1991).

Kohl and Genscher returned in triumph from the Caucasus. Final steps toward completion of unification followed rapidly: the definitive Polish frontier was set in a "Two plus Four" meeting of mid-July; the treaty of legal and constitutional unification between the Federal Republic and the GDR was completed 31 August and went into effect on 2 October; and the Treaty on the Final Settlement with Respect to Germany was signed in Moscow by the "Two plus Four" on 12 September 1990.[26]

For the future, Moscow attached great importance to insuring a broad and multifaceted relationship with the powerful new German state. To outline such a relationship, the Soviet Union and the Federal Republic on 13 September initialed a "comprehensive treaty" prescribing "good neighborly" relations and partnership and designating a wide range of fields of cooperative efforts.[27] Article 3 of the treaty provided that, if either side were attacked, the other would render the attacker no assistance, a commitment that some foreign commentators thought might one day come into conflict with the Federal Republic's NATO obligations. The treaty was hailed in Germany as opening a new era in German-Soviet relations.

SOVIET MOTIVATIONS

Why did Gorbachev agree, in less than a year, to a complete reversal of previous Soviet policy that had long been based on the division of Germany? Two reasons stand out.

First, the Soviet Union shared with West Germany, France, Britain, and the United States a common interest in quickly bringing the upheaval in East Germany and the resultant political and societal instabilities under international control. Underlying this consideration was the instinctive understanding that once the Berlin Wall went down in November the popular movement toward unification was inexorable, that it would occur with or without foreign governments' approval, and that it could always be stimulated and reinforced from West Germany if external countries tried to block it. Since the Soviet Union could not block the movement, it had no choice but to join it.

Second was the absolute priority which Gorbachev had assigned to his domestic reform agenda and his conviction that that agenda's success required the Soviet Union to be kept open to Western and particularly German advice and assistance. It was essential, therefore, for the Soviet president to gain German goodwill and cooperation for the future, an assurance that was given form in the comprehensive treaty of 13 September. The German leadership, particularly Foreign Minister Genscher, was sensitively attuned to the Soviet Union's wish not to be isolated or excluded from Europe, to its desire that its strategic setback be somehow cloaked, and to its aversion to any sign of defeat or imposition of humiliating conditions.

West German diplomacy, therefore, sought to assure Gorbachev that his country, despite its military withdrawal from the center of Europe, would continue to play a leading role on the continent. Bonn laid stress on the CSCE, a structure which had originated in USSR proposals of the late 1960s, as a forum for a leading Soviet role. West Germany was best able to meet Gorbachev's needs to demonstrate at home that the Soviet retreat had brought not only a diminishment of power but also tangible economic and security benefits.

SOVIET GAINS AND LOSSES

Considering the progressive weakness of his government's domestic position and the steep decline in Soviet authority in its former East European empire, Gorbachev was able to play a weakened hand surprisingly well. He gained for the USSR a long-term relationship with the rising European power which, had he tried to oppose unification, he might have lost for some time to come. A popular West German publicist put it as well as any political scientist:

> Gorbachev's dream partner abroad for [his] revolution from above is the Federal Republic. It has decisive weight in the North Atlantic Alliance. It offers political stability. It is an economic superpower. Even under Chancellor Kohl it has a moderating effect on the U.S. The Kremlin's leader hopes for cooperation from Bonn in solving his security problems and economic stimuli for his reforms.[28]

So far, such calculations look good. The West Germans have been careful to avoid causing Gorbachev difficulties with his most pressing security problems in the Baltic countries. They now champion Soviet causes with their friends and allies. Against U.S. wishes, the Federal Republic successfully urged inclusion of the USSR in the new European Bank for Reconstruction and Development. At the 1 July 1990 summit at Houston of the leading seven industrial countries, the G-7 meeting, West Germany (together with France) advocated immediate Soviet membership in the International Monetary Fund and World Bank. Within the European Community, the Germans have backed economic and emergency food assistance for the USSR. And at Christmastime, Kohl encouraged a widespread public CARE package campaign in his country to alleviate food shortages in Soviet cities. On 27 February 1991, and in order to create an even greater incentive for the Supreme Soviet to ratify the "Two plus Four" treaty, Bonn declared its willingness to negotiate with Moscow on compensation for the more than eight million forced laborers brought to Hitler's *Reich* in World War II.[29]

Moscow can also count on concrete economic advantages from its relationship with the new Germany.[30] Unless traditional patterns change radically, commerce between the two, now about 15 percent of Soviet foreign trade turnover, may eventually rise to between 17 and 20 percent. Germany will surely continue to be the Soviet Union's largest foreign trade partner, far ahead of other countries. Even more important will be the technical, managerial, and administrative skills which Germans can provide, as they did for centuries when Russia was ruled by the Romanov dynasty.

In the security field too, Soviet gains are not inconsiderable. Limitations on the size of the *Bundeswehr,* effective denuclearization and partial demilitarization of the eastern part of the united Germany, and a definitive settlement of all German frontiers in the east work to the USSR's security advantage. For all the rhetoric of Germany's attaining "full sovereignty," its 13 September 1990 treaty with the Four Powers restricts it in many ways, which enhances Soviet security. Most important of all, Germany reaffirms (Article 3), as it has many times in the past, its renunciation of "the manufacture or possession of and control over nuclear, biological, and chemical weapons." For the USSR, which possesses them all, this pledge must be very welcome.

These gains, however, cannot mask the essence of German unification as far as the Soviet Union is concerned. On this point Gorbachev's conservative, nationalist critics have it right: the rise of a new powerful Germany and the corresponding collapse of USSR power in Central and Eastern Europe represents a setback of historic dimensions. Within only one year, the Soviet Union abandoned its most loyal and strongest ally, the GDR, and witnessed the disappearance of the communist system there with its party-led institutions and its membership in Soviet-dominated organizations, such as the

Warsaw Treaty Organization and the Council for Mutual Economic Assistance, themselves now vanished. More bitter yet and potentially dangerous, it had to assent to the absorption of this ally within what remains an adversarial military alliance. In countries such as Poland, Czechoslovakia, and Hungary, German cultural influence is now displacing Russian, and German investors and businessmen the economic bureaucrats from Soviet ministries and foreign trade organizations.

FUTURE GERMAN-SOVIET RELATIONS

As long as the Federal Republic, which was established in 1949, existed, its friends in the West could easily forget that there was more to "Germany" than the West Germany to which they had become accustomed. They could easily forget too that Germany had always been a Central and Eastern European rather than a West European country, a country with strong historical links to Poland and especially to Russia. These links are now being restored, and the USSR and Germany have additional new ways of influencing each other as well. Until the 360,000 or so remaining Soviet troops finally leave the eastern German states, Moscow still retains some leverage in Germany deriving from its World War II victory. Security relationships of a different kind have developed between Germany and the Soviet Union, chiefly within the frameworks of the CSCE and the negotiations on conventional troops in Europe.

Economics will play a major part in defining future German-Soviet relations. German banks are far and away the USSR's largest foreign credit source, with almost DM 20 billion outstanding, three-quarters of it guaranteed by the German government, a sum far greater, for instance, than German bank credits to all of Latin America.[31] Even though trade with the Soviet Union will certainly be less than 10 percent of the total for Germany, it remains of decisive importance for Moscow and even crucial in certain sectors, where German firms supply close to half of USSR imports.

Emigration of ethnic Germans, who number over two million in the Soviet Union, and of a surprising number of Russian Jews who want to settle in Germany provides a new dimension to the relationship. In its comprehensive treaty with the USSR of 13 September 1990, the Federal Republic has been given certain responsibilities for the ethnic Germans who, under German law, are entitled to full German citizenship. In 1990, close to 150,000 of these so-called Volga Germans emigrated to Germany from Central Asia, where they have lived since Stalin expelled them from European Russia in World War II.[32] Hundreds of thousands more want to come. The fear of a wave of all kinds of emigrants from the Soviet Union (and Poland) driven westward by economic need today constitutes a potent subsurface fear in Germany and at the same time a powerful force for German assistance to help keep potential emigrants from leaving their Soviet homelands.

The new German-Soviet relationship enjoys solid public support in both countries. Communist party conservatives, who may be skeptical about Gorbachev's dealings with the United States and continued as late as March 1991 to attack his concessions in the Federal Republic during the unification process, do not challenge the need to build up economic and trade relations with Germany. A poll by the magazine *Argumenty i fakty* in April 1990 showed that 60 percent of the respondents supported German unification.[33] Admiration for Gorbachev and warm feelings for the USSR are characteristic of German public opinion, at least in the western part of Germany.

Soviet-German relations in the future will not develop at the expense of other European countries, as has been the case so often in the past. Twenty years of West German *Ostpolitik* (Eastern policy) have permitted Germany's allies to grow used to the relationship. The comprehensive treaty of 13 September 1990, therefore, came as no surprise to the world, as did the Rapallo Treaty of 1922 or the Hitler-Stalin agreement of 1939. It emerged instead from multinational processes, the CSCE and the "Two plus Four," in which Germany was one participant among many. Today's weakened USSR also can no longer offer Germany any substantial political or strategic advantages that Bonn has not long since obtained through its integration into western institutions, which has been the driving force of West German foreign policy over more than four decades.

New all-European security structures, probably arising out of the CSCE, may gradually replace the alliances which defined international relations on the continent during the Cold War. Germany and the Soviet Union (if it survives) will surely be among the central, supporting elements in such structures, a happier function for both than they have fulfilled during a long mutual history which has often been steeped in tension, conflict, and tragedy.

NOTES

1. Mikhail Gorbachev, *Perestroika: New Thinking for Our Country and the World* (New York: Harper & Row, 1987), p. 200.
2. Hans-Peter Riese, "Die Geschichte hat sich ans Werk gemacht: Der Wandel der sowjetischen Position zur Deutschen Frage," *Europa Archiv* (Bonn), Folge 4 (2 February 1990), pp. 117-118. See also Jurij P. Dawydow and

Dimitrij W. Trenin, "Die Haltung der Sowjetunion gegenüber der Deutschen Frage," *Europa Archiv*, Folge 8 (25 April 1990), pp. 251-253.

3. Hannes Adomeit, "Gorbachev and German Unification: Revision of Thinking, Realignment of Power," *Problems of Communism* 39, no. 4 (July-August 1990), p. 4. This is the best summary of this issue in English.

4. Adomeit, ibid., p. 5, points to the significance of this wording within the context of West German policy toward the GDR since the 1950s.

5. For a concise description of the present and future economic factors in the Soviet-German relationship, see Heinrich Vogel, "Die Vereinigung Deutschlands und die Wirtschaftsinteressen der Sowjetunion," *Europa Archiv*, Folge 13-14 (25 July 1990), pp. 408-414.

6. This assessment is to be found in the best surveys of the time, for instance, Edwina Moreton, ed. *Germany Between East and West* (Cambridge: Cambridge University Press, 1987). See also Elizabeth Pond, *After the Wall: American Policy Toward Germany* (New York: Priority Press Publications, 1990), pp. 4 and 10.

7. "Dann erhebt sich das Volk: SPIEGEL-Gespräch mit dem Moskauer Politologen Wjatscheslaw Daschitschew," *Der Spiegel* (Hamburg), no. 4 (21 January 1991), pp. 136-143.

8. Gerhard Wettig, "The Soviet Union and German Reunification," *Berichte des Bundesinstituts für ostwissenschaftliche und internationale Studien* (Cologne), no. 38-1990, pp. 6-7.

9. Adomeit, op. cit., tends to believe that the Soviets were essentially in control. For a somewhat different view, see Wettig, op. cit., and for a starkly contrasting one, see William E. Odom, "Germany, America, and the Strategic Configuration of Europe," Gary L. Geipel, ed., *The Future of Germany* (Indianapolis: Hudson Institute, 1990), pp. 190-217.

10. Pond, op. cit., pp. 13-14.

11. Author's interview with Egon Bahr, an SPD member of the West German parliament, 17 October 1990, Washington, D.C.

12. Fred Oldenburg, "Sowjetische Deutschland-Politik nach der Oktober-Revolution in der DDR," *Deutschland-Archiv*, no. 1 (January 1990), pp. 75-76.

13. Pond, op. cit., pp. 41-42; Riese, op. cit., p. 117; Gerhard Wettig, "Der Wandel des sowjetischen Standpunkts zur Vereinigung Deutschlands," *Aktuelle Analysen* (Cologne), no. 26/1990 (4 April 1990), p. 5; and Gerhard Wettig, "Stadien der sowjetischen Deutschland-Politik," *Deutschland-Archiv*, no. 7 (July 1990), p. 1073.

14. Lecture at the American Institute for Contemporary German Studies, Washington, D.C., by Robert Blackwill, former member of the National Security Council staff, 15 February 1991.

15. *Pravda*, 7 March 1990; cited in Wettig, "The Soviet Union and German Reunification," p. 17.

16. Pond, op. cit., p. 51.

17. *Pravda*, 7 January 1990; cited in Dawydow and Trenin, op. cit., p. 256. See also Riese, op. cit., p. 125, and Alexander Rahr, "Conservative Opposition to German Unification," *Report on the USSR* (Munich), 11 May 1990, pp. 15-17.
18. Wettig, "The Soviet Union and German Reunification," op. cit., p. 19.
19. Daniel Hamilton, *After the Revolution: The New Political Landscape in Eastern Germany*, German Issues no. 7 (Washington, D.C.: American Institute for Contemporary German Studies, 1990), pp. 14-15 and 46-47.
20. Wettig, "The Soviet Union and German Reunification," op. cit., p. 32.
21. Pond, op. cit., pp. 44-46.
22. Adomeit, op. cit., p. 22. See also "Excerpts from Speeches at the Communist Party Congress," *The New York Times*, 4 July 1990, p. 6.
23. Author's interview with Egon Bahr, Washington, D.C., 17 October 1990.
24. Anne-Marie le Gloannec, "Change in Germany and Future West European Security Arrangements," Geipel, op. cit., p. 132.
25. "Haushaltsausschuss entscheidet über 'Jumbo-Kredit,'" *Frankfurter Allgemeine Zeitung*, 22 June 1990.
26. U.S. Congress, Senate, *Treaty on the Final Settlement with Respect to Germany: Report of the Senate Committee on Foreign Relations to Accompany Treaty Document 101-20* (Washington, D.C.: U.S. Government Printing Office, 1990), 101st Congress, 2nd Session.
27. Text in *Süddeutsche Zeitung* (Munich), 14 September 1990, p. 11. For commentary, see *Neue Zürcher Zeitung* (Zurich), 15 September 1990, p. 1; *Frankfurter Allgemeine Zeitung*, 14 September 1990, p. 1.
28. Klaus Liedtke, "Vorwort," *Der neue Flirt: Russen und Deutsche auf dem Weg zu veränderten Beziehungen* (Hamburg: Stern Verlag, 1989), p. 11.
29. *Frankfurter Rundschau*, 28 February 1991, p. 1.
30. For informed forecasts of how German-Soviet economic relations are likely to develop, see Vogel, op. cit.
31. *Handelsblatt* (Düsseldorf), 12 December 1990, p. 10.
32. A. D. Horne, "2 Million Volga Germans Pose Settlement Issue for Bonn, Moscow," *The Washington Post*, 4 February 1991, p. A-6.
33. Poll cited in Michael Dobbs, "Soviets Reluctantly Accepting Idea of a Unified Germany in NATO," *The Washington Post*, 31 May 1990, p. A-27.

6

"New Thinking" in Soviet–Yugoslav Relations

Robin Alison Remington

In October 1990, the tornado of change that brought down the Berlin Wall and swept the hegemonic East European communist parties out of power is still swirling around the Soviet Union and Yugoslavia. The media and serious scholars alike are divided on the most fundamental question: Do the Soviet Union and Yugoslavia still exist, or have these multiethnic, federal political systems de facto collapsed into their component parts?

In July 1990 the committee preparing the League of Communists of Yugoslavia (LCY) "congress for democratic and program renewal" could not adopt the documents for such a convocation, because representatives from Slovenia, Croatia, Serbia, and Montenegro did not attend the meeting.[1] As this is being written, Mikhail S. Gorbachev appears to have abandoned the major surgery envisioned in the Shatalin 500 Day plan to introduce a market economy and opted for less radical intervention under the direction of his new, conservative prime minister, Valentin S. Pavlov. There is no guarantee that even the scaled-down version will be acceptable to Soviet consumers, who must pay more under conditions of rising inflation and unemployment, or the workers who must work harder if the Soviet economy is not to collapse. Indeed, the panic and confusion that came with the effort to curb black marketeers by taking 50- and 100-ruble notes out of circulation[2] suggest otherwise. Moreover, if the Russian Republic keeps to its declared intention to adopt the 500 Day plan with or without the rest of the country, the road to a market economy will detour into political polemics.

Soviet and Yugoslav federal politicians alike must deal with regional challengers who have declared "sovereignty and independence" of earlier clearly subordinate subunits. What that means is being determined on a case-by-case basis in a confusing choreography of political struggle. Possible futures for the Soviet Union and Yugoslavia alike range along a spectrum of drastically restyled federalism, confederation, disintegration, military coup, and civil war. Where either partner falls on that spectrum will change the nature of these relations. In short, what one thinks about the future of Soviet-Yugoslav relations is directly tied to what one thinks about domestic outcomes still in the process of development. This author has not yet made up her own mind, and given the precedent of 1989, considers prediction the province of prophets, not scholars.

Notwithstanding the above disclaimer, this chapter is a tentative, preliminary, analysis of Soviet-Yugoslav relations in the Gorbachev era. It focuses on the changed context of that relationship and attempts to identify a five-year trend line.

RETHINKING THE SOVIET-YUGOSLAV EXPERIENCE

Ever since World War II, Soviet-Yugoslav relations have largely been a function of Moscow's shifting East-West and intracommunist foreign policy priorities interacting with domestic factional struggle. During the brief flourishing of domesticism associated with the theory of "people's democracies,"[3] while Stalin still hoped for substantial allied reconstruction aid, Tito's regional revolutionary ambitions were an embarrassment that could be tolerated. When it became clear that there were too many strings attached to the Marshall Plan to make it viable from a Soviet perspective, the "two camp theory" mandated that the East European peoples' democracies turn the corner into dictatorships of the proletariat Soviet style. Quite apart from ideological/revolutionary ambitions, the economic imperatives of reconstruction required the Stalinist interstate system.[4] Yugoslav resistance to Soviet penetration devices, doctrinal challenge to proletarian internationalism as a one way street, and closeness to Leningrad Party Secretary Andrei A. Zhdanov became unacceptable.[5]

Stalin was right that the problem involved conceptions different from his own. He was wrong in believing that he could solve that problem by ostracization and the threat of force.[6] To the contrary, Stalinist tactics escalated doctrinal differences that might have been resolved to a sustained challenge to Soviet hegemony within the international communist movement and strategy toward the Third World. Once articulated, the Yugoslav alternatives of socialist self-management and nonalignment became core elements of the Soviet-Yugoslav relationship.

Nikita S. Khrushchev's efforts during 1955-1956 to woo Tito back into the socialist camp were tangled in his obsession with East-West summit diplomacy and the post-Stalin succession struggle. It was an explosive combination. Not surprisingly, Khrushchev retreated from commitment to national roads to socialism in the Belgrade Declaration, once he defeated the "antiparty group" in June 1957. The Yugoslav reaction to the Soviet reassertion of Moscow's leading role at the subsequent Moscow meeting of ruling communist parties in November 1957 was equally predictable. There followed the reaffirmation of the Yugoslav road to socialism and the open attack on Soviet "etatism" in the 1958 Ljubljana LCY party program, thereby setting off the second Soviet-Yugoslav dispute.

However, Khrushchev's preoccupation with the sins of Belgrade did not survive the Sino-Soviet schism. Improved relations with Yugoslavia became an index of credibility for "peaceful coexistence" of the 1960s. Tirana rejected Moscow for Beijing. Subsequent Sino-Soviet esoteric, proxy polemics created a tacit alliance between Belgrade and Moscow, notwithstanding ongoing tensions in the relationship.

The reign of the Brezhnev clique spans almost two decades of Soviet-Yugoslav relations. That story has not been written. For our purposes, it is enough to keep in mind three key dividing lines that determined the nature of relations between Moscow and Yugoslavia in that period: the 1968 invasion of Czechoslovakia and the elevation of the "Brezhnev Doctrine" to a principle of limited sovereignty within the socialist commonwealth; the Euro-communist victory at the 1976 Pan-European conference of communist and workers' parties; and transition from Tito's charismatic authority to the post-Tito collective leadership of Yugoslavia in 1980.

Tactically, this period reflected a "carrot and stick" approach flowing from Soviet détente imperatives and ambivalent strategies designed to contain the Euro-communist challenge within the intracommunist movement. Long before Tito died, there had been rumors that the Soviets were dabbling in Croatian separatism, angling for a naval base at Split or Pula.[7] A possible Soviet move to regain influence or territory figured prominently in post-Tito scenarios discussed in and outside of Yugoslavia. Such analyses often were linked to ethnic civil war or an army coup.[8]

Meanwhile, Moscow sent contradictory signals in the form of Brezhnev's personal renunciation of the "Brezhnev Doctrine" during his September 1971 visit to Belgrade[9] and what was seen as simultaneous pressure for a closer relationship with the Warsaw Pact.[10] In 1972, Tito was awarded an "Order of Lenin" and a Soviet sabre. These gifts had more than a little irony considering the godfather of Yugoslav communism's subsequent battle with Fidel Castro over the issue of a "natural alliance" between the nonaligned movement (NAM) and the forces of socialism at the 1979 Havana summit of NAM leaders.

To sum up, we can say that by the time Mikhail Gorbachev's "new political thinking" became a factor in Soviet-Yugoslav relations, Moscow had learned to live with the Yugoslav alternative model of socialism and nonaligned foreign policy. Secondly, USSR policy toward Yugoslavia reflected important domestic foreign policy linkages. In foreign policy terms, it was a complex, shifting—at times contradictory—mix of ideological/strategic considerations vis-à-vis the West, the intracommunist arena, and the Third World.

From the Yugoslav perspective, Moscow was the "significant other" whose rejection determined Yugoslavia's socialist and nonaligned identities alike. Moreover, the perceived Soviet threat in 1948, 1958, and 1968 had produced an artificial cohesion, papering over deep disagreements about political/economic direction. Thereby, the warning signs of road blocks on the path to market socialism, evident in resistance to the Yugoslav economic reform of 1965, were ignored. Tito himself euphorically, prematurely as it turned out, declared the "national question" resolved.[11] He set about stage-managing his own succession via the abortive 1971 constitutional amendments that, notwithstanding the Croatian crisis, lived on as the heart of the star-crossed 1974 constitution.

When Tito died in 1980, Moscow avoided the predicted destabilization scenarios and treated the issue of consolidation in post-Tito Yugoslavia as an internal affair.[12] This correct Soviet, hands-off policy undoubtedly lowered strategic anxieties among Tito's successors. However, it also deprived the struggling collective leadership of the legitimacy that comes from an external threat. There was more than a little truth to the apocryphal story that when Brezhnev arrived in Belgrade for Tito's funeral, he was warned that any Soviet attempt to take advantage of the situation would be met with united Yugoslav resistance. To which he replied, "and if we make no attempts?"

Brezhnev was already in poor health. The Soviet leader survived Tito by only two and a half years. During the Andropov-Chernenko interlude that followed his death in 1982, Yugoslavia was not a major concern. Thus, the Gorbachev chapter in Soviet-Yugoslav relations opened at a time when Yugoslav politicians were no longer protected either by Tito's charisma or Moscow's intimidation. They had inherited the Titoist myth, an awkward political machinery that no one was sure would work, and some $20 billion in hard-currency debt. Hard choices could not be avoided.

THE GORBACHEV ERA[13]

Less than a month after Mikhail Gorbachev took over as head of the CPSU in March 1985, he signed his East European allies up for another twenty years in the Warsaw Pact. There is no reason to think that the new general secretary ranked Soviet-Yugoslav relations alongside alliance cohesion as a top policy priority. There was a conciliatory Soviet response to Yugoslav concerns that Moscow had been deliberately downgrading the Yugoslav national liberation struggle and a major *Pravda* article on the thirtieth anniversary of the Belgrade Declaration.[14]

To whatever extent the *Pravda* article foreshadowed a Gorbachev strategy toward Yugoslavia, it undoubtedly led to mixed feelings among Yugoslav readers. Although the article recognized the importance of indigenous features of socialist development, it also stressed that the Belgrade Declaration recognized the need to "creatively" apply the teaching of Marx, Engels, and Lenin on the road to socialism. Just what the reference to Leninism meant was open to interpretation, but by no stretch of imagination could the Titoist solution, reluctantly reaffirmed at the 12th LCY Congress in 1982, be considered Leninist. Moreover, when Yugoslav Prime Minister Milka Planinc visited Moscow in July 1985, neither Gorbachev nor her Soviet counterpart, Nikolai A. Tikhonov, responded to her insistence that the spirit of the Belgrade Declaration remained "irreplaceable" in Soviet-Yugoslav relations.

Still, the new CPSU draft program[15] omitted attacks on Yugoslav "revisionism," leading to cautious hopes in Belgrade that Gorbachev might be more open to genuine dialogue than his predecessors. From an outsider's perspective, at a minimum the new Soviet party chief appeared to be keeping his political/ideological options open.

Politically, Yugoslavia continued to call for the withdrawal of foreign troops from Afghanistan and to polemicize against the concept of a "natural alliance" between socialist countries and the nonaligned. At the same time, the squeeze created by the imperatives of debt-servicing made economic nonalignment less and less of a reality. When Gorbachev took over in the Kremlin, the USSR was already Yugoslavia's largest trading partner with a $40 billion equivalent trade turnover projected for 1986-1990. Given the Iran-Iraq war and Yugoslav dependence on Soviet oil, the corresponding political vulnerability could only increase.

At the same time, Moscow responded to the increasingly decentralized post-Tito political system by negotiating directly with regional politicians. In March 1985 CPSU politburo member V. I. Vorotnikov held discussions on economic cooperation with Serbia and Montenegro, while later in the spring a delegation of the CPSU audit commission visited Serbia. In June 1985 the chairman of the Ukrainian SSR Council of Ministers was the guest of high-ranking party and government officials in Croatia. It is not clear to what extent these republic-level contacts were coordinated with the Yugoslav federal secretariat of foreign affairs or for that matter by its Soviet counterpart. Such contacts may or may not have represented an effort to fish in troubled waters. But combined with the official visit of the Soviet deputy defense minister, General A. N. Efimov, to Belgrade in November,[16] it is safe to say that tactically the Gorbachev strategy vis-à-vis Yugoslavia sought to develop contingency channels for political, possibly strategic, influence.

In the two years leading up to Mikhail Gorbachev's visit to Belgrade, economic considerations dominated interstate relations. On the Yugoslav side, the primary issue was reducing the price of $27 a barrel that was being paid for Soviet oil to something closer to world levels. There was also some tension surrounding the $1.5 billion trade surplus with the USSR that former Prime Minister Branko Mikulić bluntly characterized as an "interest-free loan."[17]

Although the issue of the trade surplus was still on the agenda when Gorbachev arrived at Belgrade in March 1988, the Soviet side had moved to establish an appropriate political atmosphere for improved relations. On his October 1986 visit, as head of a Supreme Soviet delegation to Belgrade, First Deputy Chairman Petr N. Demichev praised Yugoslavia's role in the victory over fascism at the end of World War II. His positive reference to the nonaligned summit in Harare was then upgraded by the Soviet foreign minister to recognition of the nonaligned movement as an "authoritative force" in world affairs,[18] when Eduard A. Shevardnadze came to Belgrade to discuss bilateral relations in June 1987.

Other high-ranking visits during 1986-1987 included a delegation of Soviet security officers led by politburo member and KGB chief Viktor M. Chebrikov, virtually on the heels of the December 1986 trip by LCY party president Milanko Renovica to Moscow. Whether or not this was a part of the "all around cooperation" referred to during Renovica's discussions,[19] the visit led to ambivalent reactions among some Yugoslav observers. Military contacts also continued in the form of talks on interarmy cooperation between Yugoslav Defense Minister Branko Mamula and his USSR counterpart, Dmitrii T. Iazov, while Mamula was "vacationing" in the Soviet

Union. Reportedly the Yugoslav defense minister also met with members of the USSR State Committee for Foreign Economic Relations to discuss unspecified issues of military economic cooperation.[20]

Politically, Gorbachev's 1988 visit went beyond post-Tito politicians' most optimistic expectations. The Soviet leader replayed the scene of Khrushchev's admission in May 1955 of USSR responsibility for the 1948 Soviet-Yugoslav split. Gorbachev used the opportunity to share his "new political thinking" with the parliament in Belgrade.

Still, more significantly, the Soviet-Yugoslav "Declaration of Principles" was one of the early statements renouncing the Brezhnev Doctrine and repeating a joint commitment to socialist pluralism. In fact, Gorbachev's public recognition that "no one has a monopoly over truth" dated from his speech to the 27th CPSU Congress in February 1986.[21] However, to raise this to the status of a joint declaration with the Yugoslavs was a substantial step beyond the level of commitment to noninfererence in internal affairs that the Soviet leader had been willing to give Planinc during her 1985 visit to Moscow. In and outside of Yugoslavia this was news.[22] Coupled with Gorbachev's pledge to leave Afganistan, the joint declaration essentially removed any vestige of tension from the Soviet-Yugoslav political relationship.

On the economic side, plans were made for cooperation until the year 2000. Moscow agreed in principle that something must be done about the trade surplus, to tie Soviet raw material prices to world market prices, and to buy more Yugoslav equipment and machinery. Notwithstanding these good intentions, by 1989 the trade surplus with the Soviet Union had grown to $1.7 billion and continued to adversely affect the Yugoslav economic crisis. To reduce these negative repercussions, Yugoslav Prime Minister Ante Marković's antiinflation package included the provision that the government would withhold payment to Yugoslav firms dealing with the Soviet Union until Moscow paid its bills.[23]

In January 1990 there were reports that an estimated $2 billion trade surplus would be dealt with over the next two years in the context of the $30 billion five-year trade turnover between the two countries.[24] By mid-year, Yugoslav and Soviet negotiators had made progress on the practical question of just how to whittle down what both sides described as "the debt." The time frame had expanded to four years, beginning in January 1991. According to the Tanjug account of talks between Yugoslav Deputy Prime Minister Aleksandar Mitrović and his counterpart, who also served as chairman of the USSR Foreign Economic Committee, Stepan A. Sitarian, the Soviet side agreed to pay back its debt in goods over a three-year period. If that deadline is not met, there will be a one-year grace period, after which hard currency payment is required.[25]

To facilitate a Soviet settlement, the Yugoslavs agreed to early repayment of $230 million of commercial and $650 million of interstate, government credit. This means that Yugoslav firms, borrowing from the USSR, are expected to pay their own federal government instead of the creditor. Or to put it differently, the Belgrade government must now collect $230 million from Yugoslav enterprises.

Other aspects involved Yugoslavia taking over an unspecified amount of debt securities that Soviet banks had been buying in London and Paris, increased USSR deliveries of goods, and Soviet construction of a natural gas pipeline system in Yugoslavia. A separate protocol agreed to shift to hard-currency payments for services as of August 1990; in general the transfer to hard-currency payments in Soviet-Yugoslav economic relations was set for January 1991. At the close of the talks, Mitrović referred to a current annual value of $6.2 billion in clearing payments and 700 million dollars in hard currency payments. The Yugoslav negotiator did not mention the Belgrade subway project that reappeared in Sitarian's interview on returning to Moscow,[26] raising the possibility that the nature of Soviet construction projects linked to eliminating the debt remains on the agenda.

In the wake of the East-Central European revolutions beginning in 1989, there has been a sea change in Soviet-Yugoslav political relations that may well come from the feeling of being in the same political boat. Apparently when Mitrović came to Moscow for the January 1990 meeting of the Yugoslav-Soviet Economic and Scientific and Technical Council, there was "an exhaustive exchange of information" about internal developments. Both sides concluded that an "even wider exchange of views" about their efforts at economic and political reforms would be useful, with then Soviet Prime Minister Nikolai I. Ryzhkov asking "a whole series" of questions about Yugoslav reforms.[27]

This theme was repeated during the five-day visit by a delegation of the USSR Supreme Soviet under Aleksandr S. Dzasokhov, chairman of its International Affairs Committee, to discuss international developments with the Yugoslav parliament's Foreign Policy Committee. The foreign policy dimension of these talks focused on European security, superpower relations, disarmament, German reunification, and nonalignment. However, the Soviet delegation also expressed "special interest in the forms of pluralist democracy being set up in Yugoslavia."[28]

In retrospect, if what Ryzhkov heard from his Yugoslav counterpart influenced the former prime minister's alternative to the 500 Day Plan, it may have been less useful than he hoped. But, nonetheless, this type of exchange underlines a sense of shared fate that informs Soviet reporting on Yugoslavia and Yugoslav discussions of national/ethnic dilemmas in the USSR alike. Soviet correspondents reporting from Ljubljana emphasize that the majority of Slovenes are not secessionists and stress the need for patience.[29] The demise of the Slovene-LC and its rebirth as an independent communist party, the League of Communists for Democratic Renewal, appeared in the form of a short factual account without editorializing.[30] Conversely, reporting on Kosovo raises the specter of civil war as a consequence of collapsing party unity.[31] The unstated analogies are obvious.

On the Yugoslav side, the lack of international recognition of Lithuanian independence undoubtedly encouraged federal policy makers as to their country's future and their own job security. It sent a negative signal to Slovene politicians about the prospects for going it alone, notwithstanding which Slovenes continued to identify with Lithuanians even as they recognized the differences between their situations.[32] Soviet media reports on the virtual disappearance of the League of Communists of Yugoslavia from the political scene have been straightforward. The coverage of the 1990 midsummer merger of the Serbian League of Communists with its own Socialist Alliance into the Socialist Party of Serbia quoted the "bitter conclusion" of the delegates to the Serbian congress that "a unified all-Yugoslav political party no longer exists. . . . The League has not withstood the blows of separatists."[33] Indeed, Soviet politburo members who assumed their positions in July 1990 may well have felt less secure in their new quarters, when they read about the decision of the LCY Central Committee to solve its financial problems by leasing out eight floors of their building in New Belgrade.[34]

Moreover, to whatever extent Mikhail Gorbachev considered substituting his new cabinet and security council for the politburo as the decisive voice in Soviet policy-making, he also has a vested interest in the outcome of efforts by Prime Minister Ante Marković to build a government party to compete in the remaining 1990 Yugoslav republic elections and the still-to-come federal election. Thus, it is not surprising that Soviet coverage of the founding meeting of the Alliance of Reform Forces praised Marković as a "pragmatic politician" reminding readers of his dramatic statement, when the 14th LCY Congress broke up, that "Yugoslavia will continue to function with or without the party."[35]

Military cooperation continued in October 1990, with the visit of a USSR delegation led by Colonel General Nikolai I. Shliaga, head of the Main Political Administration of the Army and Navy. Reportedly the talks between Yugoslav Defense Secretary Veljko Kadijević and the head of the Soviet delegation "noted that interarmy cooperation was developing successfully" in line with the good relations between the two countries.[36] There was no mention of just what such cooperation entailed.

Given the political nature of his job, one might expect that General Shliaga would be more than a little interested in how the Yugoslav armed forces dealt with the twin problems of depoliticization and cohesion on the road to a multiparty political system. Logically, the sensitive domestic questions of separatist tendencies and interethnic conflict also might have come up, although there is no public evidence that these topics were discussed. However, there is somewhat more basis for speculation in terms of foreign policy issues. From the Tanjug account of the June 1990 talks with the Supreme Soviet delegation that referred to Moscow's belief in the need for all-European institutions "to guarantee military as well as other aspects of German reunification,"[37] one can assume that, at a minimum, consultation on the military component of European security is an official component of current Soviet-Yugoslav relations.

The USSR decision-making process vis-à-vis Soviet-Yugoslav relations has clearly featured Mikhail Gorbachev's visible personal diplomacy. Yet Gorbachev's visit in March 1988 was the culmination of ongoing negotiations in the joint Commission for Economic, Scientific, and Technical Cooperation and had been preceded by the visit of Soviet Foreign Minister Shevardnadze. It has been followed up by further work in the joint commission as well as by the already mentioned June 1990 visit of the USSR Supreme Soviet delegation, led by the chairman of the Soviet parliament's International Affairs Committee, who himself became a member of the CPSU politburo in July 1990. In this writer's view, it means that Soviet-Yugoslav relations reflect the importance of the USSR foreign ministry and the growing role of the Supreme Soviet in the Soviet foreign policy process.

When the Gorbachev chapter of Soviet-Yugoslav relations commenced in 1985, Moscow appeared to be keeping its options open with respect to post-Tito Yugoslavia. The latter was still seen at the far end of the spectrum in terms of deviation from Soviet-style socialism. USSR policy makers may well have been divided on whether their interests lay in encouraging the forces for separatism or cohesion. Ideological/political differences remained a core component of the Soviet-Yugoslav relationship for policy makers in both countries.

By 1990 the economic element of relations dominated Yugoslav concerns. Political difference on Afghanistan and nonalignment had faded. There was substantial agreement on the security aspects of a "common European home." Still more significantly, Soviet politicians now identified with the nature of the Yugoslav federal dilemma, fearing that the fate of the LCY may be the handwriting on the wall for the CPSU. There is no doubt but that the currently perceived vested interest of Gorbachev and his increasingly conservative supporters is for Yugoslavia to stay together, not to fall apart.

In tentatively ordering the reasons for the changes that have occurred, this author would put as number one Mikhail Gorbachev's change in the rules of the game for intracommunist relations from insistence on "real socialism" Soviet-style to socialist pluralism in which "unity has nothing to do with uniformity" and no party has "a monopoly over what is right."[38] When Gorbachev called for "pooling efforts" and studying each other's experiences in building socialism,[39] he implicitly accepted the Yugoslav understanding of proletarian internationalism as a two-way street. His renunciation of the Brezhnev Doctrine in the joint Soviet-Yugoslav declaration of 1988 put into practice the already existing ideological restructuring of relations among socialist countries.[40]

Secondly, radicalization of *perestroika* and *glasnost'* within the Soviet Union, and the dramatic unintended consequences of that process for Yugoslavia's neighbors in East-Central Europe, traumatized Soviet and Yugoslav communist politicians alike. The latter policy makers slipped from being the engine of East-Central European reform movements to the position of caboose. As seen in Moscow, the Yugoslav model had become the least threatening alternative out there. Moreover, the substantial success of Ante Marković's antiinflation package was undoubtedly more appealing to Soviet economic planners than the Polish shock-therapy transition to capitalism.

Thirdly, ethnic strife and demands for a multiparty system in the USSR itself have substantially increased Soviet interest in the post-Tito search for political solutions.

Fourth, with German reunification there is a substantial convergence of Soviet interests in what had been a long-standing neutral and nonaligned (N + N) agenda for multilateralizing European security.

NEAR-TERM PROJECTIONS

This author's near-term projections in October 1990 were based on two assumptions:

1. that Mikhail Gorbachev would continue in power in the Soviet Union and continue his commitment to "new thinking" for the USSR and the world;
2. that despite some violence, clashes associated with demands of the Serbian minority for autonomy within Croatia, Yugoslavia would not collapse into civil war or an army coup.

Given these assumptions, the near-term projections were predicted to hold whatever the results of the remaining Yugoslav republic elections scheduled for November and December.

First, there was likely to be an ongoing convergence of Soviet-Yugoslav political/military interests that increases the stake of policy makers in Moscow in Yugoslavia's transition to a viable federal system. When federal elections do come, from the Soviet point of view, if Marković can consolidate his new Alliance of Democratic Forces, that will be just fine. The USSR also could live with a Yugoslavia dominated by the Socialist Party of Serbia, under the presidency of Slobodan Milošević, perhaps with some mixed feelings, given what might be seen as an analogy with Boris Yeltsin's position in the Russian Federation. There is no evidence that anyone in Moscow was betting on the "renewal" of the LCY.

Secondly, whatever the dynamic at the federal level, Soviet-Yugoslav relations will increasingly reflect initiatives from republic political actors. In July 1990, Serbian Premier Stanko Radmilović went to Moscow to establish relations with the Russian Federation.[41] Slovenia and Croatia also will likely establish parallel relations with other Soviet republics and vice versa. In short, the number of players will increase on both sides. One will not be analyzing a strictly Soviet-Yugoslav relationship so much as complex, overlapping federal- and republic-level relationships.

From the economic perspective, today the Soviet-Yugoslav agreement that Mikhail Gorbachev signed off on does not look as good to Yugoslavia as it did in 1988. The recent Persian Gulf crisis cost Yugoslavia an estimated $3 billion and put roughly a fifth of Yugoslav oil imports at risk. In these circumstances, the USSR's reluctant acceptance of the principle that Soviet raw material prices should reflect the level of world prices will potentially increase Soviet influence and economic advantage in the 1990s. In the near term, this will mainly result in decreasing the USSR's $2 billion debt faster.

However, there is an interesting twist. Yugoslav-Soviet relations were supposed to be on a hard-currency basis after January 1991. Yet there is an area of ambiguity concerning republic-level relations here. Tanjug reports of Serbian talks with the government of the Russian Federation referred to an opportunity for Serbia to export 600,000 tons of wheat in a barter arrangement and construction of a gas pipeline though Serbia in return.[42] The wheat could be an advance payment on the pipeline which, no matter when the wheat is sent, will undoubtedly not be finished by January 1991. Whatever the fine print in this arrangement, republic level exchanges may be a loophole that both sides resort to down the road as the pain of exchanges based on convertible currency becomes too much to bear.

Finally, it was assumed that if the blockade of Iraq did not work and the "line in the sand" was wiped out by a regional war in the Persian Gulf, current Soviet-Yugoslav positions would put them on the same side of that confrontation if it was a United Nations' operation, thereby not changing the direction of near-term projections.

By January 1991 both assumptions one and two were in doubt. The conflict in the Baltics had gone from threat of force to use of force. The question became not *whether* the Red Army and Ministry of Interior security forces would be used but *how far* they would be allowed to go. There was fear that the independence-minded Baltic republics and the center-right coalitions in Slovenia and Croatia alike would become victims of the Washington-led coalition's battle to get Saddam Hussein out of Kuwait.

However, according to early results of the 17 March 1991 Soviet referendum, "a safe but less than overwhelming majority" of voters gave Gorbachev a slim victory on the question of preserving the Soviet Union.[43] Conversely, an estimated 83 percent of Ukrainian voters also voted for the republic's declaration of sovereignty, while 73 percent of the Russian Republic supported his rival Boris Yeltsin's initiative for a popularly elected president of the republic.

Hence, Gorbachev's victory could hardly be considered a mandate to push through the draft union treaty that the Soviet leader wanted in order to hold the line against those national/separatist movements that mounted successful boycotts of the referendum in the Baltic republics, Moldavia, Georgia, and Armenia. Within less than a month—on the second anniversary of the death of 19 civilian protesters in Tbilisi—the parliament of the Republic of Georgia voted unanimously for independence.[44]

The Georgian declaration of independence coincided with Mikhail S. Gorbachev's presentation of a "crisis program," to a meeting of those republic leaders still willing to listen, that called for a year-long moratorium on strikes and demonstrations. Predictably, the Baltic republics and Georgia boycotted the session. Still, despite his running battle with Gorbachev, Boris N. Yeltsin sent his deputy, Ruslan I. Khasbulatov, while Gorbachev responded with a conciliatory tone to what he described as "calls for cooperation [that came] from the Russian Federation Congress."[45]

Mikhail Gorbachev's attempt to restore economic and social discipline came as Soviet rank and file miners rejected the agreement made by their trade union representatives to receive double pay and continued to call for the resignation of the prime minister and the USSR president himself, as a virtual general strike called to protest sharp price hikes went forward as planned in the Belorussian city of Minsk.[46]

Although Gorbachev has survived against the odds of a long line of media predictions, he is the lightning rod of popular frustration over shortages, chaos, and insecurity associated with the attempted transition to a market economy. Calls for his resignation are more strident. To force him out would take a two-thirds vote by the Congress of Peoples' Deputies, and it is not likely that 1,500 members of that body would vote against him.

Yet, despite his own denials and former President Richard M. Nixon's assessment that the Soviet president has not used the last of his nine political lives,[47] Gorbachev personally might decide to give up what has become an increasingly thankless position. Still more likely, a coalition of party, army, and security apparatus conservatives could persuade or force the father of *perestroika* into declaring martial law.

Indeed, throughout this 1990-1991 winter of discontent, the Soviet Union has attained all of the prerequisites for a classic military coup scenario: declining civilian government legitimacy, political chaos, economic crisis, social disorder, and threats to military and corporate interests.[48] The stark comparison with Poland in early December 1981, on the eve of martial law, can not be discounted.

Meanwhile in Yugoslavia, Slobodan Milošević's attempt to force the collective presidency to give emergency powers to the Yugoslav army failed by one vote, while massive demonstrations against his heavy handed political tactics and economic mismanagement appeared to have weakened his control within Serbia itself.[49] There followed a reversal of political roles in which Dr. Borisaw Jović, the Serbian representative and president of the SFRY Presidency, resigned. Milošević refused to recognize the authority of the federal presidency,[50] and the "sovereign" republics of Slovenia and Croatia came to the defense of Yugoslav unity with calls for a meeting to preserve the federation.[51]

Undoubtedly the European Community played a constructive role. The European parliament reiterated its concern for Yugoslav unity and integrity. According to Yugoslav sources, the parliament is ready to back up its verbal support with a $1.1 billion loan on "very favorable" conditions and, most important, open negotiations for the possible acceptance of Yugoslavia as an associate member of the European Community.[52]

After ten days of brinksmanship, that had appeared to many observers as the prelude to a military takeover or the withdrawal of Serbia from Yugoslavia, the political storm subsided. The High Command of the Yugoslav National Army issued a statement assuring the country and the world that the armed forces would stay out of politics, but would not tolerate armed interethnic conflict or civil war.[53]

On the eve of the summit meeting of republic presidents, Milošević and the Croatian leader, Dr. Franjo Tudjman, held a secret meeting on the border of their republics at Karadjordjevo "to eliminate options which could pose a threat to the interests of both Serbs and Croats [a euphemism for civil war] with full respect for the historical interests of both nations [to] determine a time frame within which Yugoslavia's pressing problems must be solved."[54] Supporters of Ante Marković's Alliance of Reform Forces have charged that the Tudjman-Milošević meeting was part of a concerted plot by these two republic presidents to "eliminate" the prime minister.[55] However, whatever the motive of their meeting, the fact that it took place at all, gave hope that polarized confrontation among republic leaders could give way to political dialogue.

External incentives for cohesion continued with a visit to Yugoslavia by a delegation of the U.S. Congress CSCE Commission, headed by Senator Dennis DeConcini, who held open talks in a spirit of "mutual respect and understanding" with Serbian President Milošević[56] and met with federal President Jović and Prime Minister Ante Marković as well. The deConcini message of U.S. concern for Yugoslavia was reinforced by a letter from President Bush to Prime Minister Ante Marković, stating bluntly:

> ...it is our wish that the differences among the peoples [of Yugoslavia] be solved within the framework of a united, democratic Yugoslavia, and we will not encourage or reward those striving to disrupt the country.[57]

Given that the key players in the choreography of political struggle about the confederal or federal nature of Yugoslavia in postcommunist East-Central Europe are now on speaking terms and the presidents of the Yugoslav republics are engaged in a dialogue, rather than polemical attacks, this writer's near-term projections regarding the Yugoslav half of the equation that determines Soviet-Yugoslav relations remain the same as presented in the foregoing.

Whatever the situation at the end of the two months in 1991 of scheduled negotiations among republic leaders and results of the planned national referendum, the process is moving in the direction of solutions based on mutual advantage. Undoubtedly, that process could be derailed by an outbreak of violence in the self-declared independent Serbian region of Krajina (part of Croatia) where rebel leaders announced at the beginning of April 1991 that they had decided to unite with Serbia.[58] Yet with federal army troops maintaining order in the region, republic leaders talking to one another, and the European Community holding out the carrot of associate membership, the odds appear to tilt toward one Yugoslavia.

Where the Soviet Union will be several months from now on the spectrum of federation, confederation, military coup, or disintegration is a Delphic question. In terms of the range of possibilities that will impact on Soviet-Yugoslav relations, in this writer's view there are three scenarios, in addition to the earlier near-term projection that Mikhail Gorbachev will somehow muddle through.

1. Gorbachev the reformer becomes Gorbachev the dictator; the Soviet Union continues under de facto martial law, falling into the category that scholars who write on civil-military relations refer to as a guardian regime.

In this event, the level of interest expressed in the Yugoslav move toward a multiparty political system would decline. There might be some effort to restrict independent foreign policy initiatives by USSR republics with their Yugoslav counterparts, in order to reassert federal foreign policy prerogatives. Such a transformation would have few near-term repercussions for Soviet-Yugoslav economic relations, while strategically the USSR interest in networking to establish European security arrangements outside of NATO could be expected to increase.

2. Mikhail Gorbachev resigns, is replaced, or assassinated. Vice President Gennadii I. Ianaev becomes the front man for an armed forces' Council of National Salvation or the military rules through its own collective leadership, i.e., the Soviet Union becomes an authoritarian military regime. If this scenario stops short of precipitating civil war or, if that war ends quickly and successfully represses the opposition to recentralizing the USSR, the repercussions for Soviet relations with Yugoslavia are essentially the same as in scenario number one. The one addition might be increased interest in Moscow for army to army contacts as a political rather than strictly military conduit.

3. The USSR collapses into prolonged civil war with an attempted revolution from below. In the near-term, as during World War II, Yugoslavia would be at the periphery of Soviet attention. In this case Yugoslav political and economic relations alike would be disrupted in a major way. Given its geography, demands to shelter the refugees from such a civil war or revolution would be less of a problem for Yugoslavia than for some other East-Central European neighbors of the Soviet Union. Nonetheless, if the outcome were the collapse of the USSR, Yugoslav relations would be reestablished with the states to emerge from the ashes of empire.

Politically, scenarios one and two could be expected to increase the hopes of Yugoslav centralizers and the fears of those who look to a confederal Yugoslavia. Scenario two also would logically increase the perception of the importance of the armed forces' role in Yugoslav politics, whether or not that corresponded to reality.

Strategically, all three scenarios would increase unpredictability with respect to Yugoslav national security. If the Soviet Union abandons *perestroika* to restore economic and social discipline (scenarios one and two), there is the danger that the Soviet military might want to reestablish influence in East-Central Europe or develop an uncomfortably close military interest in Yugoslavia to compensate for losses in the former Warsaw Pact member states.

With respect to scenario three, civil wars and revolutions in the region are never healthy. Whereas one can assume that Yugoslavia would not have any direct strategic involvement, the strategic outcome would be quite unpredictable.

Who knows what would be the status of Soviet strategic weapons along the way? Moreover, economically, scenario three could spill over into Western Europe, thereby pushing Europe 1992 off track and hindering EC economic relations and commitments to Yugoslavia.

Politically, scenario three could influence both directions. Depending at what point it came in the ongoing effort of Yugoslav nations to work out a compromise, the Soviet civil war/revolution could give those republics which wanted to do so an incentive to break away. Or, in this writer's view more likely, witnessing the cost and bloodshed of violent alternatives could serve as a sober warning to Yugoslav nations and ethnic groups of the advantages of peaceful solutions.

In the meantime, one can only say that by the time of this writing in mid-May 1991 the moving targets of this analysis were moving faster. The fate of their relationship continued to hang on the direction of domestic transformations that can accelerate or go into reverse with no regard for publication schedules.

NOTES

1. Tanjug (Belgrade), 26 July 1990; FBIS-EEU-90-145 (27 July 1990), p. 35.
2. Serge Schmemann, "Rubles' Recall Add Hardship...," *The New York Times*, 24 January 1991, pp. A-1 and C-5.
3. Z. K. Brzezinski, *The Soviet Bloc: Unity and Conflict* (Cambridge, MA: Harvard University Press, 1971), p. 45 ff.
4. Paul Marer, "Soviet Economic Policy in Eastern Europe," in U.S. Congress, Joint Economic Committee, *Reorientation and Commercial Relations of the Economies of Eastern Europe* (Washington, D.C.: U.S. Government Printing Office, 1974), pp. 135-163; further expanded in his chapter, "Has Eastern Europe Become a Liability to the Soviet Union? (III) The Economic Aspect," in Charles Gati, ed., *The International Politics of Eastern Europe* (New York: Praeger, 1976), pp. 59-80.
5. See Milovan Djilas, *Conversations with Stalin* (New York: Harcourt, Brace, 1962).
6. *White Book on Aggressive Activities by the Governments of the USSR, Poland, Czechoslovakia, Hungary, Rumania, Bulgaria, and Albania towards Yugoslavia* (Belgrade: Yugoslav Ministry of Foreign Affairs, 1951).
7. *The Times* (London), 19 April 1971.
8. Paul Lendvai in *The Financial Times* (London), 25 May 1971.
9. *Borba* (Belgrade), 26 September 1971, p. 1.
10. "Vera v možnost napredka," *Delo* (Ljubljana), 5 October 1971, p. 4. For a more detailed analysis, see Robin Alison Remington, "The Warsaw Pact and Soviet Policy in the Balkans" in Phillip A. Petersen, ed., *Soviet Policy in the Post Tito Balkans* (Washington, D.C.: U.S. Air Force, 1979), pp. 79-88.
11. B. Milašović, "Sotsialistički Savez...," *Borba*, 22 September 1969, p. 17.
12. See George Klein, "Soviet Foreign Policy Options in the Contemporary Balkans," in Petersen, ed., op cit., p. 142 ff.
13. This analysis of the Yugoslav perspective of relations with the Soviet Union during the Gorbachev era benefits greatly from the author's discussions with scholars and policy makers during a 1988-1989 study in Yugoslavia under the auspices of a Fulbright Faculty Research Abroad Grant and a University of Missouri-Columbia research leave. Matters of interpretation and mistakes are the author's alone.

14. V. Sharov, "Kurs druzhby i sotrudnichestva," *Pravda* (Moscow), 1 June 1985, p. 5. For more detail, see Robin Alison Remington, "Yugoslavia," in Richard F. Staar, ed., *1986 Yearbook on International Communist Affairs* (Stanford, Calif.: Hoover Institution Press, 1986), p. 382.
15. "Programma Komunisticheskoi Partii Sovetskogo Soiuza (novaia redaktsiia)," *Literaturnaia gazeta* (Moscow), 30 October 1985, pp. 1-6.
16. "S ofitsial'nym vizitom," *Krasnaia zvezda* (Moscow), 19 November 1985, p. 3.
17. Tanjug, "I suficit može da zabrinjava," *Borba,* 26 August 1987. For analysis, see *RFE Research,* 16 September 1987, p. 3.
18. "Prebyvanie v Iugoslavii," *Pravda,* 21 June 1987, p. 4.
19. TASS, "S druzhestvom vizitom," *Izvestiia* (Moscow), 11 December 1986, p. 1.
20. Tanjug, 7 July 1987; Mikhail Gorbachev, "Political Report of the CPSU Central Committee to the Congress of the CPSU," FBIS-EEU (8 July 1987), pp. 13-48, at p. 39.
21. Mikhail Gorbachev, "Political Report of the CPSU Central Committee to the Congress of the CPSU," English language text in *New Times* (Moscow), no. 9 (March 1986), pp. 13-48.
22. Tanjug, 18 March 1988; John Tagliabue, "Soviet Gives Security Vow as Yugoslav Visit Ends," *The New York Times,* 19 March 1988, p. 28. For a more detailed analysis see Jim Seroka, "Yugoslavia," in Richard F. Staar, ed., *1989 Yearbook on International Communist Affairs* (Stanford, Calif.: Hoover Institution Press, 1989), p. 412.
23. "Program ekonomske reforme i mjera za njegovu realizaciju u 1990 godini," *Borba,* 19 December 1989, p. 4. Emphasized in conversations with Yugoslav colleagues, while this writer was in Belgrade during 13-30 December 1989.
24. Tanjug (in English), 18 January 1990; "Economic Talks with Soviets End," FBIS-EEU-90-013 (19 January 1990), p. 77.
25. Tanjug (in English), 1 July 1990; "Moscow Agrees to Convertible Currency Payments," FBIS-EEU-90-127 (2 July 1990), pp. 70-71.
26. *Pravda,* 20 July 1990; "Agreement on Debts Reached with Yugoslavia," FBIS-SOV-90-144 (26 July 1990), p. 20.
27. Tanjug (Domestic Service), 16 January 1990; "USSR's Ryzhkov Meets with Mitrović," FBIS-EEU-90-013 (19 January 1990), pp. 76-77.
28. Tanjug (Domestic Service), 27 June 1990; "Assembly President Receives Soviet Delegation," FBIS-EEU-90-125 (28 June 1990), p. 74.
29. V. Khlystun, "Chem bogache...," *Komsomol' skaia pravda* (Moscow), 27 March 1990, p. 5; "Slovene Reluctance to Secede from SFRY...," FBIS-SOV-90-061 (29 March 1990), p. 22.
30. TASS, "Samostoiatel'naia partiia?" *Pravda,* 6 February 1990, p. 7; "Serbian Communities...," FBIS-SOV-90-026 (7 February 1990), pp. 42-43.
31. E. Vostrukhov, "Iugoslaviia...," *Izvestiia,* 28 January 1990, p. 4; "Newspaper Reports...," FBIS-SOV-90-026 (7 February 1990), pp. 35-37.

32. D. Košir, "Topic of the Day," *Delo*, 12 March 1990, p. 1; "Commentary...," FBIS-EEU-90-051 (15 March 1990), p. 75. See also comments of Peter Bekeš, a member of Slovenia's restructured communist party, "The economic power of Slovenia is too important to permit the other republics of Yugoslavia to say simply goodbye," *The New York Times*, 6 April 1990, p. A-6.
33. E. Vostrukhov, "Sozdana edinaia partiia," *Izvestiia*, 21 July 1990, p. 5; "Yugoslav Republic's Communist Parties Merge," FBIS-SOV (26 July 1990), pp. 20-21.
34. E. Fadeev, "Zdanie TsK SKIU v agendu," *Pravda*, 4 August 1990, p. 5; "Yugoslav Central Committee Building Rented," FBIS-SOV-90-151 (6 August 1990), pp. 31-32.
35. E. Fadeev, "Pravitel'stvo ob''ediniaet sily," ibid., 31 July 1990, p. 1; "Pragmatic Marković Launches New Yugoslav Party," FBIS-SOV-90-150 (3 August 1990), p. 28.
36. Tanjug (in English), 24 October 1990; "Kadijević, USSR Military Delegation Hold Talks," FBIS-EEU (25 October 1990), p. 60.
37. Tanjug (in English), 25 June 1990; "Foreign Policy Talks Held With USSR," FBIS-EEU-90-123 (26 June 1990), p. 59.
38. Statement to 27th CPSU Congress. English translation in *New Times* (Moscow), no. 9 (March 1986), pp. 13-48, at p. 39.
39. Mikhail Gorbachev, *Perestroika: New Thinking for Our Country and the World* (New York: Harper & Row, 1987), p. 64.
40. Ibid., p. 42.
41. Tanjug (in English), 27 July 1990; "Serbian Republic, Russian Federation Hold Talks," FBIS-EEU-90-147 (31 July 1990), p. 75.
42. Ibid.
43. Francis X. Clines, "Gorbachev Given a Partial Victory...," *The New York Times*, 19 March 1991, p. A-1.
44. Francis X. Clines, "Free From Soviets...," *The New York Times*, 10 April 1991, p. A-8. The vote came nine days after a republic wide referendum in which reportedly 98 percent voted for independence. It is unclear to what degree that report reflected the votes of Armenians (9 percent), Russians (7.4 percent), Ossetians, and other minorities. It is not likely that Osssetians (roughly 65,000), engaged in escalating gang warfare with the Georgian majority because their own demands for autonomy and protection were not recognized in the campaign for Georgian independence, voted in favor of independence.
45. Ibid.
46. With 64 major enterprises shut down for the day and tens of thousands demonstrating at Minsk, coal miners in their sixth week of strike, and bus drivers in Kemerovo—a main center of the Siberian unrest—refusing to work in solidarity with the miners, western observers expressed doubt that Gorbachev had the authority to implement the reform package he had put forward along with the demand for a moratorium on strikes and demonstra-

tions. Serge Schmemann, "Thousands Ignore Gorbachev's Call...," *The New York Times*, 11 April 1991, p. A-1.
47. Serge Schmemann, "Visiting Gorbachev...," *The New York Times*, 4 April 1991, p. A-8.
48. See Eric A. Nordlinger, *Soldiers in Politics: Military Coups and Governments* (Englewood Cliffs, N.J.: Prentice-Hall, 1977), pp. 63-106.
49. For the Tanjug (Domestic Service), 19 March 1991, English language version of Milošević's stormy meeting with Belgrade University students in the wake of the 9 March clash between Serbian police and opposition demonstrators that left two dead and 200 wounded, see "Serbian President Milošević's Political Views," FBIS-EEU-91-054 (20 March 1991), pp. 50 ff. Shortly after this meeting, Milošević's Interior Minister Radmilo Bogdanović resigned under pressure from the opposition and students. *The New York Times*, 11 April 1991, p. A-3.
50. English language text of Jović's 15 March resignation statement and Milošević's 16 March speech are given in *Politika: The International Weekly* (Belgrade), 23-29 March 1991, p. 4.
51. Zagreb Domestic Service, 18 March 1991; "Croatian, Slovenian Leaders Propose Crisis Talks," FBIS-EEU-91-053, 19 March 1991. For an analysis, see David Binder, "Yugoslavia Edges Away...," *The New York Times*, 21 March 1991, p. A-3.
52. *Politika: The International Weekly*, 23-29 March 1991, p. 2.
53. Statement by the Armed Forces Supreme Command Headquarters. Belgrade Domestic Service, 19 March 1991; "Armed Forces View Defense Issue," FBIS-EEU-91-053, 19 March 1991, p. 5.
54. Dragan Bujošević, "Secret Talks Tudjman-Milošević," *Politika: The International Weekly*, 30 March - 5 April 1991, p. 1. Summary of Communiqué, "Interests of Entire Nations...," in ibid.
55. Tanjug (in English), *Borba*, 28 March 1991; "Trying to Eliminate Marković," FBIS-EEU-91-060 (28 March 1991), p. 39. On 19 April Marković devalued the dinar by 30 percent and presented his new economic plan to the federal parliament; see Stephen Engelberg, "Feuds Crippling Yugoslav...," *The New York Times*, 20 April 1991, p. A-17. Whatever the reluctance of parliament or "conspiracies" of Tudjman and Milošević against him, the prime minister is probably right that IMF flexibility on the $4.5 billion owed by Yugoslavia in 1991 depends on returning to the path of austerity and economic reform. *Politika: the International Weekly*, 6-12 April 1991, p. 2.
56. Report of communiqué between Milošević and Senator DeConcini. These meetings were cited by Yugoslav sources as evidence that there would be no need for the CSCE Center for Conflict Resolution scheduled to open in Vienna to "get in on the act" with respect to the differences among Yugoslav nations. Stevan Nikšić, "After the Storm," *Politika: The International Weekly*, 30 March - 5 April 1991, p. 1.
57. Reportedly sent 26 March 1991. Quoted by Milica Stamatović, "Future Lies in Democracy," *Politika: The International Weekly*, 6-12 April 1991, p. 2.

58. Chuck Sudetic, "Rebel Serbs' Move....," *The New York Times*, 2 April 1991, p. A-3.

7

Poland and the Soviet Union

Roger E. Kanet and Brian V. Souders

A recent analysis of USSR-Polish relations began as follows: "Short of an unexpected decline in Soviet power, politics in Poland toward the end of this century will continue to operate within the same international framework of domination as in the previous four and a half decades."[1] This statement illustrates the view among specialists concerning the nature of the Soviet-East European relationship that still dominated in 1988. Despite changes already evident in Soviet foreign policy and despite the growing evidence of the vitality of internal opposition in the communist-ruled countries, two "truths" continued to underlie Western analysis: that communists would never give up political power without a fight and that the Soviet leadership would never permit the collapse of communist regimes in Eastern Europe.

In this chapter, the authors are especially interested in explaining the rapid collapse of communism throughout Eastern Europe and the willingness of the Soviet leadership to accept that demise. Moreover, they examine the role of Poland in this process and the probable nature of future relations between an independent democratic Poland and the USSR.

THE CENTRAL EUROPEAN REVOLUTIONS OF 1989

The year 1989 was one of historic importance for Poland, Eastern Europe, and the entire international community as well as comprising a watershed in the history of Europe. At the beginning of the year, political leaders in Poland and Hungary gave enthusiastic support to Soviet leader Mikhail S. Gorbachev's reform programs. Yet even in Poland the impetus for successful reform seemed to have stalled. By the end of the year a Solidarity government ruled Poland, the Berlin Wall had fallen, and German reunification was but a matter of time, Ceauşescu's dictatorship had been overthrown in Romania, and the world-renowned dissident playwright Václav Havel had been elected president in Czechoslovakia. Revolutionary change, in the full sense of the term, was occurring throughout the region, as the basic structures of domestic political power, including the formal institutions of governance, and the structures of the European interstate system were radically changing.

Central to the dramatic changes throughout Eastern Europe were those that resulted during September 1989 in the creation of the first noncommunist Polish government since the 1940s. In the past any movement toward reform met with strong Soviet resistance. By 1989 the USSR's policy had shifted to the point where it encouraged reform and was even willing to accept expanded pluralism and the demise of communist dictatorships, as the price for economic efficiency and political stability in the region and enhanced long-term political and economic relationships with the West.

The radical changes that occurred in Eastern Europe during 1989 must be viewed in the context of Soviet-style state socialism, which consisted of a highly centralized economy emphasizing heavy industry, authoritarian political structures to ensure political control by miniscule and illegitimate communist party elites, and a strong dependency relationship between the USSR and the smaller communist states. However, ever since Stalin's death in 1953 evidence mounted that demonstrated both the political and the economic weaknesses of the system. Sporadically, and unsuccessfully until 1989, attempts were made in various of the countries concerned to reform portions of the state socialist system inherited from Stalin.

After the signing of the Helsinki Accords in 1975, organized movements committed to the protection of political and human rights were active (and under pressure) in several European communist states. Evidence also mounted about the economic stagnation and the fact that the communist economies were falling behind their capitalist counterparts in the development and adaptation of modern technology. Moreover, the growing shortages of consumer goods and housing and the inability to halt the degradation of the environment contributed to growing dissatisfaction with the existing political system and to the demand for political reform that would extend effective political participation beyond the narrow circle of the communist party elite.

Even before the rise to political prominence of Mikhail Gorbachev and the introduction of "new thinking" in the USSR, evidence existed of a growing awareness of the nature of the problems facing communist-ruled states, the imperatives of initiating economic and political reform, and expanding flexibility in relations between the USSR and its East European allies. Thus, by the 1980s the situation throughout much of the region was ripe for political change. However, only after 1985 did the efforts at reform expand to the point of dismantling essential elements of the traditional state socialist system—from the dominance of central planning to the emergence of officially sanctioned pluralism and the demise of the communist *nomenklatura*.

GORBACHEV REFORMS AND THE CENTRAL EUROPEAN REVOLUTIONS

Since Gorbachev's reforms were central to the revolutionary changes that have occurred throughout Eastern Europe, it is important to outline their most prominent contours. First, the USSR was already in the throes of a major crisis when Gorbachev became general secretary. The Soviet GNP had stagnated; the population suffered from increasing political ennui and withdrawal; alcoholism and incompetent medical care resulted in reduced life expectancy and in a higher infant mortality rate.[2] The USSR's "allies" in Eastern Europe suffered from similar problems and were a growing drain on the Soviet economy; Third World clients had proven incapable of establishing stable political or economic systems and contributed to the growing "costs of empire" for Moscow; the exponential growth of USSR military capabilities had occurred at the expense of other sectors of the economy; and many of the assumptions that undergirded Soviet foreign policy during the Brezhnev years had proven false.

In this environment Gorbachev proposed dramatic reforms as a means to rejuvenate the USSR's economic and political system. In effect, the initial Gorbachev message can be summarized as follows: the USSR faced an economic and political crisis that undermined its ability to provide basic goods and services to its population and threatened to erode its position as a global power. Revolutionary changes were required within the economy to deal with these problems and to increase efficiency, enhance quality, and reduce the technological gap with the West. Such reforms, however, would generate opposition within the party-state bureaucracy, which benefits greatly from the perquisites associated with the present system. To overcome this opposition *glasnost'* and democratization were to create an alliance between the reform-minded leadership and the masses of the population aimed at exposing the corruption, incompetence, and inefficiencies of the current system and, thus, contributing to the success of the reform effort.

Thus, *perestroika,* openness, and democratization were interrelated from the beginning of the Gorbachev reform effort. Moreover, "new thinking" and new behavior in foreign policy were also an integral part of the reforms. The nature, scope, and cost of domestic reform would require a peaceful international environment in which Soviet leaders would be able to devote more of their attention to the issues associated with reform. Moreover, the costs of Soviet foreign policy would have to be reduced dramatically to cover the expanded investment demands of a successful revitalization of the economy. Since past commitments of extensive resources to allies and clients in Eastern Europe and the Third World had not resulted in politically stable and economically productive states, those commitments would have to be reconsidered. Since the expansion of Soviet military capabilities had not resulted in enhanced security, efforts would be essential to achieve security through accommodation and assurance strategies toward the West and, thus, to reduce the military burden.

Soviet policy after 1985 underwent more than mere rhetorical change. The dramatic shift in the USSR's position on a number of issues concerning nuclear weapons and arms control was essential to the agreement to scrap all intermediate-range nuclear weapons in Europe and Asia. The announcement in December 1988 that the USSR would unilaterally reduce its military strength in Central Europe and the implementation of the first stage of that withdrawal represented yet another shift in policy.

An important component of Gorbachev's foreign policy initiatives concerned bilateral relations with the countries of Eastern Europe. By 1987 his response to the growing economic and political problems of the region was to call upon the East European leaders to reform their own political and economic systems. Unlike past Soviet rulers, Gorbachev argued that ultimately the decision on reform, as other major decisions, must be made by the East Europeans themselves. Moscow no longer viewed itself as the final arbiter of ideological orthodoxy for its clients, according to the new interpretation of socialist internationalism.

At first Gorbachev hoped that East European communists could reform their economies and political systems to make them viable and productive. However, after they failed in this task, he accepted the idea of a region of stable, economically efficient, though noncommunist states as preferable to a continuation of the effort to maintain politically illegitimate and economically stagnant communist regimes by force or threat of force. Policy was changed in the expectation that mutually beneficial relationships can emerge in the future between the Soviet Union and Europe's dominant economic power, Germany, and a revitalized set of "Finland-like" states in Eastern Europe.

Several important points emerge from the discussion to this point. First, the revolutionary changes that occurred in all the Soviet-dominated communist states were interconnected and had common roots in emerging social groups which placed increasingly greater demands for participation on the communist elites which dominated the systems. Authoritarian elites were no longer able to suppress these groups nor to ignore their demands, with the result that during the last months of 1989 they were overthrown.

In addition to similar origins, the 1989 revolutions were also influenced by changes in Soviet policy toward the region and by the "demonstration effect" of developments throughout the area. Gorbachev's repeated assertion that East Europeans should determine their own fate and that the USSR would not intervene to undermine the process of long-needed political reform contributed to the radical political changes.[3] This "hands off" approach regarding challenges to the ruling party elites in Eastern Europe—in fact, Gorbachev openly advocated political reform in some countries—encouraged those advocating political change to press forward their demands more openly.[4] The success of the Polish Solidarity movement in challenging communist party domination, winning an election, and taking over political power—all without Soviet intervention—exerted a powerful influence elsewhere in Eastern Europe.

Events in the region after mid-1989 went far beyond anything envisaged in Gorbachev's initial reform program for the USSR. He was committed to retaining communist party dominance, while expanding some political liberties, and to making an essentially state socialist economic system more efficient and more responsive to public needs—though developments in the Baltic states in early 1991 seem to indicate that whatever was left of a commitment to reform has been abandoned in the effort to reassert central control. The East Europeans, however, moved far beyond those positions. The new Polish government has already dismantled most of the infrastructure of the centralized economic system; almost everywhere throughout the region, pluralist governments committed to political democratization and economic privatization are now in place.

As Poland pursues its independent path and as the USSR seemingly stands on the verge of disintegration or a return to the authoritarian policies of the past, what are the prospects for relations between these countries? That is the question to be addressed, after developments in Poland that led to the 1989 revolution are outlined.

POLAND IN THE 1980s: BACKGROUND TO THE REVOLUTION

The irony of developments in Poland is that of a society which moved the farthest toward genuine political pluralism during the communist era, despite the imposition of martial law during 1981-1983. Moreover, events in Poland served as a stimulus to (or at least catalyst for) reform elsewhere in Eastern Europe. Autonomous societal initiatives for reform had begun long before Solidarity became synonymous with Polish opposition. In the pre-Solidarity years analysts identified three main currents from which society would press reforms on state authority: intellectuals and students, industrial workers, and the Catholic Church. Initially these groups were isolated from one another. In 1968 students and intellectuals presented demands for greater freedom of expression, but remained isolated from workers, while in 1970-1971 workers struck en masse for economic demands and confronted state suppression without the support of the intellectuals and students.[5] As the economic and social situation worsened throughout the country, the center of gravity of reform shifted from limited circles of intellectuals to a broader social strain involving thousands prepared to engage in public protest. A social movement gradually evolved which shifted its strategy from attempting to influence the system by exerting pressure from within the party to an emphasis on social pressure from outside designed to transform the relationship between state and society.[6]

Some analysts contend that postwar Poland suffered crises of identity, penetration, and participation most severely among all European socialist countries.[7] While these crises escalated during the 1970s, a significant number of autonomous civic organizations, such as the Workers' Defense Committee (KOR), came into being because existing official institutions had failed to realize their objectives and could not meet citizen needs. It was up to new groups to limit the state's decision-making power and to introduce innovation into the social system.[8] In the legal Solidarity period of 1980-1981, a full range of societal groups developed a successful coalition strategy of "consolidated pluralism" that mobilized the majority of society against the regime.[9] This effort had the direct impact of diminishing the preeminence of the Polish United Workers' Party (PUWP) as the leading and guiding communist force in Polish society during the years following the suppression of Solidarity. Subsequent efforts to promote a political dialogue between nonparty organizations and PUWP-sponsored associations such as PRON (Patriotic Movement for National Revival) failed—made all the worse by steadily deteriorating economic conditions.

While the PUWP faced increasing challenges to its dominant position in Polish society, the USSR continued to make clear its overriding interest in the maintenance of that domination. Because of its geographic location within the staging area for the second echelon of Warsaw Pact troops facing NATO countries, the western region of Poland was of major military significance to the USSR. Besides serving as the primary logistic link to the twenty-odd Soviet divisions deployed in East Germany, Poland was also expected, in case of war, to function as a staging area from which Soviet naval infantry would move against the Danish islands and the West German port of Kiel. In 1981 Warsaw Pact commander in chief Marshal Viktor G. Kulikov reportedly attempted to convince President Brezhnev that Soviet armed forces should invade and occupy Poland because of the threat of Solidarity activities to local communist authority.[10]

Rather than risk the use of military force, Kremlin decision makers first applied psychological pressures to contain the dissident movement in Poland. During spring and summer 1981 extended Warsaw Pact military exercises on Polish territory and Soviet military exercises near Polish borders served as threats that the USSR might invade to suppress the Solidarity movement.[11] Later Polish armed forces became the surrogate occupation authority for the USSR. Invoking martial law on 13 December 1981, the government of General Wojciech Jaruzelski implemented a plan drawn up under the supervision of the head of the Soviet military mission in Warsaw. By then the ruling PUWP had lost all credibility and much of its membership, as political authority and economic power gravitated toward the 12-million-strong urban and rural *Solidarnosć* labor unions.[12]

Nineteen months of military rule officially ended on 21 July 1983. After the ban on Solidarity as a legal organization, however, many martial law controls were permanently institutionalized through additions to the penal code. Regime spokesmen admitted holding 190 political prisoners (nongovernment estimates placed the total at between four and five thousand). The last 225 individuals were not released until the September 1986 amnesty.[13]

Gorbachev's initial statements about Poland did not diverge appreciably from past justifications of martial law. Though he admitted, in the course of his speech to the tenth congress of the PUWP on 30 June 1986, that the crisis of the late 1970s and early 1980s had involved a protest against "distortions of socialism," he added "that to attack the socialist system, attempt to subvert it from without, to tear away this or that country from the socialist community—means to encroach not only on the will of the people but also on the entire postwar settlement and, in the last analysis, on peace."[14] Two years later, during a trip to Poland, Gorbachev attempted to convince the Poles of their good fortune that "at this stage of history there has appeared a man like General Jaruzelski."[15]

Within Poland until 1986-1987 there was a discernible weakening of opposition efforts, as the number of independent activists declined markedly after the lifting of martial law and the issuance of an amnesty for political prisoners. Yet, pluralist ideals and hoped-for reforms were at an all-time high among citizens.[16] The veritable explosion of civic activity in 1988-1989 was the direct outcome of a seriously weakened state, disastrous economic problems, including a severe decline in living standards, and an increasingly well organized and determined civil society which not only survived the crackdown of December 1981, but benefited from the communist party's venal image. In fact, the opposition in the post-1981 period became considerably diversified.[17]

The explosion of autonomous political groups and the failure of the Jaruzelski government to generate support for its policies led the PUWP Central Committee in January 1989 to pass a "pluralism resolution" in an attempt to build support for needed economic reforms. However, the resolution was approved amid heated debate and apprehension among officials that legalizing independent trade unions could prove to be suicidal. Less than a month later politburo members deliberated the prospects for a multiparty system, where the PUWP might give up its leading role if ousted by a "legitimate successor."[18] While the regime did not define clearly what type of alternative party would be considered "legitimate," some officials expressed the desire for competing socialist parties vying for the voters' favor in free elections. Nonetheless, a variety of parties representing different ideological positions either appeared or, in the case of precommunist parties, attempted to reestablish themselves.

Another important development which spurred reform efforts was the establishment by independent groups of umbrella organizations that could defend them more effectively against the state. Government officials agreed to accept the establishment of separate public groups to deal with economic problems, a tacit admission of the party's inability to respond adequately to continuing economic deterioration.[19] These initiatives, along with many others including the spring 1989 negotiations between the regime and Solidarity, were undertaken by organized citizens, and not by officials, elites, or specialists.

In Poland, more than in any of the other East European countries, the spontaneous growth of independent activity and its polarization were fueled by the failure of a highly centralized system. The programs of autonomous groups aimed at pushing the country in a pluralist direction with a functioning parliamentary system; an illegitimate communist leadership could offer nothing to stem the growing tide of demands.

Unlike the situation of the hard-line regimes of East Germany and Czechoslovakia, however, Poland's relationship with Gorbachev's USSR was convivial to the extent that the Soviets showed understanding of the complexity of the Polish situation. The Jaruzelski leadership was less concerned about the spillover effects of Soviet reforms than with the positive endorsement that such reforms lent to Poland's own reform efforts.[20] Gorbachev was praised for showing "energy, boldness, and farsightedness" in pursuing reforms and also for taking a realistic stance about the nature and limits of intrabloc relations. Until Jaruzelski stepped down from power, however, there were no overt gestures of concern about the prospects for substantial economic and political instability in the immediate future. Moscow remained calm during the Round Table discussions between the Polish government and Solidarity that, in the face of growing civil disobedience, led in April 1989 to the legalization of the independent labor movement and major electoral reforms; a month later, the Roman Catholic Church was granted full legal status.

The Polish election of 5 June 1989 stood as the most far-reaching manifestation of the reform process in Eastern Europe until the upheavals of fall 1989. In terms of formal political power, the new electoral laws were meant to limit the power of the opposition. Only 35 percent of the 460 seats for the Sejm, or lower house, were filled through competitive contests, while the elections for the newly established 100-seat Senate were open. The results proved a stunning defeat for the ruling Polish United Workers' Party. Its candidates failed to win a single seat for which there was a contested race, while Solidarity candidates took all but one of the seats lost by the PUWP. Moreover, all but two of 35 key PUWP personalities who ran unopposed failed to gain the required majority of the votes cast to ensure reelection. Government efforts to limit the impact of the new electoral system failed, largely because the voters were able to strike off so many officials from the ballot.[21]

Over summer 1989 much political maneuvering occurred before the emergence of a Solidarity-led government in September. In July the issue was the selection of a new president. Only after once withdrawing from the race and pushing the candidacy of the interior minister, General Czesław Kiszczak, was Wojciech Jaruzelski eventually elected president on 19 July by the margin of a single vote. After his election to the presidency, Jaruzelski fulfilled an earlier pledge to resign as head of the PUWP in favor of long-time Solidarity nemesis Mieczysław Rakowski. Though the communists successfully pushed through parliament General Kiszczak's candidacy for the premiership, he failed to form a grand coalition government, and on 24 August Tadeusz Mazowiecki was selected as the new prime minister. Mazowiecki, a Catholic intellectual with extensive political experience, had played a major role in the creation of Solidarity in 1980.[22] He was editor in chief of *Tygodnik Solidarnosć*, the communist bloc's first truly independent weekly.

After decades of the most intense and tenacious opposition activity in the region, the Poles had broken the political dominance of the communist party. For the first time since World War II, they had a noncommunist prime minister and a true coalition government (in which communists held but four of 23 cabinet-level appointments)—but one faced with imminent collapse of the economy and problems of generating effective public support for economic reform policies.

INDEPENDENT POLAND: THE PATH TO DEMOCRACY AND PROSPERITY?

The new government was committed to establishing and strengthening democratic political processes and within weeks opted for wide-ranging and radical economic reforms that would create the foundations for a market economy. In January 1990 the remnants of the PUWP abolished the old movement to form the renamed Party of Social Democracy of the Republic of Poland. This new organization, however, found virtually no support within the country. By spring it lost its stranglehold on political organizing of factories and offices, and most of its property was confiscated by the Sejm. This decision and the debate that preceded it demonstrated the irrelevance of the PUWP's successor for contemporary Poland.[23]

Despite the successes of Mazowiecki's government in laying the foundations for economic reform, by spring and summer of 1990 serious political divisions threatened the unity of the Solidarity movement. Mazowiecki was strongly criticized for the continuing role of communists and former communists in important political and administrative positions. But even when he fired ex-communist cabinet members in July, a parliamentary faction committed to Lech Wałęsa blocked the approval of Mazowiecki's nominees to replace the communists. Only mediation by the Church that brought the two Solidarity leaders together resolved the parliamentary crisis.[24]

With the defeat of the common enemy of communism, the various factions that made up Solidarity since its inception in 1980 found it increasingly difficult to hold together. The problem faced by Mazowiecki was the need to balance the demands of economic reform with those of maintaining social tranquility. The fact that Solidarity's roots are in the labor union movement and that those loyal to Wałęsa had had a different political agenda from that of the government became clear during 1990. The strike of railway workers for wage increases to balance inflation highlighted the problem. Moreover, the political divisions in Poland were complicated by personal rivalries among key personalities. While the Wałęsa political base remained in the labor movement and among the locally based citizens committees, Prime Minister Mazowiecki's support was concentrated among the intellectuals.

The divisions within Solidarity were formalized by summer 1990 with the emergence of two de facto parties, the Center Alliance formed by close associates of Wałęsa, and the Civic Movement-Democratic Action (with the Polish acronym of ROAD) committed to Mazowiecki.[25] The depth of the split became evident during the fall presidential election campaign between Wałęsa and Mazowiecki to select a replacement for President Jaruzelski. They attacked one another in an especially bitter manner, providing the opportunity for a complete outsider, political emigré Stanisław Tymiński to run a strong second in the initial round of the 25 November election and to force a runoff with Wałęsa on 9 December, won decisively by the latter (74.25 to 25.75 percent).

In the face of the potential for political polarization, it is unclear whether, as president, Wałęsa will be able or willing to pursue the policies required to establish a stable democracy. However, his appointment as prime minister of Jan Krzysztof Bielecki, an economist committed to continuing the economic policies of his predecessor, argues well for Wałęsa's commitment to healing political divisions. Moreover, the retention in cabinet posts of central figures from the Mazowiecki government—especially Finance Minister Leszek Balcerowicz, the architect of the drastic program of economic reform—reinforces this assessment.[26]

Intertwined with the political issues have been those associated with the economic crisis. The first task facing the new Solidarity government, when it took power, was the need to bring inflation under control as part of a program of stimulating an economy on the verge of total collapse. During 1989, inflation had reached an estimated 640 percent. The economic reform package, initiated on 1 January 1990, called for a four-phase program of action based on shock therapy to turn around the economy: 1) a three-to-four-month period to break the inflationary spiral; 2) decontrolling of consumer goods' industries and the introduction of some privatization; 3) the much more difficult restructuring of heavy industry; and 4) by late 1993, making Polish currency convertible. The first stage of the program was introduced on New Year's Day with the elimination of price controls and subsidies on about half of all goods (and an additional 30 percent by May). By mid-1990 these stiff measures had brought inflation down to about 4 percent per month and stabilized the foreign exchange rate; however, by the end of the year, it was estimated that the rate of inflation for the entire year had reached 250 percent. By March 1990 a plan for privatizing the economy was in place and, by May, Poland was generating a foreign trade surplus. The costs of this success, however, were very high: industrial output of state industries dropped more than 30 percent; gross domestic product for the year fell by an estimated 13 percent; official unemployment reached over one million or 8.1 percent of the total work force by the end of the year; and real wages dropped by almost a third. On the other hand, there were positive indicators that the shock therapy was working: hard-currency reserves were at a record $4.1 billion, and substantial positive balances were recorded in trade with both the East and the West—four billion rubles and $4.5 billion respectively.[27]

THE SOVIET UNION AND INDEPENDENT POLAND

To this point the background relevant to an assessment of Soviet-Polish relations has been presented. In this final substantive section of the chapter, the specifics of Soviet policy toward Poland in the recent past and likely future developments in relations between the two countries will be discussed. As noted, an essential element in the revolutionary transformation that swept over Eastern Europe since summer 1989 was the reassessment of USSR foreign policy goals and methods that influenced not only the Soviet view of its neighbors, but the very nature of the sociopolitical systems of the region.

After the imposition of martial law on 13 December 1981, Soviet-Polish relations stabilized. With this stabilization came the interpretation that USSR officials held toward the labor unrest and near collapse of Poland's communist government. Elements hostile to socialist rule, tools of Western propaganda machines, and puppets of antisocialist movements were charged with responsibility for the manipulation of the labor troubles.[28] This strongly negative interpretation of events in Poland as the result of Western intervention lasted until 1988; in response to the series of price increases and strikes that rocked Poland early that year, *Pravda* noted that the "enemies of socialism" backed the strikes.[29] By portraying the strikers as hooligans or as stooges of Western imperialism, the Soviets could continue to present the Polish crisis along traditional ideological lines.

By September 1988, when the Polish government finally accepted the strikers' demands for the first set of discussions, the Soviet position had shifted. Solidarity was referred to simply as "the opposition." Later, the Round Table agreements of 5 April 1989 which led to the competitive elections that brought down the communist government were received in Moscow as an example of Poland's struggle for the renewal of socialism. The legalization of Solidarity and the promise of at least partial representation in the Sejm by members of the opposition was presented as the "development of the Polish People's Republic as a state of socialist parliamentary democracy and as a society based on political and trade union pluralism."[30]

Soviet reaction to the overwhelming defeat of the PUWP in the parliamentary elections of June 1989 proved to be much calmer than would have been expected. The initial election reports lamented the humiliation of the PUWP at the polls, and the formation of the first noncommunist government in Poland since the imposition of communist rule in 1944 did meet with some notes of concern from the Soviet media. But, in line with "new thinking," the Poles were presented as having the right to try to find a solution to their own problems.[31] After the swearing in of the government of Prime Minister Mazowiecki, the Soviet press emphasized the USSR desire to maintain cordial relations and cautioned against efforts at thinking in terms of revenge.[32]

In the first 16 months after the emergence of the Solidarity government, Polish foreign policy underwent changes as far-reaching as those in the domestic political and economic realms. Most important were the assertion of Polish independence and the working out of a new relationship with the Soviet Union, the concerns about the implications for Polish security of the reunification of Germany, and the entrance of Poland into the new integrated Europe. The relationship with the USSR underwent several important changes during 1990. Of symbolic importance was the public admission by Moscow, after almost five decades of denial, that about 15,000 Polish officers had indeed been murdered by Soviet secret police at Katyń Forest and elsewhere early in World War II. Probable graves were identified, and President Gorbachev turned over to the Polish government documents relevant to the case.[33]

Though the Polish government made no attempt to leave the Soviet alliance system during 1990, it announced a new defense doctrine that, in effect, annulled Poland's adherence to a joint military doctrine within the Warsaw Treaty Organization (WTO). Pressures mounted in Poland to speed up the withdrawal of Soviet troops from the country. Some 20,000 soldiers were scheduled to depart by the end of 1990, with an additional 58,000 still stationed in Poland. In a wide-ranging debate within the Senate in early September 1990, the entire foundation of relations with the USSR was questioned. Although Senate resolutions are only advisory, they do point to the strength of public sentiment in Poland for a substantial change in the terms of the relationship with the USSR. Yet the Polish government remained sensitive to the need for great care in not pushing too rapidly in its new relationship with the USSR.[34] Throughout this period Foreign Minister Krzysztof Skubiszewski outlined on various occasions the central elements of the foreign policy of the Polish state. He characterized relations with the USSR as "normal interstate and intergovernmental relations," no longer based on ideological considerations.[35]

Trade has emerged as an area of increasing concern in Soviet-Polish relations. Despite contractual obligations, problems in the USSR's petroleum industry have resulted in a decline of Soviet oil deliveries to Poland. Three times during the first eight months of 1990, the USSR unilaterally changed the terms of trade, canceled guaranteed supplies of petroleum, and demanded that the Poles pay for contracted imports in hard currency, rather than through settlement procedures long in place within the Council for Mutual Economic Assistance (CMEA). The issue of trade relations with the USSR is of great importance for the Poles, since the revival of their own economy depends to a great extent on their ability to restructure and develop their economic relations with the USSR and their other neighbors. One result of the visit to the USSR by Foreign Minister Skubiszewski in October 1990 was to sign an agreement for delivery of 10 million tons of Soviet oil in 1991—2.7 million tons less than agreed upon in the past and only 70 percent of Poland's needs.[36]

Another issue of special importance in Poland's foreign policy was the concern about the implications of German reunification for Poland's western boundary and the initial refusal of Chancellor Helmut Kohl to give permanent guarantees about the Oder-Neisse border. The general agreement signed at the "Two plus Four" talks on German unification in Paris in July and the bilateral treaty between the Federal Republic and Poland signed on 14 November 1990 put this issue to rest and, thus, reduced the perceived security need of the continued presence in Poland of Soviet forces.[37]

Throughout 1990 the Polish democratic government also engaged in efforts to establish special ties with Czechoslovakia and Hungary, the two other emerging democracies in East-Central Europe. In part the efforts to forge these special contacts were related to the desire to change the nature of relations within the WTO and to strengthen Poland's position in relationship to its major, long-term objective of full entry into a new and integrated Europe.[38]

CONCLUSIONS

After this examination of the domestic and Soviet-related sources of change in Poland and of the impact of these changes on relations with the USSR, a brief effort will be made to assess likely developments in Polish-Soviet relations in the near future. This assessment is based on several assumptions about developments in both countries. First of all, on the USSR side the discussion is predicated on the assumption that the leadership will continue to be engaged in dealing with domestic economic and political problems that will be virtually all-engrossing—the attempts to rejuvenate a moribund economy, the prevention of civil war among hostile ethnic communities, and the working out of new constitutional relationships among the republics that comprise the USSR. Closely related to these concerns will be the continuing effort to strengthen relations with the West, especially the United States, in order to ensure the international stability required to focus on these domestic problems and to acquire the capital needed to rebuild the economy. However, given the military crackdown in the Baltic states and Gorbachev's general retreat from reform by early 1991, the international environment in Europe may rapidly deteriorate. Should that occur, the picture painted below may be too sanguine.

On the Polish side, we assume continued rapid movement toward a free economy, the commitment to strengthening Polish independence vis-à-vis the USSR, and the objective of integrating Poland within the economic and political structures of a united Europe. We assume that, despite the centuries-old hostilities between Poland and Russia and the oppressive and exploitative nature of the Soviet-Polish relationship from 1944 to 1989, for reasons of enlightened self-interest Warsaw's policy toward Moscow will not be based on efforts to gain revenge or to pursue openly anti-Soviet initiatives.

Based on these assumptions, a brief discussion follows of the likely evolution of the Soviet-Polish relationship over the next few years. In the military sphere, it is most likely that all USSR troops will be withdrawn from Polish territory by late 1992. Not only in Poland, but throughout the entire Warsaw Pact region, the Soviets have already committed themselves to withdrawal, and the demise of the Warsaw Pact as a military alliance reinforces the reduced Soviet military role. As Vladimir Kusin has argued, the end of the superpower confrontation and of the USSR's commitment to controlling all developments within East-Central Europe have deprived Soviet forces stationed in the region of any *raison d'être*. The collapse of the system of communist internationalism directed from Moscow has eliminated the mission of the USSR's troops stationed in East-Central Europe.[39] In fact, given Soviet troop withdrawals, the disappearance of the German Democratic Republic and its army, and the decision by several member countries to reduce their role within the Warsaw Pact, the decisions were to be expected that converted the Pact, along with the CMEA, into predominantly political organizations whose purposes relate to ensuring stable political relations within the region. What emerges from these changes will depend primarily on political developments within the USSR and on the European-wide political and security system that evolves over the next decade. The main point, however, is the fact that Poland will no longer be bound militarily to the USSR and that Warsaw Pact mechanisms will no longer exist through which Soviet leaders will be able—as they were for some 40 years—to control Poland.

Closely related to this issue is the fact that the disappearance of the PUWP and the effective disappearance of the CMEA as a functioning organization have removed two additional mechanisms that have been important to the ability of the USSR to exert strong influence, even control, over developments in Poland. Current, and future, relations will parallel those that exist between other countries; that is, they will be based on negotiated agreements in which both sides attempt to accomplish key objectives.

Yet, this does not mean that Soviet-Polish relations will not experience serious problems. Wrongs of the past are neither easily nor quickly forgotten. Behavior patterns of the past are not easily modified. Thus, antagonisms toward Russia and the USSR are likely to be an important element in the Polish foreign policy debate and may even, on occasion, influence policy decisions themselves. In such cases, we can well expect friction in relations. Related to this is the loudly expressed concern in Poland about the rights of Polish compatriots living in the Soviet Union—especially in Lithuania and Ukraine.[40]

On the other hand, Poland is likely to continue to try to establish political and, especially, economic ties with the western republics of the USSR. The decentralization of economic decision-making in the Soviet Union and the emergence of at least semiautonomous republics within the constitutional framework of the USSR has resulted in an expansion of mutually beneficial activities at this level. It is not clear to what extent the crackdown in the Baltic states portends a return to the centralized decision-making that for more than half a decade has characterized the USSR. At the same time, from the Polish perspective the restructuring of the framework within which economic relations occur with the USSR is essential. Since 1989 the USSR has tended to behave in the economic realm with heavy-handed disregard for the interests of former clients similar to that displayed in the past. Until a new more equitable framework is created, trade relations are likely to remain a source of friction in relations between the two countries.

While the Poles have already restructured their security and political relationship with the Soviet Union and are also committed to major changes in their economic relations, they also seek major changes in their relations with the West.[41]

Of major concern is the establishment of relations with the EC that will result in Poland's full reentry into the European community of nations. Yet, this process will depend on the Polish ability to establish a stable political system and a successful and productive economy. Given the level of Warsaw's continuing economic dependence on Moscow—for both raw materials and markets—the long-term solution of economic problems depends on success in restructuring economic relations with the USSR, as well as on the willingness of the West to provide substantial financial support.

There are many well-known historical reasons why relations between independent postcommunist Poland and the Soviet Union/Russia may be tense and conflictual. Yet, there are just as many reasons, beginning with economic and security concerns, that call for the two countries to overcome past differences and work out a relationship that will be mutually beneficial. In the course of the first 16 months after the creation of the Solidarity government, they made substantial progress in this direction, and leaders such as Gorbachev and Wałęsa seem committed to continuing this effort. Though it is impossible to predict with any degree of certainty the outcome of current developments, one can only hope that stability and mutual benefit will predominate in relations between the two countries.

NOTES

1. Arthur R. Rachwald, "Poland: Toward the Year 2000," in Richard F. Staar, ed., *United States-East European Relations in the 1990s* (New York: Crane Russak, 1989), p. 83.
2. The following discussion is based especially on Mikhail Gorbachev, *Perestroika: New Thinking for Our Country and the World* (New York: Harper & Row, 1987); Abel Aganbegyan, *The Economic Challenge of Perestroika* (Bloomington/Indianapolis: Indiana University Press, 1988); and Edward

A. Hewett, *Reforming the Soviet Economy: Equality versus Efficiency* (Washington, D.C.: The Brookings Institution, 1988).

3. During his address to the parliamentary assembly of the Council of Europe in Strasbourg on 6 July 1989, Gorbachev said the following:

    Social and political orders in one country or another have changed in the past and may change in the future. But this is exclusively the affair of the people of that country and is their choice. Any interference in the domestic affairs and any attempts to restrict the sovereignty of states—friends, allies, and others—are inadmissible.

    M. S. Gorbachev, "Obshcheevropeiskii protsess idet vpered," *Pravda*, 7 July 1989, p. 2.

4. Speaking against charges by CPSU conservatives that Gorbachev's policies had resulted in the "loss" of Eastern Europe, then Foreign Minister Eduard Shevardnadze responded:

    Perestroika is not responsible for the destruction of the political structure of Europe. It was destroyed by the will of peoples no longer willing to put up with oppression. The undermining of faith in socialism based on suppression and violence began in the 1940s, not in 1985. . . . Remember the Czechoslovak Spring? Surely the Czechoslovak Spring could not be viewed as imperialist intrigues. And how many examples of that kind are there?

    E. Shevardnadze, "Vystupleniia na plenume TsK KPSS," *Pravda*, 8 February 1990, p. 3.

5. Jacques Rupnik, "Dissent in Poland, 1968-78," in Rudolf Tokes, ed., *Opposition in Eastern Europe* (Baltimore: Johns Hopkins University Press, 1979), p. 60.
6. David Ost, "Towards a Neocorporatist Solution in Eastern Europe," *Eastern European Politics and Society* 3, no. 1 (Winter 1989): 164.
7. Andrzej Korbonski, "Nationalism and Pluralism and the Process of Political Development in Eastern Europe," *International Political Science Review* 10, no. 3 (July 1989): 254-259.
8. Peter Raina, *Independent Social Movements in Poland* (London: Orbis Books, 1989), pp. 13-21.
9. See the chapters by Maria Halamska, Barbara Wejnert, Paweł Kuczyński, and Krzysztof Nowak in Louis Kreisberg, Bronisław Miształ and Janusz Mucha (eds.), *Research in Social Movements, Conflicts and Change* (Greenwich, Conn.: JAI Press, 1988), vol. 10. On pluralism in European communist systems see Alexander C. Pacek and Roger E. Kanet, "Revolutionary Change in Eastern Europe," in Ilpyong Kim and Jane Shapiro Zacek, eds., *Reform in Communist Countries* (Washington, D.C.: Washington Institute, 1991), pp. 103-140.
10. Cited by Drew Middleton in "Poland's Geography: Russia's Gateway to West," *The New York Times*, 6 April 1981, p. A-11. Former General S. Prochazka stated that 45,000 of his Czechoslovak troops had been poised to invade Polish Silesia in coordination with Soviet movements from the USSR and a token East German presence in the West. The planned attack

was canceled on 5 December 1981. See Leszek Mazan's interview, "Już siedzieliśmy w czołgach," *Polityka* (Warsaw), no. 37 (15 September 1990), p. 13.

11. Military maneuvers on Polish territory lasted 22 days until 7 April, the longest in Warsaw Pact history. The USSR itself conducted exercises during 4-12 September 1981 in Belorussia and along the Baltic sea coast. See Major General A. I. Skryl'nik, chief editor, *Zapad-81* (Moscow: Voenizdat, 1982).
12. General A. F. Shcheglov, head of the 800-member Soviet military mission to Warsaw, oversaw the development of the plan. For a discussion of the martial law decision by an insider, see R. J. Kukliński, "Wojna przeciw narodowi," *Kultura* (Paris), May 1987, pp. 3-57. Some 800,000 members officially left the communist party during 1980-1982, according to Józef Barecki, et al., *Rocznik polityczny i gospodarczy, 1981-1983* (Warsaw: PWE, 1984), p. 151.
13. Amnesty International, *Report* (London: Amnesty International, 1984), pp. 293-297; editorial, "Freedom as Seen from Poland," *The New York Times,* 23 August 1986, p. 22.
14. "Vystuplenie Tovarishcha Gorbacheva, M.S.," *Pravda*, 1 July 1986, p. 1.
15. Cited in Jackson Diehl, "Gorbachev Plays It Safe—and Makes No Gains—in Polish Visit," *The Washington Post*, 15 July 1988, p. A-15. Information in notes 10 to 15 comes from Richard F. Staar, *Foreign Policies of the Soviet Union* (Stanford: Hoover Institution Press, 1991), Chapter 8.
16. The survey "Studenci Warszawy, 1983" documents these views. It was administered in the first half of that year with a sample of 650 students from Warsaw University and the Warsaw Polytechnic. Cited by Maurice D. Simon, "Citizenship in a New Polish Context," in Charles J. Bukowski and Mark A. Chichock, eds., *Prospects for Change in Socialist Systems: Challenges and Responses* (New York: Praeger, 1987), pp. 87-94.
17. A. Smolar and P. Kende, *The Role of Opposition: The Role of Opposition Groups on the Eve of Democratization in Poland and Hungary, 1987-1988* (Munich: "Projekt," 1989), pp. 11-34; and Jiří Pehe, "Independent Movements in Eastern Europe," *Radio Free Europe Research* (hereafter *RFER*), RAD Background Research (hereafter BR)/22 (17 November 1988), pp. 1-21.
18. Jan B. de Weydenthal, "PUWP Accepts the Prospect of Legalizing Solidarity," *RFER*, Polish Situation Report (hereafter SR)/2 (20 January 1989), pp. 3-6; and Roman Stefanowski, "Poland's Economic Results in 1988," *RFER*, Polish SR/4 (3 March 1989), pp. 33-35.
19. Louisa Vinton, "Is Dialogue More Likely After the Strikes?" *RFER*, Polish SR/9 (7 June 1989), pp. 3-8.
20. Karen Dawisha, *Eastern Europe, Gorbachev and Reform* (Cambridge: Cambridge University Press, 1988), p. 167.
21. Vladimir V. Kusin, "Voting Communism out of Office Polish Style," *RFER*, RAD BR/108 (19 June 1989), pp. 1-5.

22. Two days before the vote, President Gorbachev reportedly convinced Polish party leader Rakowski over the telephone that he should cooperate with Solidarity. See Richard F. Staar, "Poland: Renewal or Stagnation?" *Current History* 88, no. 541 (November 1989): 373-376.
23. See J. B. de Weydenthal, "Communists Dissolve Party, Set Up New Social Democratic Group," *Report on Eastern Europe* (hereafter *REE*) 1, no. 7 (1990): 23-27; Louisa Vinton, "The Politics of Property: Divesting the Polish Communist Party of Its Assets," *REE* 1, no. 17 (1990): 17-28.
24. Speech of Tadeusz Mazowiecki to parliament, "Premier apeluje," *Gazeta wyborcza*, 7-8 July 1990, p. 1. See also Louisa Vinton, "Government Contends with Collapse of Governing Coalition," *REE* 1, no. 30 (1990): 29-35; and Richard F. Staar, "Transition in Poland," *Current History* 89, no. 551 (December 1990): 401-404, 426-427.
25. On these political divisions, see the reports by Louisa Vinton, "Solidarity's Rival Offspring: Center Alliance and Democratic Action," *REE* 1, no. 38 (1990): 15-25; "Political Parties and Coalitions in the Local Government Elections," *REE* 1, no. 26 (1990): 26-30; and "Upheaval in Solidarity's Parliamentary Caucus," *REE* 1, no. 47 (1990): 24-27.
26. See Stephen Engelberg, "New Prime Minister's Cabinet Is Approved," *The New York Times*, 13 January 1991, p. 4.
27. See Vlad Sobell, "Shock Therapy as a Tool of Economic Reform," *REE* 1, no. 31 (1990): 49-53; and Louisa Vinton, "Privatization Plan Prepared," *REE* 1, no. 14 (1990): 28-32. For data on the state of the Polish economy see *Statystyki Polski,* supplement to *Rzeczpospolita*, 30 July 1990; *Gazeta wyborcza*, 24 August 1990; and the report of Krzysztof Lutostański of the Main Statistical Office, as cited in *RFE/RL Daily Report*, no. 240, 19 December 1990, p. 1.
28. "Between the Bug and the Odra," *International Affairs*, no. 6 (June 1986), pp. 123-24. On Soviet policy see Roger E. Kanet, "The Polish Crisis and Poland's 'Allies,'" in Jack Bielasiak and Maurice D. Simon, eds., *Polish Politics: Edge of the Abyss* (New York: Praeger, 1984), pp. 317-344; and Arthur R. Rachwald, *In Search of Poland: The Superpowers' Response to Solidarity, 1980-1989* (Stanford: Hoover Institution Press, 1990).
29. A Soviet political commentator traced the history of efforts by "imperialist circles and the antisocialist forces still intact in those countries" to rouse counterrevolutionary forces in the 1950s, 1960s, and 1980s. The strikes unleashed by Solidarity were undermining efforts at democratization in Poland, he maintained. Vitalyi Korionov, "Zemlia vos'midesiatykh: V poiskakh novogo 'dinamita,'" *Pravda*, 6 September 1988, p. 4.
30. "Urok kompromissov—V Varshave zakonchilas' vstrecha za 'kruglym stolom,'" *Izvestiia*, 6 April 1989, p. 5.
31. "Nuzhna shirokaia koalitsiia—Pol'sha posle vyborov," *Izvestiia*, 22 June 1989, p. 4; "Pol'sha—Oppozitsiia: Razdeliat', chtoby vlastvovat'," *Izvestiia*, 11 August 1989, p. 4; and "V press-tsentre MID SSSR," *Pravda*, 12 August 1989, p. 4.

32. Viktor Shutkevich, "Premiery i kaskadery," *Komsomol'skaia pravda*, 22 August 1989, p. 3.
33. Karen Lemiski and J. B. de Weydenthal, "Soviet Officials Identify Probable Graves of Polish Officers," *REE:* 1, no. 32 (1990), pp. 27-29.
34. See Anna Sabbat-Świdlicka, "Senate Calls for Changes in Eastern Policy," REE: 1, no. 39 (1990), pp. 21-26, and Aleksandr Os'kin, "A esli glazami Poliakov: . . . vzglianat' na prebyvanie Sovetskikh voisk v ikh strane," *Ogonek*, no. 40 (1990), pp. 30-31.
35. See Vladimir Matović, "Vlastima—ne aplaudiramo," *Borba* (Belgrade) 21-22 April 1990, p. 6; translated as "Skubiszewski Interviewed by SFRY Paper," FBIS-EEU (20 April 1990), pp. 46-47.
36. J. B. de Weydenthal, "Prospects for Soviet-Polish Trade," *REE:* 1, no. 44 (1990), pp. 23-25. The Soviet trade position is outlined by Jerzy Osiatyński, director of the Central Planning Office, in "Przykręcanie kurka," *Rzeczpospolita*, 14 September 1990, p. 5. On Skubiszewski's visit to Moscow, see "Ofitsial'nyi vizit K. Skubishevskogo v SSSR," *Vestnik Ministerstva Inostrannykh Del SSSR*, no. 21 (21 November 1990), pp. 3-5.
37. J. B. de Weydenthal, "Settling the Oder-Neisse Issue," *REE* 1, no. 31 (1990): 46-48. For the treaty see "Historyczny akt," *Rzeczpospolita*, 15 November 1990, pp. 1, 7.
38. See J. B. de Weydenthal, "Poland and the Soviet Alliance System," *REE* 1, no. 26 (1990): 32 and his "Poland: Finding a Place in Europe, *REE* 1, no. 52 (1990): 23.
39. Vladimir V. Kusin, "The Soviet Troops: Mission Abandoned," *REE* 1, no. 36 (1990): 37-38.
40. During his visit to Moscow in November 1989, Prime Minister Mazowiecki discussed two major issues with his Soviet counterparts, trade relations and conditions of the Polish minority in the USSR. See Tomasz Łubieński, "Kartki z Rosji," in *Tygodnik Solidarność*, 8 December 1989, p. 5. On the call for dual citizenship for Poles in the USSR and the opening up of Polish-language schools and churches, see Krzysztof Leski, "Negocjacje Polska—ZSSR," *Gazeta wyborcza*, 23 November 1989, p. 1.
41. See the interview with Foreign Minister Skubiszewski who noted: "But most of all, we see cooperation as embracing all of Europe, with emphasis on rebuilding the link with the EC, with which we are interested in political cooperation, though we are primarily concerned about economic cooperation." Krzysztof Leski, "Wywiad z ministrem Krzysztofem Skubiszewskim: Rewidujemy Układ Warszawski," *Gazeta wyborcza*, 26 July 1990, p. 3.

8

The Changing Character of Soviet-Czechoslovak Relations in the Gorbachev Era

Carol Skalnik Leff

HISTORICAL CONTEXT

Relations between the USSR and Czechoslovakia have been shaped by two landmark postwar events—the February 1948 coup and the 1968 Warsaw Treaty Organization (WTO) invasion; both of them can now be publicly interpreted in Czechoslovakia as national tragedies, signposts to the quelling of sovereignty by Soviet coercion.[1]

The communist seizure of power in 1948 had a dual meaning: the sovietization of Czechoslovak politics, and the lost promise of the interwar First Republic. Not merely an interval of independence and parliamentary democracy, the First Republic became, retrospectively, a talisman of economic success, when Czechoslovakia was one of the world's leading industrial economies. It was thus invoked as a yardstick to measure the depths of economic deterioration under communism, but also a promise of returning prosperity after communism.

The 1968 Prague Spring, the second landmark event in Soviet-Czechoslovak relations, was an abruptly truncated experiment in autonomous socialist development. The abuse of the country's sovereignty by WTO troops later appeared, in 1989 and 1990, as the starting point from which to redefine international relationships; the official repudiation in December 1989 of the 1968 invasion by the governments involved was heralded in

Czechoslovakia as the benchmark for rethinking the past and reordering the present. Most concretely, of course, the invasion provided the rationale for the withdrawal of Soviet troops "temporarily" stationed in Czechoslovakia since August 1968 on the grounds that the original occupation was now agreed to be "null and void."[2] Domestically, 1968 and 1969 have also been a yardstick, a measure of merit and demerit. Commissions have been organized to study the culpability of the communist political leadership,[3] as well as to provide a means of redressing the wrongs of communist rule. Rehabilitations of previous victims facilitated their return to universities, to the military, politics, the Academy of Sciences, journalism—even the security police—and to any field from which reformist activism had previously been a disqualifier. The settling of debts a generation and more old continues to be a keynote of contemporary politics.

CHANGING PATTERNS IN THE SOVIET-CZECHOSLOVAK RELATIONSHIP

Continuities and Changes under Gorbachev: Political Relations

The Czechoslovak response to *perestroika* was conditioned by one central political reality. Gustáv Husák and a hyperstable politburo that would change in composition only marginally—and grudgingly—before 1989, all owed their ruling positions to the postinvasion "normalization" process that convulsed the Communist Party of Czechoslovakia (KSČ) between 1969 and 1971. Miloš Jakeš, who succeeded Husák as secretary general in 1987, was the same man who had supervised the purge of about 500,000 supporters of reform communist Alexander Dubček some 19 years earlier.

Ruling under the tenuous supposition that the invasion had been a legitimate rescue operation to preserve socialism from the "right-wing forces" of counterrevolution, the regime served perforce as a most loyal Moscow vassal. It was true in East-Central Europe generally that the aging rulers of the bloc would find it difficult to critique and reconstruct polities over which they themselves had presided; in Czechoslovakia, the linkage between current authority and past responsibility became a particularly sensitive issue.

How could Husák undertake genuine *perestroika* without fatally undermining his own claim to govern? "Was Dubček wrong in substance or merely in timing? How big and reprehensible a sin is being prematurely correct?" Was Soviet *perestroika* a vindication of 1968? Thus succinctly did Otto Ulc pose the delicate issues facing the KSČ before November 1989.[4] The party's solution was to preach *perestroika* without seriously attempting to practice it—what Michael Shafir called the "simulation of reform,"[5] selectively appropriating a vocabulary that only increased the gap between regime pronouncements of progress and the political-economic reality of declining performance and credibility. Instead, the party's message to Moscow was verbal compliance and the promise of continued stability, with tightly controlled change focused on the economy. It was a bargain that Gorbachev probably felt compelled to accept.

Symptomatic of the tensions generated by this awkward accommodation was the Soviet inability to respond fully to mounting international and domestic interest in reassessment of the Brezhnev Doctrine and its concrete manifestation in the 1968 decision to invade. Over time, Polish and Hungarian voices in particular joined those of Czech and Slovak dissidents in demanding a reckoning; official repudiations of the invasion by Hungary and Poland in August 1989 predated the general reassessment. As Gorbachev increasingly emphasized Soviet willingness to respect the sovereignty of socialist states and the noncoercive resolution of differences, the failure to confront 1968 decisively became ever more pointed. Yet his advisors conceded that it was impossible to carry through a comprehensive reevaluation as long as the historically implicated Husák regime remained in power. Before 1989, the Soviet stance represented something of a political death-watch, waiting for the older generation of KSČ leaders to pass on before attempting a definitive revision of the interventionist credo of 1968. Hence, the Czechoslovak case looked like something of a general obstacle in the reordering of bloc relations. Until the November/December 1989 transfer of power, however, official Moscow shied away from direct confrontation, appearing to pursue a policy of critique by proxy.

Party-to-party relations between the CPSU and the KSČ were thus rather strained after 1985, as the latter served as both partner and problem for Moscow. Defenders of the normalized Prague regime were reduced to decrying the "opportunism" of critics who seized on the Soviet parallels to the Prague Spring, "socialism with a human face," and—most ironically—to chiding outside disavowals of the invasion as unwarranted interference in Czechoslovak internal affairs. In fact, resistance to significant reform, in defiance of the Soviet example, was often couched in terms of applying *perestroika* "creatively," to meet the individual needs of Czechoslovakia. Although Soviet officials urged "the need for a plurality of views" within the KSČ,[6] they clearly faced a stalemate.

The Politics of Czechoslovak-Soviet Relations After the Revolution

After ten days of successive demonstrations that grew in size to half a million participants, the ruling communist politburo resigned on 24 November 1989. Three days later, a general strike brought all activities to a halt at noon and forced the government to negotiate with the opposition Civic Forum. Noncommunists were admitted into the government. Before year's end, dissident playwright Václav Havel had become president of the country. A high-level message, reportedly sent through USSR Ambassador Viktor P. Lomakin, warned the local communists that delay in political change would mean trouble.

Since this dramatic upheaval, the Soviet Union has had to deal with a transformed political regime that is evolving its own distinctive features and its own distinctive approach to dealing with Moscow. This section will deal first with the character of the regime, to provide a context for the new foreign policy relationship that has evolved.

One of the distinguishing features of postcommunist Czechoslovakia, now renamed the Czech and Slovak Federative Republic (hereafter ČSFR), is that it has had a clear national leader in Václav Havel, who continues nineteenth- and twentieth-century Czech traditions of intellectual activism in politics epitomized by his great predecessor, interwar president and professor Tomáš G. Masaryk. Havel, now in his mid-fifties, gained domestic and international standing as a founder of Charter 77 and as a three-times incarcerated martyr to the cause of a free society.[7] His credentials as a critic of communist power, and his activist moral philosophy gave definition to the "velvet revolution." After his accession to the presidency, Havel's foreign visits helped restore a sense of national identity for Czechoslovakia.

Perhaps equally as important, he has been a force for cohesion at home, consolidating the dominant position of the Civic Forum (*Občanské Forum* or OF) and its sister Public Against Violence (Verejnost' proti násiliu or VPN) in Slovakia, which captured 46 percent of the vote against 13.6 percent for the KSČ in the June 1990 parliamentary elections.

Havel's has been a voice for compromise and tolerance, once the velvet fabric of the revolution inevitably started to fray. Championing a pluralism that extends even to include the communist party, Havel has struggled to modulate pent-up anger and the spirit of revenge. No other transitional system in East-Central Europe has just this sort of political balance wheel.

Havel's political dominance is not a certain recipe for political effectiveness, nor have his moral imperatives made for political surefootedness. The ethos of tolerance has led him in foreign policy where the public was hardly enthusiastic to follow—in his apologies to the Sudeten Germans evicted from Czechoslovakia after World War II, for example. Even Havel's supporters worry that the presidential advisory circle is strong on moral credentials and weak on practical expertise.[8]

Nonetheless, to a marked degree, Havel's weaknesses are an extension of his political strengths. The country's foreign policy and its relationship with the Soviet Union bear the clear imprint of his thinking and that of the dissident community that came to power with him, most notably Foreign Minister Jiří Dienstbier, journalist turned boiler stoker as retaliation for his role in Charter 77. In the context of Soviet-Czechoslovak relations, perhaps the most striking thing about a broad-gauged European and global vision that developed under previous communist persecution is the extent to which the USSR remains central to government thinking. The starting point of the Havel-Dienstbier approach is a recognition of the continuing regional significance of that faltering superpower. Playing with paradox, President Havel told the U.S. Congress in February 1990: "you can help [Czechoslovakia] most of all if you help the Soviet Union on its irreversible, but immensely complicated, road to democracy."[9] A cooperative, economically solvent USSR would clearly benefit the region as well as itself.

To emphasize the centrality of Soviet viability and cooperation is not to say that *Realpolitik* is the unique vantage point for defining the political essentials of Czechoslovak-USSR discourse. On the contrary, the same government of former dissidents that responds with understanding to the Soviet plight could also champion the Baltic cause and host dissident conferences in which Georgian, Latvian, Lithuanian, and Armenian nationalist opponents of the Soviet regime participate.

In addition to the personal standing of the president and his colleagues, the second significant feature of the Czechoslovak decision-making context is the nature of the Civic Forum/Public Against Violence movements. Originally conceived as a "political incubator" to breed a party system for the 1990 elections, the loosely organized OF/VPN remained a monument to "the great aversion of citizens to being organized in the traditional [partisan] structures."[10] In charting a transition from ad hoc orchestrator of the velvet revolution to parliamentary holding company, this umbrella organization has groped for a formula of internal cohesion powerful enough to provide policy cohesiveness as well. Both Civic Forum and Public Against Violence faced an identity crisis in the summer and fall of 1990, characterized as "fuzzy" and "barely legible" by its own adherents. In October 1990, Civic Forum unexpectedly elected a new, more organizationally minded chairman, Finance Minister Václav Klaus, launching a continuing attempt to build a more disciplined vehicle for governance that culminated in the Civic Forum's transformation from movement to party in January 1991 amidst continuing schismatic tendencies.[11]

Meanwhile, the party system that contested the June 1990 elections is still in its infancy, imperfectly reflecting the range of possible options. During the campaign, significant ethnic and regional variations of emphasis notwithstanding, all parties looked to a marketization of the centrally planned economy, the pluralization of politics, and the return to Europe—vague and flexible formulations offering no definitive orientation for the voter even for the seven parties that surmounted the 5 percent electoral cutoff and achieved parliamentary representation.

Party-to-Party Relations after November 1989

Is the KSČ still an entry point for Soviet relations with Czechoslovakia? Forced to cede power and to abandon its leading role in late November 1989, the KSČ did an about-face, and within one week produced a draft Action Program that both condemned the 1968 invasion and castigated the recently ousted leadership for paying mere lip service to *perestroika*. For the party, the Soviet Union was to remain the "chief guarantor" of Czechoslovakia's security. The dismissal of the old guard did eliminate some of the most serious tensions that had strained CPSU/KSČ relations. However, party-to-party relations have lost their capacity to produce authoritative results; even the CPSU may no longer speak with the certainty of legislative acquiescence. As the only left-wing party to achieve representation in the Federal Assembly, the KSČ does, however, have a platform to speak for its program, even though spurned by all as an acceptable coalition partner.

However, the party is besieged from within and without. The membership base hemorrhaged from 1.7 million members in November 1989 to an aging remnant of perhaps 300,000 to 500,000 active members in October 1990, according to then KSČ chairman, Vasil Mohorita. The desertion of at least one million communists did not even offer the consolation of greater unity among a remnant riven by ideological divisions. A further source of differentiation was the KSČ's federalization at its 18th Congress in November 1990, according the Slovak Communist Party (*Komunistická strana Slovenska* or KSS) a confederal status equal to that of a parallel Czech branch.

Even a unified self-assertive communist party would be a questionable pathway of influence for Soviet interests. Although maintaining a base of electoral support, the KSČ faces scarcely repressed virulently anticommunist and also anti-Soviet sentiment sufficient to promote suggestions that it be banned altogether. Impatient with party foot-dragging on the issue of its large and murkily acquired assets, the ČSFR Federal Assembly acted in October 1990 to seize the remaining disputed property. Even Havel cannot always offer protection. In October 1990, KSČ chairman Vasil Mohorita was ousted from the presidium of the Federal Assembly, while communist Defense Minister Miroslav Vacek was dismissed from this sensitive post. Ex-communist Prime Minister Marián Čalfa faced continuing pressure to resign as well.[12] The Soviet Union is attempting to maintain correct government-to-government relations in a situation where party-to-party relations are subject to intense scrutiny. Gorbachev accordingly responded to Mohorita's overtures for a new relationship cordially, but with the proviso that "mutual solidarity and the broad possibility of common operation" proceed in the context of respect for noninterference in the internal affairs of sovereign states.[13]

Changes in Military/Security Policy

The efficacy and reliability of non-Soviet WTO forces in fulfilling Soviet strategic plans was canvassed by Western military experts and found wanting, even before the Gorbachev era. These important studies emphasized the necessity, from the Soviet perspective, of an integrated command structure; "corseting" of indigenous forces with a high ratio of Soviet troops; limited duration of military engagements; and concentration of non-Soviet troops in defense of their own borders.[14]

The Czechoslovak People's Army (*Československá lidová armáda* or ČLA, since renamed the Czechoslovak Army) considered part of the strategically vital northern tier, was buffeted by a series of weaknesses: serious difficulties in officer recruitment, increasingly evident into the late 1980s in falling enrollments for military academies; tensions in army-society relations, reflected both in low military status and in local discontent over disruptive military exercises; and concomitantly low levels of morale.

The end of communist rule therefore only formalized the termination of an already suspect ČLA contribution to Warsaw Pact effectiveness, the most important component of which may well have been the country's arms production. The future military posture of the reconstituted army will necessarily depend on the overall redefinition of a broader European security framework. Certain elements of the country's defense orientation, however, are already fairly clear.

The most pressing imperative that emerged in the fall of 1989 was the evacuation of Soviet troops from Czechoslovak soil; by February 1990, negotiations with USSR military officials produced a timetable for full troop withdrawal by the end of June 1991. The issues surrounding the withdrawal are not merely symbolic, but also practical matters of compromised sovereignty. Still outstanding is the problem of compensation for the environmental damage left after the withdrawal; cleanup costs are estimated to run to some $2 million per site (USSR troops occupied about 150 military installations in the ČSFR), and Soviet willingness and ability to pay are still not fully resolved. A general protocol covering these financial claims, not scheduled to be concluded until 1993, augurs a protracted period of bargaining and disagreement. The troop withdrawal has also been marred by controversy over the treatment of Red Army soldiers wanting asylum, and pronounced Czechoslovak ambivalence about permitting the transit of Soviet troops from Germany.[15]

Looking beyond the waning Soviet military presence, which by February 1991 had been cut by over three quarters,[16] ČSFR officials have also begun to respond to two additional imperatives. The first is the reorientation of defense policy within the context of an—as yet undefined—multilateral European or larger international context. Both Havel and Dienstbier have articulated long-range proposals for a new security system that look beyond bipolarity to collective security, preferably with headquarters in Prague. The ČSFR's current defense posture emphasizes the even deployment of troops across the territory of the state without targeting any specific security threat, which entailed an eastward shift of troops to Slovakia, scheduled for completion as early as March 1991.

In the immediate future, it is important to recognize that the vigor and speed with which the new government negotiated the withdrawal of Soviet troops does not mean that the current civil-military leadership of the ČSFR was immediately eager to bury the corpse of the Warsaw Treaty Organization, which in Czechoslovakia is frankly and emphatically declared moribund as a combat force. The organizational shell, however, retained utility for the Havel government as "an instrument to keep the Soviet Union within the European process" and as a framework for arms control negotiations. Czechoslovakia initially was less eager to push for the immediate dismantling of the Warsaw Pact than was neighboring Hungary, for example. The Czechoslovak security conception garnered support at the WTO Political Consultative Committee meeting in June 1990, where a Czechoslovak draft statement emphasizing the alliance as a "treaty of sovereign states," and the need to strengthen the role of the Conference on Security and Cooperation in Europe (CSCE) was accepted as the basis for the final joint communiqué.[17]

Popular anti-Soviet sentiment and the desire for nonalignment would surely have been permissive of a harsher, more abrupt or more neutralist approach to managing the security transition than the one that has been adopted.[18] Only in winter 1991 did Polish, Hungarian, and Czechoslovak security concerns begin to converge in the face of unrest and the conservative backlash in the USSR.

Domestically, the future disposition and morale of the armed forces is conditioned by broad pressures to reduce and differentiate individual military commitments. The dissident case for demilitarization in the 1980s proved broadly attractive and politically compelling in 1990. In March of that year the transitional government, responsive in particular to student demands, reduced the term of military service from 24 to 18 months, authorized alternate civilian service, and demilitarized the curricula at the country's universities. Between the enactment of this legislation and the fall of 1990, some 14,000 soldiers and prospective inductees had applied for alternate service.[19] The possibility of resorting to a professional army by the end of the century remains under debate, although the clearer current tendency is to reduce the size of the armed forces and of the military budget.

Changes in the Soviet/Czechoslovak Economic Relationship

In economic terms, Gorbachev's initial approach to East-Central Europe was to try to harness its resources to the machinery of Soviet *perestroika,* an engineering feat that recognized the anomaly of a periphery in some cases more advanced than the Moscow metropole. The development of multilateral economic and technical cooperation that always eluded the Council for Mutual Economic Assistance (CMEA) in the past might reinforce *perestroika* at home and reduce the liabilities of an economically stagnant bloc. In this design, more industrially developed Czechoslovakia would be a key actor. A comprehensive program to accelerate scientific and technical progress, adopted at the 41st CMEA meeting in December 1985, was the first of several initiatives in this direction. By 1989, it was clear that an integrated approach to joint problems had failed to materialize and bear fruit. Declining growth rates throughout the bloc gave eloquent testimony to the persistent failure to jump-start the stalled economic mechanism.[20]

Czechoslovak foreign economic relations are now premised on a transition to a radically different economic model; internal debate over the speed and sequence of marketization, demonopolization, and privatization must of course be attuned to changing patterns of foreign economic relations as well. The changes in these trade and investment patterns, however, are not likely to be as radical in scope and pace as are the domestic transformations. This is largely a function of the limits of economic possibility.

The transitional leadership in the new ČSFR was in no position to execute an instant crash program of economic reorientation to the West. Trade with the West actually had declined in percentage terms after 1980, as Czechoslovakia tried to insulate itself from a Polish-style economic crisis by a conservative approach to the incurrence of hard-currency debts. Moreover, the rising world market price of oil necessitated increased deliveries of exports to the Soviet Union to meet energy bills. As a result, in marked contrast to Hungary for example, Czechoslovakia remained heavily dependent in the Gorbachev era on the bloc, and on the USSR in particular, for its trade. Most top officials appear to agree with Prime Minister Čalfa that the Soviet market is vitally important, pending the development of alternative Western markets.

The centerpiece of the Czechoslovak-Soviet economic relationship is the ČSFR's historical dependence on the USSR for 95 percent of its natural gas and oil. Over many years, this dependence represented for the USSR a source of leverage and a diversion of valuable resources that could have otherwise earned hard currency on the world market. Czechoslovakia in turn faces a Hobson's choice in meeting its energy requirements. Reliance on nuclear power raises the specter of Chernobyl and strains relations with neighboring Austria. Domestically produced brown coal is a prime culprit in the country's terrible pollution problem. Hence, fuel imports are indispensable. However, Soviet fuel supplies are increasingly uncertain and more expensive. A pattern of repeated delays and shortfalls in deliveries commenced with January 1990. In light of this continuing problem, and a Czechoslovak aversion to dependence on a single supplier, the government hope is to develop a more balanced pattern of economic relations, with a gradual weaning from lopsided reliance on the USSR without sacrificing access to a Soviet market that may later be mutually beneficial.[21]

The dilemma of energy supply is part of larger stresses in Czechoslovak-Soviet economic relations. Slackening economic growth, and in particular the dislocations of the transition, have produced a declining Soviet demand for ČSFR industrial products at the same time that Poland and especially the former GDR were also pruning back their orders and even canceling— greatly to Czechoslovak dismay—existing contracts. This diminution of regional trade volume has had its inevitable dampening effect on growth rates of an otherwise disrupted economy, and helped to contribute to a four percent decline in industrial output in 1990 compared to the previous year.[22]

The Soviet Decision-Making Process

A few brief comments on the USSR decision-making process are pertinent to the changes analyzed above. The most striking institutional feature of this process under Gorbachev is its diversification from the narrower party elite base in previous years. While Gorbachev's "new thinking" has continued to determine Soviet international posture, often in dramatic fashion, the field of foreign policy discussion has broadened to include open debate in the USSR Supreme Soviet, more systematic expert input from research institutes, more initiative and more open reporting from the diplomatic corps, and greater controversy in media coverage.[23] In addition, the problematic devolution of power to the Soviet republics has created the potential for more diverse and decentralized foreign interactions with the USSR.

None of this institutional diversification has thus far produced a definitive challenge to Gorbachev's foreign policy initiatives, or to his choices regarding East-Central Europe, although there has been growing conservative and military criticism of the lost empire. Public opinion surveys and anecdotal evidence depict a public immersed in domestic crisis; there is no clear popular base, accordingly, to give overt policy content to conservative assault on recent choices in dealing with East-Central Europe. Soviet reportage of developments in Czechoslovakia does sometimes highlight anti-Soviet sentiment in the ČSFR, and bemoan Czechoslovak hostility to the young Red Army conscripts stationed there. But these articles appear to be written more in sorrow than in anger, and lack a clear policy thrust.

When the focus shifts to international institutional linkages, three instruments of USSR foreign policy are meeting differential fates. Party-to-party relations are no longer a policy transmission belt. Even before 1989, however, Soviet emphasis on state-to-state relations was increasing in tandem with Gorbachev's emphasis on national sovereignty. The CMEA forum for bloc economic relations was abandoned in its previous form in January 1991; prospects for the successor organization remain unclear. Finally, the WTO, its military command structure officially dismantled the end of March 1991, is destined for liquidation. Its dual functions, in providing deterrence against the West and assuring the maintenance in power of communist regimes, have both been overtaken by events. Provisional efforts to accent the political rather than the military aspects of the alliance, launched well before the fall of 1989, do not ensure even its political survival, especially in light of regional hostility to Moscow's crackdown in the Baltic states; it may not even survive to serve the transitional function envisaged for it by Havel and his government.

On the whole, the general calculations of cost, benefit, and feasibility that guided Gorbachev's trial and error policy on East-Central Europe framed the response to the specific case of Czechoslovakia as well.[24]

The differentiating factors center on the dilemma of dealing with the Husák-Jakeš regime described earlier. The trade-off between stable leadership and foreign policy reliability on the one hand, and the gains that might be realized from a potentially more productive reformed society on the other, produced a stand-off until 1989, when the USSR made a series of interlocking nonintervention decisions, the most important (non) decisions since World War II. What so startled the West was that Gorbachevian pronouncements about respect for sovereignty and the renunciation of intervention proved eventually to be genuine policy guidelines.

CAUSES OF CHANGE

The key issues outlined in the preceding sections are the following:

1. **POLITICAL.** The fluid institutional context of foreign policy decision-making in Czechoslovakia, centered on Václav Havel and the dissident intellectuals with whom he collaborated in internal exile and with whom he now governs. These decision-makers, operating at the apex of a diplomatic structure still under reconstruction, have given a distinctive imprint to relations with the USSR, an approach that accepts Soviet engagement in Europe, rather than its ostracism. At the same time, however, the paramount goal is to equalize transactions with the USSR insofar as differential resources permit.
2. **MILITARY.** The central military change is the reorientation of Czechoslovak security on a smaller budgetary and manpower base, to perform a more modest defense function. The eventual hope is to preserve sovereignty within a more inclusive European framework of collective security.
3. **ECONOMIC.** The thrust in foreign economic relations is to diversify the base of trade and investment relations, working from the current reality of extensive Czechoslovak dependence on the USSR market and its energy resources. The eventual balance to be struck is premised on maintaining a significant continuing foothold in the Soviet market.

The causes for these changes are mutually reinforcing. On the USSR side, a continuing relationship with Czechoslovakia divested of its political and economic liabilities has been the thrust of politics since Gorbachev came to power. Soviet acquiescence to the decommunization of Czechoslovakia, as in the rest of East-Central Europe, testifies to the acceptance of the fact that the long-term resolution of these liabilities was no longer possible under the hegemony of an economically floundering USSR. While these considerations may have been determinant in the decision to permit political transformation in Czechoslovakia and elsewhere, however, the same constraints also impede the reordering of the economic relationship, as diversion of USSR resources to more pressing domestic purposes has triggered a retrenchment of the exchange of energy supplies and industrial orders on which the ČSFR is still heavily dependent.

On the Czechoslovak side, certain features of the transition would have compelled a similar response by any government. A declaration of political independence, buttressed by demands for Soviet troop evacuation, were integral to the reassertion of state sovereignty under any circumstance. Moreover, domestic priorities were already trimming the defense budget; in light of popular pressures, the current direction of changes in Czechoslovakia's military posture was probably inevitable. Likewise, economic dependence on the USSR constrains any government, however much the country wishes to "return to Europe." If there is a twist to the formulation of foreign policy toward the East, it lies, as suggested, in the specific composition and attitudes of the elite who have thus far defined the course of the velvet revolution and were vindicated in the June 1990 elections. No specific foreign policy program flowed ineluctably from the generalized public support for the reassertion of the country's autonomy and the reentry into Europe. Therefore, one must attach importance to the perspective of a new generation of foreign policy architects, who have been the voices for a modulated, inclusive policy that seeks to ward off a "Soviet Versailles."

In broad outline, the irreversibility of these changes is guaranteed by popular support for Czechoslovak reassertion and by the alternative priorities that rendered the USSR relatively impotent to challenge the transformation. In specific emphasis, however, the evolution of a revitalized Soviet-Czechoslovak relationship is contingent on the course of the internal transformations occurring in both countries, the response of the West, the stability of the governing coalitions in each country, and the way in which existing stresses in the relationship are managed by those elites.

NEAR-TERM PROJECTIONS

This section will extrapolate certain current trends and introduce several factors that may complicate international relations, as the ČSFR reaches its final constitutional form over the two-year transitional period for political consolidation.

Impact Of Ethnic Factors: The Multiplication Of Foreign Policy-making Centers.

One major novelty in the political decision-making framework is the renegotiation of the federal arrangements by which the current Czech and Slovak republics have been governed since the country was federalized in 1969. The "Slovak question" has been a thorny issue for the state since its inception in 1918. Slovakia, with about one-third of the country's population, has long resented economically and politically blighting "Prago-centrism";[25] Czechs, in turn, have seen themselves as unappreciated benefactors of a less mature younger brother. A considerable consensus has developed around the devolution of a significant degree of governmental competence to the republic level, the precise character of which—particularly in the macroeconomic sphere—was heatedly debated in the fall of 1990 and will continue to be negotiated.

The foreign policy implications of this shift in the internal balance of power are not yet clear. Certainly, the prospect of the existence of a secessionist independent Slovakia on the USSR border would be of considerable moment, although at present the independence-seeking Slovak National Party holds only 15 seats out of 300 in the Federal Assembly, and suffered a heavy defeat during the November 1990 local elections. Nevertheless, the Czech and Slovak governments have each established departments of foreign relations, in anticipation of the right to take independent initiative in foreign contacts under a revised federal constitution. The prospect, therefore, is for multilateral dealings between the Czech and Slovak republics, on the one hand, and the 15 Soviet republics as they develop individual outreach efforts.[26]

Military Trends: Scaling Back of the Armed Forces.

In the summer of 1990, then Defense Minister Vacek projected that the Czechoslovak army would be reduced in size from 200,000 to 140,000 by 1993. Defense budget cuts (projected at 10 percent for 1990) and shortened terms of service point toward a restricted army on a smaller base of reserves.

Tensions over internal restructuring and the army's diminishing popular standing (reflected in the overenthusiastic conscript response to the opportunity for alternative service) point toward difficulties ahead. The provisional character of ČSFR membership in the Warsaw Pact has been discussed earlier; the Havel government's commitment to the formal discontinuation of the army's subordination to the WTO joint command intensified by Moscow's military action in the Baltic states in early 1991.

Despite the military malaise, governmental plans for military retrenchment and troop redeployment did find popular resonance in a November 1990 opinion poll indicating that 77 percent of the public saw no threat of a foreign attack. Hence, the deputy defense minister's startlingly unequivocal avowal that "Czechoslovakia has no potential enemies" echoes broad and probably enduring public support for the new developments in military doctrine.[27] Perception of heightened threat, however, emerged with a concern about the growing militarization of Soviet politics in winter 1991.

Economic Trends

The CMEA transition to convertible currency in January 1991 occurred in conjunction with, and reinforced, increasing energy costs for East-Central European buyers. Czechoslovak estimates suggest that in 1991 a ton of crude oil will cost up to four times what it did in 1990—an oil shock comparable in magnitude with those the West experienced in the 1970s.[28] Aware of the economic crisis underlying unfulfilled delivery contracts from the USSR, Prime Minister Čalfa confessed in exasperation that "we have absolutely no information available on how the Soviet Union will behave!"[29] ČSFR projections that 1991 oil delivery contracts with the USSR at the central government level will at best be capable of providing for half of Czechoslovak petroleum needs has accelerated the hunt for non-Soviet suppliers, and promoted dealings at the republic, *oblast'*, and enterprise levels in the USSR. This was manifest, for example, in the effort of Slovak enterprises to promote a countertrade exchange with the Tiumen *oblast'* of crude oil for consumer goods.[30] Czechoslovakia's flexibility in responding to the Soviet shortfall is hampered by the lack of oil storage facilities and, above all, by the structure of an oil delivery system premised on monopoly Soviet supplies.[31]

Ambiguous Impact of Change of Government

The above summary of short-term tendencies in Czechoslovak foreign policy has been predicated on the fundamental assumption that the coalition centered on the Civic Forum/Public Against Violence will continue to govern and to define foreign policy goals through the period of consitutional revision up to the parliamentary elections scheduled for 1992. The distinctive bent of the Havel-Dienstbier approach, with its efforts to accommodate Soviet integration with Europe and its accent on tolerance rather than vengeance in foreign and domestic affairs, would not necessarily represent the proclivities of a successor coalition based on a different center of gravity. Politics in the ČSFR faces an ongoing process of differentiation, in response above all to the exigencies of economic transformation. Whether ideological or nationalist forces in the state pose a real challenge to current foreign policy is difficult to judge. Nor have these forces, or centrifugal forces within Civic Forum, as yet produced an alternative international vision as clear-cut even as their often nebulous domestic programs. The hardest possible thing to gauge in such difficult democratic transitions is the elusive quality of citizens' political patience. It is already clear elsewhere in East-Central Europe that this precious resource can be squandered by political infighting and deadlock. Its importance in the Czechoslovak case is that, if Civic Forum should shatter, its distinctive foreign policy vision might also evaporate and with it any systematic forecast of the Czechoslovak relationship with the Soviet Union.

NOTES

1. The Soviet press approvingly reports the continuing refusal of the Communist Party of Czechoslovakia (KSČ) to disavow the spirit and purpose of 1948. See A. Krushinskii, "Muzhaia v ispitaniiakh," *Pravda* (Moscow), 4 November 1990, p. 5.

2. See Milan Vodička, "Temporariness Draws to an End," *Mladá fronta,* 16 June 1990, p. 5; *Foreign Broadcast Information Service* (FBIS) EEU-90-014 (22 January 1990), p. 18.

3. The USSR refused to provide the damaging letter requesting fraternal assistance, but has generally cooperated in reassessment. A joint Soviet-Czechoslovak conference dealing with 1968 is scheduled for 1991. See "Vyhovejú nášmu záujmu," *Pravda* (Bratislava), 18 August 1990, p. 1. For a critical review of the meaning of 1968, see Petr Pithart, *Osmašedesáty* (Prague: Rozmluvy, 1990).

4. Otto Ulc, "The Soviet Union and Eastern Europe: Will the Reforms in the USSR Make a Difference?" in Nicholas Kittrie and Ivan Volgyes, eds., The Uncertain Future: Gorbachev's Eastern Bloc (New York: Paragon House, 1988), pp. 119-54.

5. Michael Shafir, "Eastern Europe's Rejectionists," RFE, *Background Report*, no. 121 (3 July 1989), p. 2.
6. Jan Fojtík, cited in RFE, *Czechoslovak Situation Report*, no. 19 (20 September 1989), p. 4; Alexander N. Yakovlev, ibid., no. 22 (27 December 1988), p. 25.
7. Biographical information can be found in ČTK, 29 December 1989; FBIS-EEU-89-249 (29 December 1989), p. 23; and Václav Havel, *Disturbing the Peace* (New York: Alfred A. Knopf, 1990).
8. See especially Alexandr Kramer, "Politika s nepolitickým horizontem—sedm měsíců nové československé diplomacie," *Lidové noviny*, 3 August 1990, p. 5.
9. Havel's "Address to the United States Congress," reprinted in *The New York Times*, 22 February 1990, p. A-8.
10. Petr Kučera, OF Coordinating Center spokesman, cited in Dalibor Macha, "Incubator Heats Slowly," *Rudé právo*, 18 July 1990, p. 3; FBIS-EEU-143 (25 July 1990), p. 16.
11. Petr Pithart, cited by Dalibor Macha, *Rudé právo*, 26 September 1990, p. 8; *The New York Times*, 18 October 1990, p. A-4.
12. "V. Mohorita odvolán z předsednictva FS," *Rudé právo*, 23 October 1990, pp. 1-2.
13. The text of Gorbachev's letter is reprinted as "Očistit chápání socialismu," *Rudé právo*, 2 October 1990, pp. 1 and 5.
14. See Jeffrey Simon and Trond Gilberg, eds., *Security Implications of Nationalism in East Europe* (Boulder, Colo.: Westview Press, 1986); Condoleezza Rice, *The Soviet Union and the Czechoslovak Army, 1948-1983: Uncertain Allegiance* (Princeton, N.J.: Princeton University Press, 1984); and Daniel N. Nelson, "Measurement of East European WTO Reliability," in Nelson, ed., *Soviet Allies: The Warsaw Pact and the Issue of Reliability* (Boulder, Colo.: Westview Press, 1984), pp. 2-41.
15. "Smutný suvenyr," *Signal*, 17 December 1990; Irena Jirku, "Účet je zatím otevřený," *Mladá fronta*, 4 October 1990, pp. 1-2; and "Dopis vojína Masljajeva," *Lidové noviny*, 20 October 1990, pp. 1-2.
16. "Sovětská vojska: okupace neskončila," *Respekt*, 10 February 1991, p. 4.
17. Douglas L. Clarke, "Warsaw Pact: The Transformation Begins," *Report on Eastern Europe*," no. 25 (22 June 1990), pp. 34-37.
18. About two-thirds of those polled on foreign policy in May 1990 opted for neutrality over membership in either alliance. Poll results reported in unsigned editorial insert, *Lidové noviny*, 14 May 1990, p. 2.
19. Interview with Deputy Prime Minister Jan Čarnogurský, Prague Television Service, 1 February 1990; FBIS-EEU-90-23 (2 February 1990), p. 21; ČTK, 1 August 1990, 19:01, translated in FBIS-EEU-90-149 (2 August 1990), p. 18.
20. See especially Adam Zwass, *Council for Mutual Economic Assistance: The Thorny Path from Political to Economic Integration* (Armonk, N.Y.: M. E. Sharpe, Inc., 1989).

21. Marcela Dolečková, "Ropa (snad) bude—za boty i dolary," *Hospodarské noviny*, 18 December 1990, p. 2.
22. "Rok utrácení," *Moravskoslezký den*, 16 January 1991, p. xx.
23. See especially "The Foreign Policy and Diplomatic Activity of the USSR (April 1985-October 1989): A Survey Prepared by the USSR Foreign Ministry," International Affairs (Moscow), no. 1, 1990: 5-111.
24. For a recapitulation of, and attempt to interpret, Gorbachev's thinking on bloc policy, see George Schöpflin, "The Brezhnev Doctrine After Twenty Years," *Report on the USSR*, no. 4 (17 January 1989), pp. 1-4; and V. V. Kusin, "Gorbachev's Evolving Attitude to Eastern Europe," RFE, *Background Report*, no. 128 (4 August 1989), pp. 8-12.
25. Rudolf Filkus, "Slovenská ekonomika v nevýhode," *Národná obroda*, 31 August 1990, p. 11.
26. "Hovory v Lanoch s prezidentem V. Havlom," Radio Prague Domestic Service, 21 October 1990; Radio Free Europe, *Přehled tisku*, 21 October 1990, p. 7.
27. "67 procent za armádu," *Čas*, 2 November 1990, p. 3; "Více vojáků na Slovensko," *Mladá fronta*, 3 October 1990, p. 1; "Jsme schopni se bránit?" *Respekt*, 10 February 1991, p. 5; and "Nekrolog Varšavskej zmluvě," *Smęna*, 13 February 1991, p. 6.
28. Pavel Paral, "Are We About to Experience a Raw Materials Shock?", *Rudé právo*, 19 June 1990, p. 2; FBIS-EEU-90-121 (22 June 1990), p. 20.
29. Karel Hvizdala, "Marian Čalfa's Anxieties," *Mladá fronta*, 2 October 1990, p. 3; FBIS-EEU-90-196 (10 October 1990), pp. 20-21. See also "Ropy ještě méně?" *Svobodné slovo*, 24 September 1990, p. 1, on the "deideologizing" of Soviet foreign trade.
30. See "Výmenou za ropu," *Národná obroda*, 10 October 1990, p. 1; "Spolupráca SR a RSFR v oblasti vzájomného obchodovania," *Slovenský denník*, 5 September 1990, p. 2; and "My a ropa 1991," Rudé právo, 21 September 1990, p. 1.
31. "Na co ještě čekáme?", *Lidové noviny*, 3 November 1990, p. 1.

9

Hungarian-Soviet Relations in the 1990s: Stability Through Constant Change

Charles Z. Jokay

HISTORICAL STRUCTURE

For the past 200 years, Hungary's relations with tsarist Russia and the Soviet Union have not been good. From an empirical and a deeply felt psychological perspective, the Slavic giant repeatedly acted as an imposer of foreign political systems, an occupier, and a "non-European" influence, which contributed to Hungary's defeat in both world wars and the subsequent loss of territories. Russia and Hungary have fought each other in these wars and during two revolutions: in 1849, tsarist troops defeated the uprising against Austria, and in 1919, Béla Kun's republic of councils was inspired by the Bolshevik revolution. Hungarians fought against Russia during 1914-1918 and were defeated by the USSR in 1945. A bid for democracy and independence was crushed in 1956 during the "first war among socialist states."[1]

The list of charges also includes a record of domestic interference. After World War II the USSR supported local communists in destroying the freely elected noncommunist government by 1948; high war reparations were enforced by confiscation; prisoners of war were returned slowly, if at all; thousands were deported to labor camps from 1944 until after the uprising; severe retributions occurred after 1956, including the execution of Prime Minister Imre Nagy and his closest associates. Despite this legacy, in the

1960s Hungary became the "happiest barracks" in the socialist camp, only reluctantly invading Czechoslovakia. In the late seventies and early eighties János Kádár developed the country's role of a small nation serving as a bridge between East and West. Hungarian officials were enthusiastic supporters of M. S. Gorbachev. The ruling Hungarian Socialist Workers' Party engaged in self-destructive reforms during 1988 and negotiated its own demise with the flowering opposition movement which eventually took power two years later. The last communist government tolerated the official rehabilitation of Imre Nagy in June 1989, and later that summer opened up the Iron Curtain, which led to the downfall of Erich Honecker and the Berlin Wall in the autumn of 1989 and eventual German reunification the following year.

The history of 1989-1990 in Hungary indicates a total rejection of the Soviet model, as previously had been the case with the 1946 elections and the 1956 revolution. At first glance, the interests of Hungary and the USSR are contradictory and incompatible, and the historical record seems to represent a poor basis for good relations in the future. But since the Soviet Union has "released" the former satellite states, and needs assistance as well as advice on conducting its own economic and political transformation, there is great potential for Hungary to establish good relations with the remnants of the USSR, the Russian Republic, or with any other sovereign or semiindependent entity during the early 1990s.

RECENT DEVELOPMENTS AFFECTING HUNGARIAN-SOVIET RELATIONS

A complete transformation of the political system had taken place peacefully during 1990 in Hungary, without any purges, trials, or revenge against those in the old system responsible for the bloodshed after 1956 and the country's economic problems. The nature of the centrist Democratic Forum coalition government, which came to power on a platform of removing Hungary from the Warsaw Pact and joining the European Community after a transformation to a market economy and rule of law, has serious implications for the development of bilateral relations with the Soviet Union. These implications stem from two sources: the fundamental systemic transformation and issues directly related to military, economic, and political ties that had developed since 1945.

The solidification of parliamentary democracy in April 1990 and the last four months of the "socialist" caretaker government demonstrated to the Soviet Union and to its various republics that a communist/socialist party can peacefully negotiate itself out of power. Hungary's last communist, later renamed "socialist," government with Miklós Németh as prime minister, essentially will go down in history as gracefully having bargained away the people's republic and one-party rule. The agreement among the "three sides"[2] on elections, the partial rehabilitation of 1956, continued negotiations on Soviet troop withdrawal, increasing close ties to the EC and Germany, are some of the policy threads picked up by the Democratic Forum and its coalition partners. What happened in Hungary is essentially a model for other transitional systems. The political transformation took place without demonstrations or violence, a model not followed elsewhere since dissidents stormed into office in Czechoslovakia and East Germany as the ruling party vacated its posts, while in Romania the violent upheaval is far from complete as the "revolutionary" members of the old *nomenklatura* accumulate power. Political transformation in Hungary did not leave any communist figureheads like General Wojciech Jaruzelski nor did it come after a decade of strikes, martial law, and the imprisonment of thousands of activists, as was the case in Poland.

Military Relations

Hungary's relatively insignificant role as a staging area for a Warsaw Pact advance into Yugoslavia or up the Danube Valley was recognized, as the Soviet evacuation began under the Németh government. Even though serious disagreements continue over the financing of the withdrawal, the Soviets are expected to remove their troops, equipment, and dependents by sometime in mid-1991. With the unification of Germany and the end of the Cold War, Hungary, like several of its neighbors, felt no need for the pact, and did not take part in any of its exercises. The military function of the pact ended on 1 April 1991, as announced at Budapest by the WTO foreign and defense ministers the preceding February.

Various levels of Soviet officialdom, ranging from local garrison commanders in southern Hungary to foreign ministry negotiators, continue to demand reparations for facilities abandoned and "improvements" made since 1945. These claims are similar to those against Lithuania, for ports and railroad construction. Though the Soviet withdrawal is based upon an agreement with the previous communist government in March 1989, since then the USSR has insisted upon compensation for the construction at bases throughout Hungary. Many buildings are turned over stripped of all wiring and plumbing. Fuel spills, ammunition dumps, sanitary fills, and hazardous waste remain behind, not to mention damage caused by maneuvers and firing ranges. Areas abandoned by the Soviets often are in such condition that they have to be razed, and some military buildings have no practical civilian use. One motivation for acquiring compensation for facilities "leased" to them by Hungary in the first place is that Soviet soldiers and their families have limited opportunities for quarters back home. Slowing the withdrawal from Germany, Poland, Hungary, and Czechoslovakia eases the housing shortage in the USSR.

Hungarian officials reply that the hard currency the country needs to spend on environmental cleanup by Western firms—removing hazardous chemicals, oil- and gasoline-saturated soil, sanitary landfills, ammunition, garbage, and so on—should be paid by the USSR. In addition, Hungary wants compensation for the destruction caused mainly in Budapest by the Soviet army in 1956.

On 28 September 1990, the Hungarian minister of international economic relations, Béla Kádár, and his counterpart, Konstantin F. Katushev, signed a protocol regarding compensation for both sides. Hungary agreed to pay for Soviet improvements, after deducting "moral and physical amortization," while the USSR agreed to pay for pollution damage caused by their troops. Environmental evaluation is to be carried out by an independent group of international experts. Talks have continued on the exact terms of mutual compensation.[3] The fact that the controversial financial details of the Soviet withdrawal were discussed and negotiated by the respective international economic ministries indicates that USSR-Hungarian military relations have lost their imperial character. By January 1991, only 20,000 Soviets remained in Hungary, but the terms of mutual compensation were still being negotiated. In late December 1990, Prime Minister Antall was considering a new cooperation treaty with the Soviet Union.

A New Security Environment

With the end of a military role for the Warsaw Pact in early 1991, Hungary is left without formal allies, in an environment which has become more dangerous as the Soviet Union tends to its own internal disintegration. Budapest has conducted an intense series of bilateral discussions with all of its neighbors on issues of mutual security. It has assured Czechoslovakia and Romania that any "threat" from Hungary is purely theoretical. Security has been redefined to include protecting not only the territorial integrity of the state but also the rights of Hungarian minorities in neighboring states.

Budapest has sent an ambassador to NATO in Brussels and maintains diplomatic relations with the European Community (EC) as well. Hungary pursues its broad security objectives, not only on a bilateral level, but also in multilateral fora such as the CSCE follow-up conferences. Membership in the Council of Europe was granted in October 1990, which obligates it to a high standard of civil liberties and the rule of law. Hungary's interest is not to exclude Czechoslovakia or Romania from this body, since membership implies rights for ethnic minorities which are not currently a priority for either of these potential members.

An additional element of Hungarian security policy is the goal of joining the EC, which involves a transfer of sovereignty that policymakers have yet not fully understood.

Political Issues

Hungary's primary foreign policy intention is to join the European Community first as an associate member and then as a full member. The overall "desovietization" of foreign policy lies in its explicit East-Central European orientation, which by definition excludes the current Soviet Union. On the diplomatic front Budapest actively promotes at least four forms of such cooperation: Alpine-Adriatic (parts of Bavaria, Austria, Italy, Yugoslavia, Hungary); the Pentagonal Group (Austria, Italy, Yugoslavia, Hungary, Czechoslovakia); the newest, the Tisza-Carpathian Group (Hungary, eastern Slovakia, Transylvania, Ukraine); and finally a Czechoslovakia-Hungary-Poland group, advocated by Václav Havel. This last tripartite effort may add the Baltic states in the future. Prime Minister Antall also has called for an "East-Central European Union" to come into being, after dismantling of the Warsaw Pact, and which would be a balancer between the West European Union and the USSR.[4] Poland and Yugoslavia are expected to act as bridges to the Baltic states and the Balkans respectively.

A critical principle of Hungarian participation in these multilateral consultations is protection of the linguistic, educational, cultural, and collective rights of ethnic minorities. Yet enthusiasm for these potential forms of East-Central European cooperation does not replace the number one foreign policy goal, namely, "rejoining Europe." Prime Minister Antall has declared unequivocally that no form of regional cooperation is an alternative to all-European unity. Instead, regional cooperation simply invigorates historical and economic ties on a geographical basis. In other words, even Hungary, an enthusiastic supporter of East-Central European cooperation, will not place regional efforts above the goal of joining the European Community and other Western bodies.[5] The "Europeanization" and simultaneous "Central Europeanization" of Hungary's foreign policy orientation explicitly desovietizes these relations, by excluding the Soviets from regional associations and by abandoning organizations that the USSR established to dominate that sphere after 1945. However, some versions of East-Central European cooperation include the possibility of expansion in two directions: incorporating various regions or republics of the USSR; or inviting newly independent former Soviet republics to join, such as the three future Baltic states. Thus in the long run, confederal proposals will include what is left of the Soviet Union, after a range of independence and sovereignty has been attained.

Just as the EC legitimized and made acceptable German reunification, some form of non-EC and non-NATO confederation in East-Central Europe may legitimize total independence for various Soviet republics seeking it and allow Moscow to shed the union of restive republics while saving face, since the new association is friendly and nonthreatening to the USSR itself. As defined by Foreign Minister Géza Jeszenszky, the Soviet Union becomes one leg of a "five-legged" Hungarian foreign policy, whose other limbs include Germany, France, the United States, and Hungary's neighbors.[6]

The Soviet Union has apologized to Czechoslovakia for the 1968 invasion, and has conceded that the Molotov-Ribbentrop agreement was immoral. However no official state or party organ has apologized for suppressing the 1956 revolution, which killed thousands of Hungarians, including Prime Minister Nagy, during the fighting and several years of retribution thereafter. In August 1990 the Hungarian parliament requested that the USSR Supreme Soviet declare the 1956 intervention illegal. A delay in this awaited formal reconciliation could prevent a full redefinition of Hungarian-Soviet relations.

Popular and official frustration is growing in Hungary at the weak Soviet responses to Hungarian concerns. Soviet views on 1956 are divided. For example an article attributed to hard-line elements appeared in *Pravda* which called the 1956 invasion a "necessary and a tragic action."[7] On the other hand Dmitrii Markov, a Soviet academician who studies Hungary at the Institute on the World Economy and International Relations (IMEMO), stated that "acknowledging our sins is not only a historical and ethical necessity, but a symbol of goodwill and an indicator of good-neighborliness."[8] The diversity of opinions emanating from the USSR does not however disguise the fact that an official apology has not been made.

Potential Recognition of "Sovereign" Soviet Republics

Hungary greets the declaration of independence and sovereignty by most of the Soviet republics with enthusiasm. In other words, Budapest is willing to conduct relations directly with those republics, if they approach Hungary first. Political sympathy and solidarity is most evident with the Baltic states, where direct contacts exist and recognition is likely. The centrally planned trading system cannot deliver enough energy to Hungary and to the rest of East-Central Europe. Therefore, Hungary, Poland, and the Czech and Slovak governments are ready to negotiate directly with the local governments of the other oil-producing regions in the USSR.

There are indications that Hungary will support moves toward independence and sovereignty among various republics of the Soviet Union. After announcing bilateral relations with Ukraine, Prime Minister Antall pointed out the following in a speech to the Council on Foreign Relations:

> We support the attempts of other republics in the Soviet Union to regain their sovereignty, in particular the Baltic countries ... We trust that Mr. Gorbachev, who in his own thinking has moved away from reform of an incurable political system and now endorses democratic pluralism, will definitely adopt the thinking of those Russians, who propose sovereignty and fair relationships of [for] republics within a new kind of Soviet Union.[9]

The prime minister explicitly has hinted at the role of Hungary and other East-Central European states in reshaping the USSR into a voluntary democratic confederation of independent states.

If democracy and market economics emerge in the republics and overall in the Soviet Union, then Hungary is ready to expand friendly ties.[10] In late September 1990, Budapest and Kiev expanded consular ties in preparation for possible full diplomatic relations. The Ukrainian government also promised "cultural autonomy" for the Hungarian minority in Subcarpathia. Also in late September 1990, Estonia and Hungary agreed to establish consular ties. The possibility of a new web of direct political and economic ties among the former states of the outer Soviet empire could be interpreted as threatening by Moscow, or conversely it could form the basis of a peaceful transition to a confederation in place of the USSR. Poland has followed Hungary in signing a cooperation treaty with Ukraine on 15 October 1990, and Lithuania has formal relations with Czechoslovakia. The Lithuanian prime minister on an unofficial visit to Budapest to commemorate the 1956 revolution hinted at incipient consular relations in the near future.

Soviet Foreign Minister Eduard A. Shevardnadze's resignation and the stern warning he issued about looming dictatorship in the USSR was greeted with grave concern in Hungary. In January 1991, the crackdown in the Baltics was carefully condemned and compared to 1956 by Hungarian foreign ministry officials. In parliament, József Antall expressed support for the Lithuanian people's "heroic fight for freedom." He called on the Conference for Security and Cooperation in Europe to resolve the situation. Foreign Minister Jeszensky summoned the Soviet ambassador to express Hungary's official concern.[11]

Economic Problems

A significant and stubborn cause of controversy is the 45-year-old system of foreign trade in the USSR, based upon barter of energy for goods uncompetitive on the world market at negotiated prices in negotiated quantities. Long after Hungary has left the Warsaw Pact and removed all other vestiges of communism, socialism, and the Soviet army, the economic damage caused by CMEA will remain to haunt the transformation process.

Soviet-Hungarian economic relations in the 1990s will be influenced at first by the shock of converting the CMEA's barter system of bilateral trade in transferable rubles to a system of world market pricing in hard currency. In addition, Hungary's commitment to a full transformation to a market system is complicated by existing delivery quotas from and to CMEA partners, and the structure of industry which guarantees large-scale unemployment as CMEA trade converts to a rational system. Not only will Hungary have to pay hard currency for its imports of Soviet energy and raw materials starting in 1991, it will also have to privatize its economy, establish capital, wholesale and retail markets, as well as absorb the costs of transition: inflation from price decontrol and unemployment from rationalization. This painful recovery from the Soviet-imposed trading system, inefficient industry, high-level pollution, and totally inappropriate economic structure is complicated by an accumulated Soviet trade deficit. Heavy industries which used to export to the USSR and the former East Germany face bankruptcy, as those countries refuse to accept shoddy goods and demand hard currency for their own exports. The János Kádár and later regimes tried repeatedly to reform the CMEA from within, and to simultaneously expand Hungary's trade with the hard-currency areas. The commitment to a completely Western orientation is now total with the new government.

Once the initial shock of transition has been absorbed, Hungary will still be plagued with an energy infrastructure overwhelmingly reliant upon Soviet supplies, industrial standards designed for the USSR market, a heavy reliance upon imported raw materials, and a legacy of inferior products. In a sense, the debate over Soviet subsidization of East-Central Europe through energy prices below world market prices could be settled by determining the opportunity cost of central planning and membership in the CMEA: compare Austria to Hungary, and the former East Germany and the Czech lands to West Germany.

The Iraqi invasion of Kuwait and the consequent fluctuation in energy prices hurt the Hungarian economy by raising the cost of ever-shrinking Soviet fuel supplies, and by increasing hard-currency liabilities to alternative suppliers.

Though the sudden energy price increases nearly caused the Hungarian government to collapse after a three-day transport strike in October 1990, changes in the Soviet-Hungarian trading relationship are far more significant. Specifically, CMEA as an organization ceased to exist in January 1991. However, existing trade patterns, payment systems, and debts still were a subject of bilateral Hungarian-Soviet negotiation throughout 1990. The USSR cut its energy shipments to Hungary throughout 1990 by at least 30 percent. Yet Hungary ran a trade surplus with the Soviets at the end of 1990. The total accumulated trade surplus is 1.2 billion transferable rubles. The Soviets have agreed to convert this to $1.1 billion (U.S.). The exact terms of payment were still not decided in January 1991.[12]

In general, ruble balances would be paid off by March 1991 with Poland and Czechoslovakia, while trade with the former East Germany switched to a hard-currency basis in July 1990. Hungary's losses from switching to dollar clearing with the USSR were estimated by some to be in excess of $1.5 billion. This figure is disputed by some economists since Hungarian-Soviet trade volume had shrunk by over 30 percent since 1989, with the Soviet share of overall trade at about 20 percent in 1990, compared to 40 percent in 1988. Germany and the European Community have replaced the USSR as Hungary's most important trading partners. Calculated from the current structure of trade, Hungary's one-time losses of switching from ruble trade to dollar trade with the Soviet Union amount to $300 million.[13]

The best indicator of Hungarian-Soviet economic relations for 1991 is the reduction of Soviet oil shipments from 6.5 million metric tons in 1990 to only 1 million tons in 1991. In the 1991 trade protocol the Soviets will ship $2.1 billion of goods, while Hungary will export $1.7 billion's worth. The protocol specifically calls for Hungary to make up its needs through direct contacts with individual republics and enterprises. The trade agreement puts economic relations on three levels: Hungarian-All Union, Hungarian-republic, and interenterprise. This treaty sets a precedent for the other East-Central European countries as well, and acknowledges that individual republics have economic needs of their own, a stance that supports Hungary's approach to independence-minded republics.[14]

East-Central Europe Outruns the USSR Decision-Making Process

Soviet policy after 1988 was uncoordinated, badly timed, and implemented only in reaction to initiatives taken by parties, governments, and populations alike in East-Central Europe. Gorbachev's approach to Hungary and the other radical reformers during 1988-1989 revealed a new version of the "Common European House" (CEH) slogan. The laissez-faire approach of 1990 was preceded by two other versions.

L. I. Brezhnev's interpretation of the CEH was expansionist, i.e., it was intended to separate the United States from Europe and to reorganize the continent under Soviet leadership. The neutron bomb debate, the initial Pershing II and cruise missile decision, and the reluctance of the West European countries to take part in the grain and pipeline embargo were exploited to promote the CEH as a pragmatic West European defense against American extremism and ideological crusading. Reflecting the policies of K. U. Chernenko and Iu. A. Andropov, the later version of the CEH doctrine was intended to defend the status quo in Europe, i.e., promote ties between East and West Europe that would transfer technology, yet sterilize any potential political effect upon the desires for democracy within the East-Central European countries.[15]

The new Soviet interpretation of the CEH doctrine under Gorbachev is designed to give up systemic competition, and is aimed at obtaining Western aid to modernize the Soviet and East-Central European economies. In the context of Hungary, by the time this doctrine was made clear, the last communist government had decided to eventually join the EC, and did not frame its foreign or economic policy in deference to Soviet wishes.

The new USSR doctrine is aimed at obtaining favorable conditions for internal reform through reduced military expenditures, withdrawal from the Third World, reduced conflict with China, and economic cooperation with the West. In terms of ideology, this new foreign policy dropped class conflict, redefined peaceful coexistence as avoiding war and/or initiating and escalating violence, and made clear that countries have the right to choose their own path of social development.

The Brezhnevian "irreversibility of the gains of socialism" was ejected from doctrine, but in practical terms Hungary and Poland had already disregarded it in the mid-1980s. On the eve of the Hungarian Socialist

Workers' Party agreement with the opposition to hold democratic elections, which spelled the end of communist rule in Hungary, Gorbachev stated to the European Parliament that the new Common European House policy rules out violence among and within alliances. And all peoples have the right to change their political-social order if they wish.

At that point, changes in Hungary and Poland were more threatened by hostile reactions from Gustáv Husák's Czechoslovakia, Nicolae Ceauşescu's Romania, and Erich Honecker's East Germany, than by the USSR. Positive signals toward Hungary by Aleksandr N. Iakovlev in late 1988 and by Gennadii I. Gerasimov in late 1989 indicated that the USSR supported Hungary's experimentation and had no intention of intervening. Whether the USSR had the will or capability to stop the democratization process in Hungary is irrelevant when considering that tacit and explicit support for the process built up goodwill, goodwill which partially compensates Hungary for suppressing the revolutions in 1849 and 1956 by intervention from the East.

Some Soviet commentators greeted the momentous changes in East-Central Europe with great enthusiasm, calling them the end of "administrative, etatist socialism that in some places assumed the form of rigid feudal tyranny." The changes, whether demanded by crowds in the street or a result of many years of reform communism, are hailed as being legitimate. Some analysts admit USSR responsibility for imposing alien systems with "a stern hand" upon the region. There is little sense in the contention that the USSR "lost" East-Central Europe. Instead, the possibility of a pluralistic world with no clearly defined blocs and allegiances is greeted as a positive development.

Others argue that the reform attempts of various East-Central European countries starting in the 1960s offer a model for the USSR to emulate. Thus experimentation with economic transformation in Poland, Hungary, and Czechoslovakia offer a laboratory for the USSR to draw upon and positive aspects to emulate.[16]

Gorbachev alone does not deserve commendation for "letting Hungary go" in 1989. Instead, a larger, systemic factor should also be taken into account: the realization that the Soviet model and the various permutations of "existing" or "reform socialism" doomed its practitioners to inferior standards of living, and grave environmental and technological inadequacy. Peter Robejsek summarized both the new model of Soviet foreign policy and the systemic factor in the following manner:

> The efforts of Gorbachev to integrate the USSR into the world economy as quickly as possible allowed the return of the small East-Central European states

to Europe. The common denominator of this return however is *asymmetric convergence*, the one-sided approach towards the Western model of society.[17]

The Hungarian parliament passed a resolution aimed at asking the USSR Supreme Soviet to condemn and declare illegal the 1956 Soviet intervention in Hungary. Spokesman Gennadii Gerasimov earlier had called events in 1968 and 1956 "inadmissible." Some feel that an apology may be an issue, but it is not a high priority for Gorbachev, who is struggling for the economic survival of the USSR and the preservation of his own power.

In sum, earlier versions of the Common European House thesis included defensive mechanisms such as the Brezhnev Doctrine, and neutralization of the devolutionary effects of increased East-West contacts. Gorbachev's policy of laissez-faire toward Hungary and Poland must however be placed in the context of implicit condemnation and perhaps covert sabotage of the paleocommunist "embarrassments to socialism": Honecker, Husák, and Ceauşescu. Gorbachev's and the USSR's role thus shifted from preservation of the status quo to encouraging domestic opposition against the various vestiges of the Brezhnevite legacy in East-Central Europe.

EXPLAINING THE SHIFT IN USSR POLICY

Numerous global and environmental factors governed the change in Soviet attitudes toward East-Central Europe. The information revolution, USSR technological backwardness, the failure of the Soviet economy, among others, acted to alter the general world view dominating the foreign policy machinery. In addition, autonomous actions by elites and masses in the East-Central European countries themselves were factors completely beyond USSR control.

However, the major question remains: why did the Soviet Union "let East Europe go," or at least why did it not more actively and effectively resist pressures for change? Several hypotheses are presented below, which are not mutually exclusive and certainly do not offer a complete explanation. Rather they suggest possible cost and benefit calculations which may have shaped policy.

From a purely economic perspective, Hungary was a marginal buyer of Soviet energy products. Even if market prices charged in hard currency replaced the transferable ruble or barter system, this would not have any substance or impact on the USSR. The inherent "subsidy" to East-Central Europe was determined by the difference between the five-year moving average of world prices used in CMEA and the true market price for oil. The

Soviets could have sold that oil and other raw materials in theory at world market prices and for hard currency elsewhere. Thus, letting East-Central Europe go can be interpreted from a cost-cutting perspective.

The energy infrastructure, military presence, and trade in shoddy goods, among other methods, were designed to maintain the external empire. The benefit to the USSR was a string of allies who were totally dependent on it for cheap energy and as a market for goods not salable on the world market. That network of friendly states formed a barrier and a forward deployment area for a potential war against "German revanchism" and U.S.-inspired NATO imperialism. Once the mythical danger of a Western attack was disproven, the economic cost of empire became more transparent and unsustainable.

From a political perspective, tiny Hungary poses no danger to the USSR. Its involvement with potential East-Central European associations, and its improving ties to the EC could benefit the USSR as well. Surely the Soviets felt that a centrist democratic government would not be hostile to the USSR, even though it would hold firm positions on leaving the WTO and CMEA as quickly as possible. This view has been confirmed by Foreign Minister Jeszenszky as well:

> In fact, if our relationship is free of one-sided dependence and imposed alliance and friendship, we have good possibilities for establishing really fruitful economic and political relations with the USSR.[18]

Having abandoned plans to initiate a war against the West, the USSR perhaps recognized that it had nothing to fear from a Hungary firmly anchored in the Western political sphere. The USSR could benefit from an East-Central Europe with access to EC markets, hard currency, and high technology.

Renouncing the Brezhnev Doctrine coincided with another significant event in the Soviet approach to the region. In 1985 the USSR recognized the European Community as an entity independent of both the U.S. and NATO. The EC passed the Single Europe Act the following year, presaging a market of 320 million consumers. That body, with increasing political cooperation among its top government leaders and bureaucracies at all levels, occupies a significant portion of the Common European House. In May of 1985, M. S. Gorbachev indicated to visiting Italian communists that he would not oppose direct ties between the EC and various CMEA members. During Italian Prime Minister Bettino Craxi's discussions with Gorbachev later that month, the latter declared his wish to bring order to the relationship between the two economic blocs in Europe.[19]

Treating the EC as a legitimate partner for the small East-Central European states contributed toward the new Soviet approach of allowing those states to pursue their economic interests independently, and often in direct contradiction to declared Soviet and CMEA principles.

The historically Western states of Hungary, Czechoslovakia, and Poland were attracted to the EC from a cultural and pragmatic point of view. Not only did the EC offer concrete economic rewards, it held an alternative political-philosophical orientation, and offered a democratic solution to ending Soviet dominance. In the past, the leadership of the USSR tried to discipline CMEA members who dealt with the EC Commission directly, instead of using the CMEA Secretariat, but without success. Soviet recognition of the EC as an emerging economic and later political superpower, and its magnetic attraction to East-Central Europe, may have convinced the USSR leadership to "allow" the EC to absorb the outer empire into its sphere.

By separating the political, economic, and military components of security, Soviet policy makers in 1988 braced themselves for the ensuing emergence of the EC as a political actor, fortified by the future internal market of 1992. Thus global environmental factors, combined with the economic burden of empire, the declining utility of ideological conformity, and the passive and active presence of the EC, may explain the Soviet adoption of a laissez-faire approach toward East-Central Europe, and acceptance of asymmetric convergence.

THE NATURE OF SOVIET-HUNGARIAN RELATIONS IN THE 1990s

Despite the overwhelming economic, military, and political weight of an empire undergoing internal fragmentation and fundamental transformation, the USSR has slipped to a relatively low priority in Hungarian foreign policy. To completely reorient a domestic political system and the fundamental principles of foreign policy has proven easier than the economic transformation which severs energy dependence and reverses foreign trade orientation. In the near term, Hungarian-Soviet relations will continue to be dominated by trade disputes and arrangements to dismantle the CMEA system. Dependence on USSR supplies, solidified in a pipeline and power-line infrastructure, cannot be altered quickly. While Hungary will reorient its trade toward Germany and the EC, a large fraction of its energy needs will be supplied by the USSR.

Besides the inherent disputes in dismantling CMEA and the details and costs of Soviet military withdrawal, relations with the USSR have become a side show to three major concerns of Hungarian foreign policy:
1. Rejoining Europe through association and eventual membership in the EC;[20]
2. Ensuring the rights of nearly 4 million Hungarians living in areas that became parts of Yugoslavia, Czechoslovakia, and Romania after World War I;
3. Supporting new forms of cooperation through several East-Central European regional groupings.

Hungary and the USSR have to settle the untidy business of the Cold War, i.e., Soviet troop withdrawal and compensation. The burden of "socialism," inadequate infrastructure and outdated industries, will remain long after CMEA formally comes to an end. Once the shock of these nonrecurring issues settles, there is much hope for friendly relations.

Rejoining Europe

Rejoining Europe in an economic sense is both a desired result and a method of supporting transformation. As a goal, becoming a capitalist, prosperous, democratic country like Austria or the Federal Republic of Germany is paramount. EC membership is seen as a magical formula to achieve prosperity as well as economic transformation. Associate and eventual full EC membership is supposed to propel Hungarian exports, pull in capital investment, training and technology. However, painful and comprehensive reforms are required for entry into the EC. Hungary has obtained the support of several West European states for its membership effort, including Germany and Britain.[21] The goal of EC membership motivates industrial restructuring and privatization. But EC membership, or associate status alone, does not alleviate impending inflation and unemployment. Hence, privatization and the creation of an entrepreneur sector should take place regardless of potential membership. Creating favorable conditions for domestic and foreign investors and building an infrastructure to attract investors can take place without EC membership.

Membership also has a spiritual, symbolic meaning. Hungarians need recognition from the rest of Europe that they are considered a part of the Western world. Feeling emasculated by the allied powers after World War I, when the country lost two-thirds of its historical territory, Hungarians felt betrayed by the allied powers during World War II, when the awaited

Anglo-American invasion never took place, and the USSR was assigned to "liberate" Hungary. Of course, Hungarians felt abandoned to the Soviets in 1956 as the West, which had declared the doctrine of rollback, claimed to avoid nuclear war by letting Khrushchev settle matters in his sphere of influence. Membership in the EC would be a historical apology for "abandoning" Hungary to the Soviets, an expression of gratitude for allowing East Germans to escape, and a recognition of Hungary's self-liberation and dedication to parliamentary democracy. Associate and eventual full membership, thus, has emotional and psychological meaning beyond any real or perceived benefits of unrestricted access to the internal market.

Hungary and Its Neighbors

Hungary's other foreign policy priority only affects the USSR regarding Subcarpathia, a part of Ukraine since the end of the Second World War. Roughly one out of three ethnic Hungarians lives in countries surrounding Hungary. Some are concentrated in compact, homogeneous communities, while others live near the Hungarian border in cities and villages which experienced a large influx of non-Hungarians since 1920. It is clear that Hungary is intent upon enforcing the promises of the former dissidents who share power in Czechoslovakia and Romania regarding the institutionalization of protection for all ethnic and linguistic minorities. Hungary provided moral and substantive support to Václav Havel and Alexander Dubček, and refuge for tens of thousands of Romanian citizens, regardless of ethnicity, for several years before the transformations in Czechoslovakia and Romania. Foreign Minister Jeszenszky does not hesitate to point out the generous humanitarian, medical, and logistic assistance that all levels of Hungarian society provided to the Romanian revolution in December 1989, in the hope of ending the inflamed animosity exploited by the Ceaușescu dictatorship.[22]

Certain unofficial elements and government officials among Hungary's neighbors react to attempts to even discuss the situation of ethnic minorities with a chorus of accusations reminiscent of the communist days: "revisionism, fascism, revanchism, and so on." It has become difficult to conduct a rational discussion of the matter without these responses. Speaking of Hungarians outside of Hungary was taboo until the 1980s, and Hungary's neighbors introduced freedom of speech only in late 1989. Therefore nationalist emotions, which were suppressed for nearly 50 years, are all coming to the surface simultaneously. Any mention of minority rights is regarded by some as "revanchism" and an attack on national legitimacy or sovereignty.[23]

Declining standards of living inspire extremists to blame the usual suspects. In Hungary, these suspects are the Gypsies. In Romania and Slovakia, the scapegoats and targets of nationalist newspaper articles are Gypsies, foreigners, "fascists," and Hungarians.

Soviet-Hungarian relations are affected directly by the status of Hungarians living in Subcarpathia, or Transcarpathia as the Ukrainians refer to it. Although in World War II the USSR used the "Transylvania card" to entice Romania to abandon Germany in 1944, the USSR will most likely remain neutral when Hungary discusses minority rights with Romania, Czechoslovakia, and Yugoslavia.

Stability Through Constant Change

In the past, the USSR attempted to channel and deflect change in Hungary and among other Warsaw Pact members. As a consequence of changes the USSR could not moderate in the late 1980s, Gorbachev openly criticized hard-liners like Ceaușescu, Honecker, Zhivkov, and Husák, hoping to replace them with reformers like himself.

While resistance to change remained a Soviet goal through the mid-1980s, in the 1990s the USSR's interest would be best served by constant and irreversible change in East-Central Europe. Quite simply put, the Pandora's box of democracy and capitalism has been opened. Expectations are rising for higher standards of living and individual liberties as well. The Soviet leadership, realizing the economic difficulties of the new regimes in East-Central Europe, does not want to contribute to conditions ideal for a Peronist, populist backlash, or for Ion Iliescu-type neocommunist Romanian instability and shattered promises.

When rapid change does not keep up with rising expectations, as in Romania, the USSR does have cause for concern. Public worries about economic collapse can be diverted by populist-nationalist rhetoric, elements of which are present in all of the postcommunist or seemingly postcommunist societies. The danger to the USSR from domestic instability in East-Central Europe would then arise from halted or reversed reforms and the presence of either leftist or rightist extremists. Unemployment and inflation, either in the Polish shock fashion or gradual as in Hungary, drastically lower the standard of living for many potential supporters of the former "socialist" rulers of East-Central Europe. Trade unions, displaced workers, impoverished pensioners, and others may provide the mass base for demagogic movements of either right or left. The lack of change or a slowdown in progress toward free markets and democracy in Hungary pose a danger to Soviet-Hungarian relations, as long as the USSR remains on a gradual reformist path.

Hungary could play a positive role in providing global legitimacy to various Soviet republics seeking independence. The Russian Federation, represented by Boris N. Yeltsin's deputy, Ruslan I. Khasbulatov, seeks a comprehensive cooperation agreement with Hungary, an agreement which eventually will lead to the establishment of consular and then diplomatic relations.[24] Hungary naturally risks the ire of Soviet authorities in a potential backlash against sovereignty-minded republics. However, direct relations with the Russian Federation and other republics would place Hungarian relations with the remnants of the USSR on a positive note, with immense potential in trade and investment for all states involved.

Implications for United States Policy and Relations with the Soviet Union

From the perspective of U.S. foreign policy, the existence of minorities in all states of East-Central Europe should not necessarily be viewed as a threat to regional stability. If the United States were to insist upon strict enforcement of the Helsinki agreement's minority protection clauses as a precondition of significant financial assistance, in addition to existing standards of democracy and human rights, states in the region would have an incentive to stop trying to create "unitary national states" or monocultural societies at the expense of eliminating the heritage of a part of their citizens. So the United States could encourage the "spiritualization" of borders, contributing toward the efforts of East-Central European countries to prepare themselves for membership in the EC, where borders are becoming immaterial. These are also the goals of Hungarian foreign policy, and they are not incompatible with U.S. and USSR intentions for a peaceful post-Cold War arrangement in Europe.

In the interest of "stability," the United States should point out that diversity and multilingualism do not inherently and should not threaten the legitimacy of governments. Czechoslovakia and Romania, both multinational, could become East-Central European incarnations of Switzerland or Belgium, without any danger to their territory or statehood. A sign of a mature civic culture is the tolerance and promotion of diversity. Unfortunately, many levels of government and administration, as well as societal bodies such as the *Vatra Românească* movement in Romania and the Slovak

National Party in Slovakia do not support ethnic tolerance and even oppose the Swiss model of multilingualism.

From a policy perspective, the end of socialist solidarity removed the façade of peaceful relations among nationalities in East-Central Europe. However, diversity itself does not mean inevitable "instability" prophesied by many Westerners. The United States and the USSR in their new relationship could cooperate not only in assuring economic transition, but also by acting in partnership to make ethnic diversity an asset, not a threat to peace.

The Next Millennium

Hungary is a minor actor in the pantheon of Soviet foreign policy. But once the painful shocks of economic, political, and military transition have been endured, Hungary could inspire the USSR in its own transformation. Hungary will become a part of three regional systems. First, it will take its place among the associate members of the EC, and participate in the European Economic Space, essentially a free-trade zone encompassing the EC, the European Free Trade Association, and various potential members of the EC, and perhaps favored areas, such as the Soviet Union. Negotiations for Hungary's EC associate member status began in December 1990.

Secondly, Hungary will be a part of the East-Central European cooperation attempts, oriented toward the Alps and Adriatic, or toward the Carpathians, the Balkans, and the Baltic coast. Envelopment in these two regional efforts will hopefully solve the problem of ethnic minorities which are present everywhere in the region.

Thirdly, Hungary joined the Council of Europe in November 1990, offering the Soviet Union and various republics its services as an intermediary.

Besides regional participation, Hungary can offer the USSR a model of communist party retreat into parliamentary opposition. Trade with the USSR will remain as a peaceful bond, as Hungary and the various Soviet republics establish direct economic and political links, perhaps assisting the devolution of the inner Soviet empire into a genuine confederation.

NOTES

1. This term was introduced by Béla Király in *Az elsö háború szocialista országok között* (New Brunswick: Hungarian Alumni Association, 1981).

2. The three sides were represented by the Hungarian Socialist Workers' Party (HSWP), various opposition groups, and the mass organizations formerly controlled by the HSWP.
3. MTI, 29 September 1990; "Kádár Details Protocol on Withdrawal," *Foreign Broadcast Information Service: East Europe* (FBIS-EEU), no. 190 (10 October 1990), p. 43.
4. See *RFE/RL Daily Report*, no. 166 (31 August 1990), p. 2.
5. Gábor Arató, "Nem alternatívája az európai egységnek," *Magyar Hirlap*, 2 August 1990, p. 1.
6. Budapest TV Service, 9 September 1990; "Jeszenszky Queried on Foreign Policy Achievements," FBIS-EEU, no. 176 (11 September 1990), p. 29.
7. "Pravda Calls 1956 Invasion 'Necessary,'" *RFE/RL Daily Report*, no. 204 (25 October 1990), p. 1.
8. Interview with Dmitrii Markov by László N. Sándor, "A pártház ostroma csak ürügy volt," *Magyar Hirlap*, 10 September 1990, p. 2.
9. József Antall, "Hungary's Place Among the Western Democracies," transcript of speech before the Council on Foreign Relations, New York, 16 October 1990, p. 8.
10. See Csaba Poór, "Számolunk a Szovjet Unió felbomlásának lehetöségével," *Magyar Hirlap*, 2 August 1990, p. 3.
11. See "Hungarian Government's Stance on Lithuania" in *RFE/RL Daily Report*, no. 10 (15 January 1991), p. 1.
12. MTI, 10 December 1990; FBIS-EEU, no. 236 (13 December 1990), p. 28.
13. See Gábor Szabó's interview with László Csaba, "Magyar-Szovjet Kereskedelem: Átálláspénz," in *Heti Világgazdaság* 8, no. 1 (5 January 1991): 68-69.
14. See "More on Hungarian-Soviet Trade Agreement," *RFE/RL Daily Report*, no. 236 (13 December 1990), pp. 2-3; "Hungarian-Soviet Trade Agreement Signed," ibid., no. 235 (12 December 1990), pp. 2-3; "Moscow to Slash Oil Exports to Hungary," ibid., no. 223 (26 November 1990), p. 2.
15. The various definitions of the Common European House doctrine are given by Peter Robejsek in "Europapolitische Vorstellungen und Konzepte in der DDR, in Polen, der ČSSR und Ungarn," *Berichte des Bundesinstituts für ostwissenschaftliche und internationale Studien*, no. 6 (1990), pp. 1-2.
16. Eastern Europe as a model for Soviet political and economic transformation is discussed in Valeri Karavayev, "Eastern Europe is Opening Itself to the World," *International Affairs* (Moscow), no. 4 (April 1990): 35-44.
17. Robejsek, op. cit., p. 37.
18. Alfred Reisch, "Interview with Foreign Minister Géza Jeszenszky," *Report on Eastern Europe* 1, no. 30 (27 July 1990), p. 20.
19. Gorbachev's offer is analyzed in detail by Christian Meier, "Die Gorbachev-Initiative von 29. Mai 1985—Vor neuen Verhandlungen zwischen RGW und EG?" *Aktuelle Analysen*, no. 18 (20 August 1985), a publication of the Bundesinstitut für ostwissenschaftliche und internationale Studien, Cologne.

20. Alfred Reisch, "Primary Foreign Policy Objective to Rejoin Europe," *Report on Eastern Europe* 1, no. 52 (28 December 1990): 15-20.
21. For the state of negotiations and legal discussions concerning EC entry, see Péter Balázs, "Vertragsbeziehungen zwischen Ungarn und der Europäischen Gemeinschaft: Aktuelle Lage und Perspektiven," *Südosteuropa* 39, no. 6 (June 1990): 341-349.
22. Jeszenszky, op. cit., pp. 341-349.
23. Examples include the following: the Slovak National Party staged mass protests in October 1990, demanding that Slovak be made the only official language, even in areas that are populated by Hungarians, Ruthenians, Germans, and Gypsies. Public Against Violence and other parties in the Slovak government passed a law that allowed non-Slovak languages in official transactions, where the minority quotient exceeds 20 percent.

    Public opinion polls conducted in ethnically mixed areas of southern Slovakia, however, indicate that 79 percent of Hungarians in Slovakia speak both languages equally well, while only 38 percent of Slovaks speak each language on an equal basis. About 74 percent of the Hungarians prefer bilingual street names, et cetera, while only 26 percent of the Slovaks are in favor of bilingualism. About 37 percent of Slovaks in the mixed areas speak no Hungarian at all, while only 3 percent of the Hungarians are monolingual.

    There is a plurality of opinion in both Romania and Czechoslovakia with varying degrees of verbal sparring among groups representing the Hungarian minority in each country, such as Coexistence in Slovakia and the Democratic Federation of Hungarians in Romania (RMDSZ) or with press outlets in Hungary itself. See Judy Dempsey, "Bad Old Ways Spoil New-Style Rumanian Politics," *The Financial Times* (London), 23 October 1990, p. 3; Michael Frank, "Slowakisch als alleinige Amtssprache gefordert," *Süddeutsche Zeitung,* 8 October 1990, p. 9; "Slovaks, Hungarians Polled on Linguistic Ability," from *Lidové noviny* (Prague), 12 October 1990, p. 3, in FBIS-EEU (16 October 1990), p. 36; Michael Frank, "Slowaken setzen slowakisch als Amtssprache durch," *Süddeutsche Zeitung*, 27/28 October 1990, p. 2.
24. Agence France-Presse, "Russland will eigene Beziehungen mit Ungarn," *Süddeutsche Zeitung*, 22 October 1990, p. 8.

10

Bulgarian-Soviet Relations

John D. Bell

BACKGROUND

During the communist era, Bulgaria sought and earned the title of "The Soviet Union's Most Loyal Ally."[1] Georgi Dimitrov coined the slogan that Soviet friendship is Bulgaria's "air and sun," and Todor Zhivkov (born 1911, party leader since 1954) often stated that Bulgaria and the USSR share "a single circulatory system" or that "the Bulgarian watch is set on Moscow time."[2] Signs of Bulgaria's fidelity to the USSR abounded. When Dimitrov died, he was laid to rest in a mausoleum modeled on Lenin's; in the 1960s, a verse celebrating solidarity with Moscow and the CPSU was inserted in the national anthem; and the Soviet ambassador regularly took part in important state occasions and rituals alongside members of the politburo and other high Bulgarian officials. The officially sponsored Movement for Soviet-Bulgarian Friendship was reported in 1983 to have had 4,486 clubs.[3]

Bulgaria's domestic policies were as closely modeled on the Soviet example as was the postwar architecture of downtown Sofia. Within the communist world and on the larger international stage, Bulgaria served as a Soviet echo, defending the USSR against Western criticism and upholding its leading role against socialist advocates of polycentrism. So subservient did Bulgaria appear that Western observers took to calling it the "sixteenth

Soviet republic."[4] This was only a small exaggeration for, according to material that recently became accessible, in 1963 Zhivkov proposed to N. S. Khrushchev that Bulgaria actually be incorporated in the USSR.[5] Even though the Soviet leader rebuffed this offer, Bulgaria's development was closely integrated with the Soviet economic system.

Bulgaria's subservience to the USSR has been explained as a manifestation of national character: dull, passive, accustomed to obeying orders.[6] On the other hand, Bulgarian and Soviet propagandists and a number of Western commentators with some knowledge of the Balkans have pointed to the historic links between the Bulgarian and Russian peoples. Both are Slavic and linked to the Eastern Orthodox Church; Russian Pan-Slav societies supported the Bulgarian national revival; Russian armies liberated Bulgaria from the Ottoman yoke. Consequently, it has often been assumed that an unusual depth of sympathy exists between Bulgarian and Russian. This overlooks, however, a strong anti-Russian tradition that has also had a powerful influence in Bulgaria. Even at the time of Bulgaria's liberation from the Turks, the nationalist leader Liuben Karavelov qualified his gratitude toward Russia in his famous statement that: "If Russia comes to liberate, she will be met with great sympathy; but if she comes to rule she will find many enemies."[7] Dimitŭr Blagoev, the founder of Bulgarian communism, was a firm opponent of Pan-Slavism and Russian expansionism, and of course Bulgaria took the German side in the two world wars. If the argument based on the "historic ties" between Bulgaria and Russia is to have any validity at all, it should be stated negatively, i.e., that Bulgaria lacks the reservoir of hostility toward Russia present in much of Eastern Europe.[8]

The relationship that developed between Bulgaria and the USSR after World War II owed less to failings in national character or to the residue of romantic Pan-Slavism than to hard historical realities. The Bulgarian communist regime, in its full Stalinist variant, was installed with great brutality by men and women who had spent much of their lives in the USSR and who were closely monitored by Soviet authority.[9] When Stalin finally allowed Georgi Dimitrov to return to Bulgaria, he saw to it that the "Hero of Leipzig" was constantly accompanied by Soviet watchdogs.[10] The new Bulgarian constitution was drafted by Soviet experts and reportedly edited by Stalin himself.[11] Dimitrov's successor, Vŭlko Chervenkov, studied at the OGPU secret police academy in Moscow and is generally thought to have advanced his career by informing on internal Bulgarian party affairs.[12] Traicho Kostov was personally abused by Stalin and paid with his life for conducting economic negotiations with the USSR on the principle that Bulgaria was an independent state.[13] Todor Zhivkov owed his elevation to Khrushchev's direct backing.

Over the longer run, the Soviet Union has appreciated the strategic importance of Bulgaria's loyalty in a region occupied by two NATO members, Greece and Turkey; the nonaligned Yugoslavia and Albania; and the doubtful ally, Romania. In 1978 the USSR opened the Varna-Illichevsk ferry, giving it the capacity to move large military forces to Bulgaria without relying on the land route through Romania.

Bulgaria probably received more benefits than any other East European state from its membership in the Soviet bloc. Whatever else may be said about Soviet domination of East-Central Europe, it created for Bulgaria an international environment of unusual stability. The 45 years of peace that Bulgaria has enjoyed since World War II are already 19 years more than the second-longest period of peace (1886-1912) that occurred since the country's liberation. The military security afforded by membership in the Warsaw Pact has been an important factor to a country that has lost three wars in the twentieth century and whose territorial integrity is not recognized by its largest neighbors.[14]

Soviet experience provided the model for Bulgaria's economic development, and material assistance from the USSR contributed greatly to the process of industrialization. Although the exact level of Soviet economic support was never made public, extensive material and technological assistance were visible in such large-scale projects as the Maritsa-Iztok energy-industrial complex, the Kremikovtsi metallurgical combine, the Burgas petrochemical complex, and in the development of the nuclear power industry. During the 1980s the two countries signed treaties coordinating economic policies until the end of the century.[15]

Bulgaria's participation in the "scientific-technological revolution of the twentieth century," to repeat a phrase regularly employed by Zhivkov, was also aided by Soviet educational institutions. In 1980 it was reported that more than 8,500 Bulgarian citizens had received advanced education in the USSR and that more than 1,250 had defended doctoral and candidate's dissertations there.[16] Through the early 1980s, if Zhivkov was ever disturbed by the obsequious demeanor he displayed toward the USSR and visiting Soviet officials, he could console himself with the thought that his people had not experienced the ordeals suffered by Hungary and Czechoslovakia and that Bulgaria had real gains to show. So confident had he become, that he boasted to the British foreign secretary that the USSR was a "Bulgarian colony" providing raw materials in exchange for manufactured goods.[17]

THE IMPACT OF *PERESTROIKA*: INITIAL RESPONSE

The first signs of disharmony in the relations between the Soviet Union and Bulgaria came soon after the death of L. I. Brezhnev. According to rumors that circulated at the time, when Zhivkov went to Moscow for Brezhnev's funeral, he came in for sharp criticism from Iu. V. Andropov, probably over the low quality of manufactured goods that Bulgaria exported to "its colony" in return for energy and raw materials.[18] Although there was speculation that Andropov was putting pressure on Zhivkov to retire, the Soviet leader's prolonged "cold," followed by his death and the subsequent election of K. U. Chernenko appeared to restore Soviet-Bulgarian relations to their accustomed pattern. Under Soviet pressure Zhivkov abandoned the limited policy of improving relations with the West that had been associated with his daughter,[19] becoming the first bloc leader to join the Soviet boycott of the Olympics and obeying last-minute instructions to cancel a planned visit to West Germany that had been given heavy advance publicity.[20]

With the introduction of *glasnost'*, *perestroika*, and "new thinking" by M. S. Gorbachev, Bulgaria's relations with the USSR became more complex, and in fact proceeded on two levels: official relations between the two states and the unofficial influence of Soviet developments on Bulgarian society.

When Zhivkov visited the new Soviet leader in June 1985, it was reported that Gorbachev told him that "the roots of our friendship are deep and strong, but the tree must be watered and nurtured in order to bear fruit."[21] Later in the year, in describing his talks with Zhivkov at Sofia, Gorbachev stated that "We did not avoid the sharp edges."[22] Soviet concern at that point was focused on Bulgarian economic performance. Some of the details were spelled out by Soviet Ambassador L. I. Grekov during an interview published in the Bulgarian journal *Pogled*. Although he had high praise for the past record of Soviet-Bulgarian cooperation, Grekov stressed that the two countries could not rest on their laurels. Specifically, he criticized the low quality of goods that Bulgaria was sending to the USSR and the low quality of labor discipline shown by Bulgarian workers. In what was perhaps intended as a display of wit, he said that the Bulgarian working class was much less an industrial proletariat than its Soviet counterpart; that many Bulgarian workers maintained "dachas" and gardens in the countryside, leading them to look upon their factory jobs "as a period of rest following their agricultural labors."[23]

As Soviet *perestroika* gathered momentum, its effect on Bulgaria began to go far beyond purely economic issues. Zhivkov and his closest colleagues, who had for decades proclaimed their loyalty to Soviet experience, were now pressured to develop their own broad vision of reform. Zhivkov's version of *perestroika* will not be discussed here in any detail. In essence it consisted of public expressions of the need for reform combined with extravagant proposals which were implemented in such a way that everything and everyone stayed in place; nomenclature changed, but the *nomenklatura* remained the same. Bulgarians were offered the prospect of competitive local elections in 1988, but candidates lacking official approval were disqualified in four-fifths of the districts and subject to gross electoral manipulation in the rest. Leasing of land, approved in principle, was not to be put into practice until a nationwide discussion could take place. A decision on basic reforms was postponed until the next scheduled communist party congress in 1991. Until the very end, Zhivkov's regime continued to crack down on groups and individuals that demanded real reform or went beyond the official limits of Bulgarian *glasnost'*.[24]

In private, Zhivkov stated that Bulgaria had experienced all the *perestroika* it needed in 1956, when he supervised the Bulgarian version of destalinization. According to the indictment read by Slavcho Trŭnski after Zhivkov's fall, this statement greatly upset the Soviet ambassador.[25] Other signs of Soviet displeasure were visible, at least to the inner circle. Although Zhivkov continued to be received in Moscow on ceremonial occasions, according to Trŭnski, his closest politburo ally, the overbearing Milko Balev, was deliberately shunned. Praise of fraternal Bulgaria's achievements, once a minor staple of the Soviet press, entirely disappeared during Zhivkov's last two years in power.[26]

For his part, Zhivkov attempted to develop relations with the conservative communist governments of Czechoslovakia, the German Democratic Republic, and Romania. His defense of the legitimacy of the 1968 Warsaw Pact occupation of Czechoslovakia[27] was rewarded by Prague's approval for the campaign against Bulgaria's ethnic Turks. Shortly after the massacre in Tiananmen Square the foreign minister of China visited Sofia, while the Bulgarian government issued a statement supporting the Chinese action as "meant to restore order" and "protect the socialist gains of the working people."[28] Zhivkov also courted the orthodox regimes in Cuba and North Korea.

There is little doubt that Zhivkov looked to the conservative wing of the CPSU to replace Gorbachev. *Sovetskaia Rossiia*'s publication of the "Nina Andreeva letter," in March 1988, was immediately followed by the firing of a number of cultural leaders in Bulgaria and the purge of Central Committee secretary Stoyan Mikhailov for failing to insure party leadership over intellectual life. At that time Zhivkov told a party plenum that the Soviet experience would not automatically be transferred to Bulgaria.[29] The declining fortunes of the USSR's conservatives, however, and the crumbling of the Czechoslovak and East German regimes left Zhivkov more and more isolated.

Glasnost' and *perestroika* in the USSR acted as a stimulus on Bulgarian society, particularly its intelligentsia, encouraging it to promote its own interests and emboldening it to begin to challenge the Zhivkov regime openly. No East European people followed developments in the USSR more closely than did the Bulgarians. Soviet books and periodicals were a staple of Bulgarian reading matter. With a circulation of 160,000 copies, *Pravda* was one of the most widely read newspapers in the country.[30] Bulgarian television has a Soviet channel, and numerous cultural figures from the USSR routinely visited Bulgaria and were interviewed in the country's media. Many Bulgarians, particularly students, spent time in the Soviet Union where they came in direct contact with the spirit of "new thinking." Consequently, developments in the USSR influenced Bulgarians, both inside and outside the communist party, more than did events in the other East-Central European states.

One striking example involved the contrast in the way the Soviet and Bulgarian governments dealt with the Chernobyl disaster. In an example of the new *glasnost'*, the USSR government and press described the dimensions of the catastrophe with candor. In Bulgaria, although scientists established that the country had received a high level of radiation with the result that a number of agricultural products, especially vegetables and milk, contained dangerous levels of radioactivity, they were forbidden to warn the public. The government issued reassurances that no problem existed. When the truth leaked out, it revealed how far Bulgaria lagged behind the changes in the USSR.[31] Continuing reliance on Chernobyl-style reactors, which provide 30 percent of the country's electricity, created enduring anxiety.[32]

Soviet "new thinking" provided a legitimate way to criticize Zhivkov. The very names of the two most influential opposition organizations—Ecoglasnost' and the Discussion Clubs for the Support of *Glasnost'* and *Perestroika*[33]—are testimony to the radicalizing impact of Soviet experience on the Bulgarians. Their ostensible loyalty to the USSR made them difficult to attack, although Zhivkov continued to threaten.[34]

THE FALL OF ZHIVKOV

Not enough is yet known of the details surrounding the conspiracy to remove Zhivkov to allow an assessment of the extent of the USSR's involvement.[35]

At this point it seems clear at least that many in the Bulgarian leadership were aware that Zhivkov no longer enjoyed Soviet favor. The key organizers of the coup, Foreign Minister Petŭr Mladenov and Defense Minister Dobri Dzhurov, on the other hand, were well connected with the Soviet leadership.[36] According to one persistent rumor, on the eve of the coup Mladenov, who was returning from a visit to China, stopped in Moscow for last-minute consultations. He has denied this, but it does appear that judging by the reports of his departure from Beijing and arrival in Sofia his flight took several hours longer than would normally be expected.[37] Whether USSR support for the coup was direct or passive, the Soviet press quickly made it clear that the change of leadership was welcome in Moscow.[38]

If Mladenov and his allies had hoped to manage an orderly and moderate reform program, they were quickly disappointed by the demands for fundamental change that arose across the country and in the party itself. Popular demonstrations forced the promise of free elections and the legalization of opposition parties. The old guard, at least its most conservative members, were forced to retire from the communist leadership, and a number of radical factions appeared that pressed for rapid internal democratization and a reorientation of Bulgaria's foreign policy toward Western Europe.[39] Bulgaria's new leadership—President Mladenov, Prime Minister Andrei Lukanov, and Bulgarian Communist Party Chairman Alexander Lilov—all publicly stated that Bulgaria would consider itself a member of "Europe," not simply the Soviet bloc, and would seek normal, friendly relations with the West. To be sure, there seemed to be little alternative to this policy, given the crumbling of the Warsaw Pact and the inability of the USSR to maintain its past level of economic support.

At its 14th Congress (the "Congress of Renewal") in January and February 1990 the BCP took a number of steps toward democratization, its new leadership denouncing the "totalitarian past," changing the party's name from Communist to Socialist, and pledging to move toward a moderate, Western-style socialism. Alexander Lilov proposed that when the party succeeded in carrying through its program of internal renewal, it would seek membership in the Second International.[40]

THE OPPOSITION

The legalization of political parties and the communist/socialist abandonment of a claim to a monopoly of political power was followed by the rapid emergence of an effective opposition. While more than 50 parties were formed, some having no more than an ephemeral existence, the most influential ones entered a coalition—the Union of Democratic Forces (UDF). Although the UDF fell short of ousting the socialists in the June 1990 elections for the Grand National Assembly, it won more than one-third of the votes, no small achievement in the short time that it had to organize itself and find the resources to wage a national campaign.[41] Moreover, the UDF dominated Bulgaria's cities, winning 24 of 26 seats in Sofia and scoring a clean sweep in Plovdiv and Varna. It also dominated among youth and the intelligentsia. Public opinion polls after the election showed a continuing shift of sentiment toward the UDF and, in order to govern at all, the socialists were forced to acquiesce to the election of UDF leader Zheliu Zhelev as president of the republic.[42]

Even if the socialist leadership was both sincere and successful in transforming the BSP into a party of the democratic left—and at its congress in November party conservatives appeared to be making a comeback[43]—it is doubtful that the party ever could enjoy significant popular trust until it was completely separated from the state and spent some time out of power. The decline in socialist fortunes continued steadily after its electoral success. At a party congress in September, Lilov and Lukanov engaged in a mutually destructive power struggle, while Mladenov and Dzhurov, who engineered the coup against Zhivkov, were voted out of the leadership.[44] Unwilling to take full responsibility for economic reform measures that would lead to hardships among the population, and faced with a general stike led by *Podkrepa,* the opposition trade union, Lukanov's socialist government resigned on 29 November. It was replaced by a government led by Dimitūr Popov, a jurist who belonged to no political party, but who enjoyed the confidence of the opposition.[45] It is almost certainly only a matter of time before the UDF takes full charge of the country, perhaps after the next parliamentary elections scheduled for September 1991.

The UDF, as an umbrella organization uniting parties and movements with divergent points of view,[46] has experienced difficulty formulating clear and consistent positions on many issues, including relations with the USSR. On the right wing of the UDF spectrum are figures that hope to "settle scores" with their former persecutors and advocate a policy that has come to be called in Bulgarian, "McCarthyism." Their position is that a leopard cannot change its spots, that is, that communists in Bulgaria or the USSR cannot be anything other than totalitarian Marxists. Their program is complete opposition to cooperation with the socialists at home and anti-Sovietism in foreign policy. On the other hand, the UDF's "left," those elements from the Clubs for the Support of *Glasnost'* and Democracy and Eco-*glasnost'* that provide the UDF's brain trust and the bulk of its parliamentary leadership, advocate a policy of reconciliation that takes as its model Spain's transition to democracy under Juan Carlos. While they would make no compromise with the BSP *as a party,* they would be willing to deal with BSP members as individuals.[47] They are also far less inflexible in their attitude toward the USSR.[48]

President Zhelev's views are particularly interesting in that they rest on his own analysis of the phenomenon of totalitarianism.[49] Zhelev wrote that a totalitarian party cannot survive in an environment of civic freedom. It follows that it is not necessary to launch a frontal assault on the BSP; rather, the BSP's loss of influence will be the inevitable by-product of the creation of a system that guarantees basic civil and political rights to all Bulgarian citizens. Zhelev believes that such a process is taking place in the USSR, but that it is a far more difficult one owing to the facts that communism has been in place for a longer time and that the USSR is an empire rather than a national state.[50]

Zhelev has expressed the concern that a possible reactionary coup in the USSR could set back the process of change in Bulgaria by encouraging conservatives in the BSP to attempt to take power by force. Consequently, he has advocated that Bulgaria move as rapidly as possible to democratize its political and social institutions. He has added that such a transition in Bulgaria would serve the interests of the USSR, or at least the reformers there, by demonstrating that a peaceful escape from communism is possible.

Above all, Zhelev is convinced that for the foreseeable future Bulgaria's principal concerns will be internal, and that the country does not need to complicate its international situation by antagonizing the USSR. But this view is not shared by the whole opposition. As the UDF began its election campaign in spring 1990, Zhelev was invited to the Soviet embassy to make the acquaintance of the ambassador. When he arrived, he found the entrance blocked by a demonstration organized by the Independent Students' Society, a member of the UDF, demanding freedom for Lithuania. Zhelev later declared that this demonstration was "absolutely justified from a moral point of view," but that it was a complication that Bulgaria simply did not need at that time.[51]

PROSPECTS

It is unclear at the moment in what form the Soviet Union will emerge from its present travail. The institutions that regulated its relations with East-Central Europe, the Warsaw Pact and Council of Mutual Economic Assistance, are in the process of disintegration. While Bulgaria has made significant strides toward democratization, a troubled period of transition obviously is still ahead. In these circumstances, it is difficult to speculate with any confidence about the future of Bulgarian-Soviet relations.

With this caveat, some generalizations seem possible. Bulgaria will have to become less dependent on the USSR for economic and military support. The inability of the Soviet Union to meet even a reduced schedule of oil deliveries during 1990 is symptomatic of the fact that for practically all Bulgaria's economic needs, particularly those involving energy and advanced technology, the USSR has become almost irrelevant. The Soviet decision at the end of the year to barter 6.5 million tons of gasoline for Bulgarian manufactured goods left two-thirds of Bulgaria's 1991 energy needs unmet.[52] All Bulgarian political forces seem to agree that the country's future welfare depends on its ability to establish new relationships with Western governments and institutions and on the speed with which these relationships develop.

Psychologically, Bulgaria has already begun to divest itself of Soviet trappings. The national anthem is being revised and may soon be replaced altogether by the traditional *"Shumi Maritsa."* Communist and pro-Soviet symbols are being removed from buildings and public areas, and the Grand National Assembly has created a commission on renaming Bulgarian towns and landmarks. The historian Nikolai Genchev, appointed to head the commission, stated that its first decision was to replace all names of Soviet origin with their Bulgarian predecessors or with other Bulgarian substitutes.[53] The mummy of Georgi Dimitrov has been removed, surely as a prelude to the razing of his mausoleum. Public expressions of anti-Soviet feeling have become more common as the emergence of a free press has allowed greater discussion of the past Soviet role in Bulgarian affairs and as the USSR has shown itself unable or unwilling to continue its economic support.[54] The Bulgarian government has invited the United States to send arms experts to dismantle eight Soviet SS-23 missile launchers, supplied in 1986 to the Bulgarian army.[55]

Bulgaria, however, has genuine economic and security needs. When the current crisis passes, it will almost certainly express a concern regarding the treatment of ethnic Bulgarians in Yugoslavia's Republic of Macedonia. The possible break-up of Yugoslavia or the outbreak of civil war there, would recall some of the most dangerous moments of Balkan history. At the moment, Bulgarians would prefer that such problems be resolved in a European context, i.e., within the framework of Western or European structures. In an address to the United Nations, President Zhelev stated that Bulgaria's highest priority was to become a part of the democratic West. And he argued forcefully that it was very much in the interest of the West to include the Balkans in the larger European community. In his words, "The Europeanization of the Balkans is far preferable to the Balkanization of Europe."[56] It is not at all clear, however, that the countries of Western Europe or the United States will accommodate Zhelev's desire. Western nations have traditionally assigned a low priority to Bulgaria and do not now seem inclined to give it the attention devoted to the "northern tier" or to other world trouble spots.

Projections

1. The removal of Soviet trappings from the Bulgarian physical and psychological landscape and the continuing decline of the Bulgarian Socialist [communist] Party in political life should make possible the creation of a new Bulgarian-Soviet relationship based on traditional diplomacy and the rational calculation of mutual interest. The fact that neither the USSR nor Bulgaria can yet produce manufactured goods that are competitive on the world market suggests that at least in some spheres there could be an extended period in which the two countries continue to exchange goods for which other outlets are not available.

2. Many Bulgarians would like to reestablish some cultural links with ethnic Bulgarian communities in Ukraine and Moldavia. Ever since the 1930s, when thousands of ethnic Bulgarians were sent to labor camps, charged with plotting to annex Ukraine to Bulgaria, the Soviet government has not allowed its republics to establish contacts with the Bulgarian state. The Bulgarian government will seek to open this issue with the USSR or with the individual republics.

3. Bulgarians outside the former communist party would welcome the "Balkanization" of the USSR, both because they sympathize with small peoples struggling for independence and because they see this as promoting the permanent collapse of communism, at least in parts of the Soviet empire.

4. On the other hand, to the Bulgarians the most unwelcome possibility is a military/KGB crackdown on the Soviet republics or the outbreak of extensive civil conflict in the USSR that would disrupt the development of Bulgarian-Soviet relations and make Bulgaria even more dependent on the good will and farsightedness of Western Europe and the United States. The historical experience of the Bulgarians in

modern times provides no basis for optimism, should events take this course.

NOTES

1. Flora Lewis, *Europe: A Tapestry of Nations* (New York: Simon and Schuster, 1987), p. 485.
2. John D. Bell, *The Bulgarian Communist Party from Blagoev to Zhivkov* (Stanford: Hoover Institution Press, 1986), p. 142. In an interview with Western reporters on 27 November 1990, Zhivkov stated that such phrases had been "just rhetoric." He added that Bulgaria would now be much further advanced if the West had not consigned the country to Stalin after World War II, and that socialism itself was based on false premises. Chuck Sudetic, "Bulgarian Communist Stalwart Says He'd Do It All Differently," *The New York Times*, 28 November 1990, p. A-4.
3. Georgi Monev, Zoia Nesterova, and Nedialko Khadzhiev, "Mogŭsht faktor za raztsveta na rodinata." *Rabotnichesko delo* (Sofia), 10 June 1983, pp. 1, 3.
4. Nissan Oren, *Revolution Administered: Agrarianism and Communism in Bulgaria* (Baltimore: Johns Hopkins University Press, 1973), pp. 171-183; L.A.D. Dellin, "The Communist Party of Bulgaria," in Stephen Fischer-Galati, ed., *The Communist Parties of Eastern Europe* (New York: Columbia University Press, 1979), pp. 71-82.
5. Georgi Assyov, "On the Tracks of Betrayal," *Sofia News*, 11 January 1990, p. 9. Assyov suggested that it was Zhivkov's desire to become a member of the CPSU politburo that prompted his proposal. Reluctance to have Zhivkov discuss Bulgaria's past relationship with the USSR in public has been given as one reason that his successors have been slow to bring him to trial or allow him to appear before the Grand National Assembly.
6. Flora Lewis, op. cit., p. 485. This explanation is a staple of anti-Bulgarian specialists in Yugoslavia. See, for example, the article of Mihajlo Apostolski, "Nemam dokaze, ali tvrdim...," *NIN* (Belgrade), 4 March 1979, pp. 5-8.
7. Cited in Cyril E. Black, *The Establishment of Constitutional Government in Bulgaria* (Princeton: Princeton University Press, 1943), p. 41.
8. An excellent, common-sense discussion of this theme is found in Georgi Markov's essay "Liubovta kŭm 'Golemiiat brat,'" in *Zadochni reportazhi za Bŭlgariia*, vol 2 (Zurich: Georgi Markov Fund, 1981), pp. 142-157.
9. An overview of the measures taken to sovietize Bulgaria is given in Bell, *The Bulgarian Communist Party*, pp. 77-99; the reorientation of Bulgaria's foreign policy is described in Klaus-Detlev Grothusen, "Zur Frage der 'Sowjetisierung' der bulgarischen Aussenpolitik nach dem Zweiten Weltkrieg (1944-1948/49)," in Reinhard Lauer and Peter Schreiner, eds.,

Kulturelle Traditionen in Bulgarien (Göttingen: Vandenhoeck & Ruprecht, 1989), pp. 315-331.
10. Cyril E. Black, "The View from Bulgaria," in Thomas Hammond, ed., *Witnesses to the Origins of the Cold War* (Seattle: University of Washington Press, 1982), p. 83.
11. Mito Isusov, *Politicheskite partii v Bŭlgariia, 1944-48* (Sofia: Nauka i izkustvo, 1978), p. 390.
12. Peter Semerjeev, *Sudebny protsess Traicho Kostova v Bolgarii, 7-12 dekabria 1949* (Jerusalem: Hebrew University Press, 1976), p. 106.
13. Bell, *The Bulgarian Communist Party*, p. 104.
14. In 1979 Zhivkov proposed that Bulgaria and Yugoslavia sign a treaty guaranteeing existing borders, and he repeated this offer several times during the 1980s. Yugoslavia consistently rejected the proposal and has maintained that the Pirin region, the portion of Macedonia retained by Bulgaria after the Second Balkan War, ought to be united to the Macedonian Republic in Yugoslavia. Turkey has shown an active and understandable interest in defending the rights of the ethnic Turkish population concentrated in southeastern Bulgaria. The example of Cyprus is much on the minds of Bulgarians, even those well disposed toward the Turkish minority.
15. George W. Hoffman, *Regional Development Strategy in Southeast Europe: A Comparative Analysis of Albania, Bulgaria, Greece, Romania, and Yugoslavia* (New York, 1972), pp. 97-99; John R. Lampe, *The Bulgarian Economy in the Twentieth Century* (New York: St. Martin's Press, 1986), pp. 139-154.
16. E. Shevchenko, "Sovetsko-bolgarskoe sotrudnichestvo v oblasti vysshego obrazovaniia, 1966-1980 gg." in Pantelei Zarev *et al.*, eds., *Dokladi: Razvitie na naukata i obrazovanieto v Bŭlgariia* (Sofia, Bŭlgarska Akademiia na Naukite, 1982), p. 608.
17. Stephen Ashley, "A Review of Bulgarian-Soviet Relations," *Radio Free Europe Research*, 7 November 1985, p. 4.
18. Robert C. Toth, "U.S. Officials Discount 'Bulgarian Connection,'" *The Los Angeles Times*, 29 May 1983, pp. 1, 27.
19. Liudmila Zhivkova, who in the late 1970s became the chief of Bulgaria's cultural affairs, promoted Bulgarian nationalism and improved ties with Western Europe. She was popularly believed to have been in Soviet disfavor, and many Bulgarians were convinced that her death in 1981 was a KGB assassination.
20. Soviet instructions were carried to Zhivkov by Mikhail Gorbachev. Elizabeth Pond, "Conflicting Signals from Moscow: About-face on Bulgarian Visit to Bonn Puts 'Mini-détente' on Ice," *Christian Science Monitor*, 11 September 1984, pp. 1, 4; Eric Bourne, "Bulgaria Sought Wider Trade with West through German Trip," ibid., 12 September 1984, p. 9.
21. Rada Nikolaev, "Bulgarian-Soviet Relations," *Radio Free Europe Research*, 2 September 1985, p. 4.
22. "Rech na drugaria Mikhail Gorbachov," *Rabotnichesko delo*, 25 October 1985, p. 2.

23. Nikolaev, op. cit., pp. 4-5.
24. John D. Bell, "Bulgaria," in Richard F. Staar, ed., *1989 Yearbook on International Communist Affairs* (Stanford: Hoover Institution Press, 1989), pp. 299-302; henceforth cited as *YICA*. Clyde Haberman, "Bulgarian Change Barely Plods Along," *The New York Times*, 7 October 1989, p. 5.
25. Sofia Domestic Service, 17 November 1989; "Deputy Slavcho Trŭnski Denounces Zhivkov," *Foreign Broadcast Information Service: East Europe* (FBIS-EEU), 27 November 1989, pp. 6-7. That Trŭnski, a former partisan commander, included "upsetting the Soviet ambassador" in his list of Zhivkov's crimes, is itself revealing of Bulgaria's position vis-à-vis the USSR in the psychology of communists of that generation.
26. This was pointed out to the author by Stephen Ashley of Radio Free Europe during a meeting in Washington, D.C., in November 1988. It is, of course, also possible that the disappearance of reports on Bulgarian achievements was due to changing Soviet journalistic standards and did not reflect official disapproval of Zhivkov.
27. Unsigned editorial, "Po koi pŭt?" *Rabotnichesko delo*, 21 August 1989, p. 6.
28. Bŭlgarska Telegrafna Agentsiia, 13 June 1989; "Foreign Minister Approves Chinese Authorities," FBIS-EEU (14 June 1989), pp. 4-5.
29. Todor Zhivkov, "Some Problems and Tasks Related to the Restructuring of the Intellectual Sphere," *Sofia News*, 4 May 1988, special supplement, pages unnumbered.
30. L. Zhmiriov, "Gazety za dollary," *Pravda*, 4 October, 1990, p. 5.
31. Because the victims were above all infants and children, the cover-up concerning the effects of Chernobyl is considered one of the most despicable acts of the Zhivkov regime. The measures taken to suppress information about the disaster were described to the author in April 1990 by members of the Bulgarian scientific community, some of whom were directly involved in the testing of milk and vegetables. See also Liubomir Danchev, "No More Chernobyls," *Sofia News*, 10 May 1990, pp. 1, 3.
32. Paul Lewis, "Anxiety Rises in Eastern Europe," *The New York Times*, 7 April 1990, p. 5; Marlise Simons, "At East Europe Nuclear Plants," ibid., 24 June 1990, p. 6.
33. The Discussion Clubs, whose formation was inspired by Zheliu Zhelev, quickly spread from Sofia to Bulgaria's other cities. Now renamed Federation of Clubs for *Glasnost'* and Democracy, they are, along with Ecoglasnost', a principal factor in the Union of Democratic Forces.
34. Todor Zhivkov, *Preustroistvoto na nasheto obshtestvo—presvanie i otgovornost na inteligentsiiata* (Sofia: Partizdat, 1989), pp. 4-7.
35. For a discussion of Zhivkov's removal, see John D. Bell, "Bulgaria," *1990 YICA*, pp. 312-315. Some additional details appeared in "Todor Zhivkov's Resignation: the Story behind the Story," *Sofia News*, 7 June 1990, p. 5.
36. Mladenov's biography appeared in "Petr Mladenov," *Pravda*, 8 September 1990, p. 6. See also Bell, *1990 YICA*, pp. 308-318.

37. Mladenov's denial was broadcast by the BTA, 20 November 1989; "Mladenov Comments on Leadership Change," FBIS-EEU (22 November 1989), p. 6.
38. See the following reports in *Pravda:* L. Zhmiriov, "Smena lidera: Bolgariia na puti obnovleniia," 13 November 1989, p. 6; L. Zhmiriov, "Peremeny v Bolgarii," 15 November 1989, p. 6; "Kursom peremen," 18 November 1989, p. 5; "Zasedanie Politburo TsK BKP," 29 November 1989, p. 5; O. Losoto and A. Cherniak, "Shag k narodovlastiiu," 1 December 1989, p. 4.
39. One influential party faction calls itself "Road to Europe."
40. Discussion with the author in Sofia on 16 June 1990.
41. John D. Bell, Ronald A. Gould, and Richard Smolka, *The 1990 Bulgarian Elections: A Pre-election Technical Assessment* (Washington, D.C.: International Foundation for Electoral Systems, 1990) and John D. Bell et al., *An Orderly Rebellion: Bulgaria's Transition from Dictatorship to Democracy* (Washington, D.C.: International Foundation for Electoral Systems, 1990). Both may be obtained from IFES, 1620 "I" Street N.W., Washington, D.C., 20006.
42. Chuck Sudetic, "Bulgarian Opposition Leader to Become President," *The New York Times,* 2 August 1990, p. A-4.
43. Only one leader of any reform faction was elected to the party's Supreme Council. BTA, 25 September 1990; "Council Voting, Omissions Viewed," FBIS-EEU (26 September 1990), pp. 1-2.
44. John D. Bell, "Bulgaria," *1991 YICA*, forthcoming.
45. Born 25 June 1927, the son of a priest, Dimitŭr Popov served for many years as a legal consultant to the transport ministry and as a judge in the Sofia courts. He gained significant recognition for his work as a secretary of the Central Electoral Commission in preparing the June 1990 elections. BTA, 7 December 1990; "Dimitŭr Popov," FBIS-EEU (10 December 1990), p. 3.
46. The UDF was formed in December 1989 by ten parties and organizations. These included the Discussion Clubs and Eco-*glasnost'*, whose constituency came primarily from the intelligentsia; two revived traditional parties, the Social Democrats and the Bulgarian Agrarian National Union—Nikola Petkov; four human rights organizations; the Independent Students' Society; and the independent trade union, *Podkrepa*. Soon thereafter, three more organizations were admitted. Two, the Democratic and Radical Democratic parties, were revivals of precommunist political forces. The third, the Green Party, was a new formation made up of those who found Eco-*glasnost'* insufficiently radical. Several other parties, organizations, and movements also subsequently announced their solidarity with the UDF.
47. Several UDF leaders privately state their belief that a UDF-BSP coalition government is necessary to deal with the many crises the country must deal with. Some even feel that the BSP might be easier to deal with than some of their partners. They have been handcuffed, however, by their "read my lips" vows never to form a coalition with the socialists.

During his recent visit to Washington, President Zhelev suggested that the extraordinary and unforeseen developments arising from Iraq's invasion of Kuwait might now justify a coalition with the progressive elements of the BSP. Speech to the International Club, Washington, D.C., 26 September 1990.

48. The moderate wing of the UDF suffered a sharp setback when Petŭr Beron, leader of Eco-*glasnost'* and Zhelev's successor as UDF president, suddenly resigned amid charges that he had once been an informer for Bulgarian State Security. He was succeeded by Filip Dimitrov, a 35-year-old attorney and vice chairman of the Green Party. The UDF's governing council charged that the Soviet KGB was involved in an attempt to discredit opposition leaders by making compromising material about them available. BTA, 9 December 1990; "SDS Resolution on Alleged KGB Activities," FBIS-EEU (11 December 1990), p. 7.

49. Zheliu Zhelev, *Fashizmŭt* (Boulder, Colorado: Social Science Monographs, 1990). Zhelev's text was written in the late 1960s and published, through editorial inadvertence, by Bulgaria's youth publishing house in 1981. It was immediately suppressed, and has long been an underground classic. Although ostensibly concerned with the problem of "fascism," the work clearly applied to Bulgaria and other Soviet model states.

50. See the afterword to the American edition of *Fashizmŭt*, pp. 1-4.

51. Conversation with the author in Sofia, 19 April 1990. The incident suggests President Reagan's quip: "Sometimes our right hand doesn't know what our far right hand is doing."

52. Blaine Harden, "Gas Line or No Line, Either Way, It's a Problem in E. Europe," *The Washington Post*, 3 January 1991, p. A-18.

53. Discussion with the author on 16 October 1990 in Washington, D.C.

54. A. Smirnov, "Trudnoe prozrenie," *Sovetskaia Rossiia* (Moscow), 4 September 1990, p. 3.

55. These weapons were armed with conventional, not nuclear, warheads. BTA, 31 August 1990; "Missiles not Armed with Nuclear Warheads," FBIS-EEU (4 September 1990), p. 9.

56. "Bŭlgariia veche ne e komunisticheska, ne e totalitarna dŭrzhava," *Demokratsiia* (Sofia), 3 October 1990, pp. 1, 4.

11

Soviet-Albanian Relations: The Return of Russia to the Balkans

Nikolaos A. Stavrou

Three decades of intense ideological warfare against successive Soviet leaders for their alleged abandonment of Marxism-Leninism and the restoration of capitalism have come to an end in Albania. The momentous events of 1989-1990 in East-Central Europe, a dismal economic situation, a restless youth and intelligentsia, and power struggles that continue to beset the leadership of the Albanian (communist) Party of Labor, compelled the Tirana regime to abandon decades of hostility toward the two superpowers and seek normalization of relations with both. A dramatic step in that direction was taken on 31 July 1990. A formal communiqué, issued simultaneously in Moscow and Tirana, announced the restoration of diplomatic relations between the two countries which had been severed almost 30 years ago. A new era in Albanian foreign policy vis-à-vis the Soviet Union thus has commenced, for which the recent past can hardly serve as a guide for its future course.

The "bloc" which Albania abandoned three decades ago no longer exists, and Marxism-Leninism—the semireligion of the world communist movement—has fallen into irreversible disrepute. For Albania, more so than the other East-Central European countries, normalization of relations with Moscow could not mean return to the "family" because the family itself is in disarray. Moreover, there is no acceptable definition of "normal relations" among states like Albania and Cuba that still persist in calling themselves "socialist." The Eastern bloc is a thing of the past, Marxist ideology is bankrupt, and the Balkans have returned to a state of emotion-laden ethnic fragmentation. More so than in other cases, relations between Moscow and Tirana cannot rely on principles that have shaped Soviet-East-Central European relations over the past 45 years, or the ideals that made the revival of pluralism in East-Central Europe possible under Gorbachev. For almost 30 years, Albania was neither a partner nor a contributor to the development of multilateral relations among socialist states, and its experience with pluralism is almost nonexistent. The ideological foundations and structures that have assured Moscow's control over the area and promoted its strategic interests have also lost their usefulness as policy guides, and no Soviet grand strategy has emerged to take their place. The Warsaw Treaty Organization and CMEA that kept East-Central European states in line had long been abandoned by Albania. Tirana renounced the Warsaw Pact (and got away with it, thanks to its geography) in the wake of the Soviet invasion of Czechoslovakia and had ceased participating in CMEA affairs many years before that.

The collapse of communist regimes in East-Central Europe and elsewhere in the late 1980s and early 1990s brought about a new world order which is essentially responsible for setting in motion the process for normalization of relations between Moscow and Tirana. Although the evidence is preliminary and hardly sufficient to make valid generalizations, it seems that during the Gorbachev era, Soviet-Albanian relations would be influenced by two historical periods: the 1924-1940 era which, for lack of a better term, may be called the era of nostalgia, and the postwar years, dominated by one of the most intensely fought ideological battles. Before examining the domestic factors that influenced the changes in Soviet-Albanian relations and assessing the root causes of change during the Gorbachev era, a review of the historical sources of Albanian foreign policy is in order.

THE PAST AS A GUIDE FOR THE PRESENT

During the past five years, Soviet press commentaries and academic studies have shown a revived interest in "socialist" Albania's economic and political developments and factually reported all the activities of its government and communist party. Analysts and policymakers alike searched rather deeply into Moscow's early interest in Balkan affairs for positive events of cooperation and dismissed the Soviet-Albanian rift as a "misunderstanding that could have been avoided." By 1988, Soviet commentators all but blamed the whole affair on Nikita S. Khrushchev and came fairly close to offering an apology to the post-Hoxha leadership of Albania. Nina D. Smirnova, a prominent Soviet historian and Albanologist, explained the issues as follows in a commentary published by *Novyi mir:*

> It was an overreaction on our part on the stand taken by the Albanian leadership. In response to the Albanian's side fanning of ideological difference, we broke off diplomatic relations.[1]

Other publications expressed similar sentiments, including *Izvestiia,* which repeatedly termed Soviet-Albanian relations as "abnormal and we wish to correct them." Despite a USSR eagerness to forget the past, Tirana repeatedly rejected all overtures until February 1990.[2] The patronizing and occasionally glowing descriptions of Albania's attempts to build "socialism by its own means" had little impact on suspicious members of the Tirana clique who saw a plot every time the Russians or Americans said something positive about their country. On the Soviet side, there seemed to be a more positive attitude about references to the interwar period, particularly the years 1924-1939. This was an era in which the roots of Albanian communism are traceable and is viewed with nostalgia by scholars of both countries. Albanian communism was at its romantic stage then, and Moscow as well as the Comintern were pleased with the prospects of a peasant revolution in the Balkans in which the Albanians would play a "leading role," as they did in the Ottoman Empire. Albanian communist militancy and intense nationalism blended in a most effective manner during the interwar period.

Studies of Soviet-Albanian relations produced in the West have, by and large, omitted the depth and extent of Bolshevik involvement in the Balkans during the interwar period and the prominent role played by Albanian communist leaders in Comintern affairs.[3] The omissions are casually patched over by meaningless generalizations in monographs produced by nationalist advocates who, collectively, seem to treat the appearance of communism in Albania as an accident of history, and the Soviet involvement in that country's affairs as a postwar phenomenon. Invariably, the "annexation" by Italy in 1939 is offered as the "genetic" cause of Albanian communism, while the seizure of power by the Albanian Communist Party in 1944 is explained as a consequence of World War II.[4] In the era of *glasnost',* Khrushchev's role is all but ignored and emphasis is placed instead on the relevance of the prewar period of Soviet-Albanian relations, which was, indeed, free of acrimony and polemics. We shall avoid jumping to premature conclusions based on the strong similarities of the Balkans in the thirties and today. But the similarities are indeed striking. Then, the Balkan Federation—a Comintern creation—for almost a decade exploited the intensity of Albanian nationalism in Kosovo to deal a "blow to Serbian feudal reaction," which

Georgii Dimitrov saw as the main obstacle to a Balkan-wide peasant revolution. A Committee for the Liberation of Kosovo, manned exclusively by Albanians and Vlachs, was a critical component in Comintern schemes for the solution of the region's ethnic problems. Dozens of Albanian operatives were carrying out orders for the Comintern and Stalin in the Balkans, Europe, Asia, and simultaneously pursued the goal of unification of all Albanians under one flag.[5] These were the days of unrestrained Albanian enthusiasm for Moscow, duly recorded in the annals of the Comintern, and now replayed, perhaps hoping to serve as a substitute for Marxism-Leninism.[6] Not only Soviet, but also Albanian historians refer with pride to the role of their "pioneers" in the ranks of the Comintern that for ten years had made Kosovo a test case of socialist revolution based on the peasantry.[7]

The first group of young Albanians (some of whom are now old Albanians and still prominent in their country) was delivered to Moscow by an unorthodox Orthodox clergyman, Bishop Fan S. Noli, in 1927.[8] Born Stylianos S. Mavromates in Greek Thrace, Noli "discovered" his Albanian heritage in Cairo, traveled to the United States, studied divinity at Harvard University while at the same time acting as the leader of the Albanian community in Boston. He visited Albania for the first time in 1914 to lend his support for establishment of the first Albanian state ever. Gradually he drifted in the direction of Leninism.[9] In June 1924, Noli led a coup, undertaken by four Comintern-created organizations, and marched to Tirana as the head of "the Albanian bourgeois revolution."[10] An admirer of Lenin, Noli recognized that his regime caused serious concerns among his neighbors and a protest by the British government for inviting the Bolsheviks into the flammable powder keg called the Balkans.[11] He is now viewed in Albanian historiography as the "leader of the progressive forces," and by post-Brezhnev historians in the USSR as the person most likely to have introduced socialism in the Balkans had it not been for the war and the distortions of Stalinism. Even current leader Ramiz Alia has a nostalgia for the glorious days of the 1920s and admiration for the role of Noli in Albanian history. In a visit to Tropojë, just across the Kosovo border, he recited one of Noli's poems about that sacred land and the glories of one of the bishop's associates, Bajram Çuri, a Comintern operative and revolutionary of the 1920s.[12]

The Albanian communist movement of the thirties emerges as a period over which there is little disagreement about its meaning and its utility as a point of reference for the development of relations on the fundamentals of the "nation-state" system. For Albania, this era was characterized by unfulfilled national goals and revolutionary excitement over Kosovo; for the Soviets, it was an opportunity to test all available means to promote revolution, including the Orthodox Church. On that score too the role of the *Cernnii Episkop* (Red Bishop) was pivotal.

One of the primary goals of Noli was establishment of a "national Albanian church."[13] Toward this end scores of Comintern agents, some disguised as choir members, flocked to Albania to help the "Bishop" set up "his Orthodox" Church and free the believers from Greek and Serbian domination.[14]

The basic variables that influenced Noli's enthusiasm for the Comintern and the Bolsheviks are still valid today and they may, once again, influence the course of Moscow-Tirana relations. In the mid-twenties, the Comintern supported Albania's claim to Kosovo and denounced Serbian as well as Greek designs over this small country. During the Gorbachev era, the issue of Albanian self-determination looms large over the Balkans and Tirana is testing the direction of USSR policy on that issue. Kosovo was an exploitable issue in the 1920s, and it is equally useful for a "Russian" or Soviet return to the Balkans and Moscow's confirmation as a traditional power broker in this volatile region.

There are valid reasons for the Soviet Union (and perhaps Albania) to deemphasize the postwar era and look into a period when Albanian nationalism and communism were effectively blended into a powerful revolutionary movement. For the duration of the war, the Albanian communist party was de facto treated as Tito's ward and the country's sovereignty was limited to the first three years of communist rule.[15] Between 1945 and 1948, Stalin showed little regard for the interests of Albanians and even less for their national pride.[16] The Yugoslav-Soviet break in 1948 forced Tirana to ask Moscow for economic and military assistance, and the country was gradually integrated into the Eastern bloc. Scores of Soviet advisors populated the Albanian ministries and, for almost ten years, de facto ran the country. The advent of N. S. Khrushchev to power, and the ideological storm that was unleashed in 1956 after his denunciation of Stalin's personality cult, led to the Soviet-Albanian rift which lasted almost 30 years.

THE SOVIET-ALBANIAN RIFT

This break was one of the manifestations of the Sino-Soviet conflict and the Khrushchev-Mao personality clash. The restoration of diplomatic relations between Moscow and Tirana brings to an end one communist sideshow that few people took seriously.

Four fundamental causes brought about the Soviet-Albanian rift in 1961, making it the longest feud of all communist rivalries: (a) the Soviet-Yugoslav rapprochement, (b) de-Stalinization and the issue of the personality cult, (c) the issues of "war, peace, revolution, and peaceful co-existence," and (d) the Greek-Soviet rapprochement.[17] The pilgrimage of Khrushchev and Bulganin to Belgrade in June 1955 signaled Moscow's desire to seek a resolution of issues that had divided the two parties and hopefully bring Tito back into the fold. Khrushchev's presence in Yugoslavia upset the Albanian leadership. In 1948, according to Hoxha's version of history, Yugoslavia was about to swallow its neighbor with the help of the then minister of interior and Tito's protégé, Koçi Xoxe.[18] The visit to Belgrade, followed by a warming of relations in the next two years, reinforced Hoxha's worst fears, i.e., that his country would be the sacrificial lamb for Tito's return to the bloc. This was not the first time that Albania was viewed as dispensable by Moscow. In 1947, Stalin had made the same offer to Yugoslavs.[19] But in the 1950s, Tito's price for forgetting the past was a heavy one: among other demands he sought the rehabilitation of all those victims, including Xoxe, who were purged or executed as "Titoists" on Stalin's orders and insisted that those responsible for their fate be removed from power. That represented a threat to Hoxha, and he was not about to be "de-Stalinized" or commit self-decapitation. Predictably, he linked national survival with his personal survival and fought both battles by selective use of ideology. At the Bucharest and Moscow conferences in 1960, the polarization that had emerged between Moscow and Tirana became even sharper by China's adoption of a divergent view on war, peace, and world revolution as well as the concept of peaceful coexistence. That was the beginning of the Peking-Tirana axis that lasted fifteen years. Khrushchev, in his impulsive manner, charged the Chinese with "factionalism" and "dogmatism"; the Albanians joined the chorus and dismissed Khrushchev as a modern revisionist. Gradually the Soviet-Albanian rift intensified and involved state-to-state relations such as trade, cultural exchanges, and technology. On 25 November 1961, the Soviet ambassador to Tirana was withdrawn and on 3 December Deputy Foreign Minister Nikolai Firiubin asked the Albanians to close their embassy in Moscow.[20]

The fourth critical issue that generated intense anti-Khrushchev polemics was Moscow's change of position on the issue of the Greek minority in southern Albania—an issue that reinforced Hoxha's fears that Khrushchev viewed his country's integrity as dispensable.[21] Moscow's change on this claim resulted from a gross misreading of the 1958 Greek election outcome, in which the left gained 79 seats (out of 300) in parliament. The EDA or United Democratic Left (overt branch of the Greek communist party that was still outlawed) surprised everyone by electing enough deputies to become the number two party and the "loyal opposition," trouncing badly George

Papandreou's center coalition. It was a peculiarity of the electoral law that was designed to "punish coalitions." But in Moscow, the EDA "victory" was interpreted as a vindication of Khrushchev's doctrine of "peaceful transition to socialism" and efforts were made to capitalize on it. The human rights of the Greek minority in Northern Epirus (south Albania) was an issue that has bedeviled Greek communists to this day. The Greek right had successfully branded the left as "traitors" ready to make concessions even to Albanian communists for the sake of "proletarian internationalism." Khrushchev sought to correct this matter by raising the question of "oppression of the Greek minority" in Albania with the Albanian delegation during the Bucharest meeting. Earlier he had assured Sophocles Venizelos (a former prime minister and the first noncommunist Greek leader to visit Moscow since 1917) that he would seek better human rights for the Greeks in Albania.[22] Placed in the context of Greek demands for annexation of the southern part of Albania (still raised by segments of the Greek political elite), this issue also added fuel to Hoxha's concerns and reinforced his doubts about Moscow's commitment to the survival of Albania as an independent state. But in Moscow's eyes, the Greek prize loomed bigger, as compared to Albania. Hoxha took the offensive. In a major speech on the anniversary of the October 1917 revolution, he denounced Khrushchev and raised higher the nationalist flag:

> They [Khrushchevites] accuse us of not making efforts toward a Balkan understanding; they join in the chorus of Tito and Karamanlis as though we were the warmongers of the Balkan countries; they accuse us of not making efforts toward a "Balkan understanding" ... But if we have failed to criticize Khrushchev (and we made this criticism in a comradely fashion) when he raised the hopes of Venizelos for the "autonomy of southern Albania," it would have been treason on our part.[23]

Albanian-Soviet relations remained frozen until 1989. As stated earlier, repeated attempts by USSR leaders, including Gorbachev, were rebuffed without hesitation. Cryptic comments during the early years of Gorbachev, usually articulated by Foto Çami (member of the politburo and secretariat, purged in the upheavals of November 1990), were contradicted by other senior officials, confirming schisms at the top and refusal to alter the course set by the late Enver Hoxha. To put matters to rest, Alia used his report to the 9th Congress of the Albanian Party of Labor (November 1986) to assure his associates of his faithful pursuit of the Hoxha course. Gorbachev, Alia said, "was a modern-day Khrushchev" and in some respects more dangerous because of his closeness to American imperialists.

THE BEGINNING OF "REFORM"

The Polish events of 1988, a rebellious Albanian youth, and a five-year economic decline compelled Alia to search for "new policies" without the necessity of restoring relations with the superpowers. For several years Albania was busy establishing economic and diplomatic ties with Western countries, including the Federal Republic of Germany. By 1988, relations with all East-Central European regimes were upgraded to ambassadorial level, and economic agreements were routinely signed following the familiar barter trade pattern. But still, Tirana refused to adhere to principles of the Helsinki Accords and kept up a barrage of antiimperialist and anti-Soviet rhetoric. Gorbachev's visit to the United States and Reagan's return visit to Moscow were denounced as "superpower collusion" to subjugate the weak states. Domestic reforms in the Soviet Union and open discussion (*glasnost*) of public issues were dismissed by the Albanian press as psychological diversions by which the Gorbachevians were trying to "foster the illusion" that the new political line is the product of extensive public discussion.

As late as January 1990, the Albanian leadership gave every indication that it was preparing for the long haul. However, economic issues complicated matters. A five-year decline in productivity, coupled with a population explosion in the brackets seeking employment (ages 15 to 25), caused serious concerns in the leadership. An attempt at a "mini-cultural revolution" a year earlier had failed to stem the decline in productivity and the lack of employment for a growing population.[24] During the 7th Central Committee plenum (1-2 February 1989), called for the sole purpose of discussing Prime Minister Adil Çarçani's report on agriculture, Alia surprised everybody by announcing the replacement of half the cabinet members. Although it initially appeared that the main purpose of the change was to deal with economic problems (complicated by the worst drought in 40 years), he had multiple objectives in mind. The central one involved strengthening his control of the politburo and neutralizing opponents who saw signs of Alia's wavering in his commitment to Hoxha's legacy. By early 1989, it was quite obvious that several power centers were unwilling to accept even minor reforms, fearing that they could lead to massive demonstrations.

The critical change that occurred in February 1989 involved the Ministry of the Interior, which was given to Simon Stefani, a member of the Secretariat and, by all previous accounts, a reform-minded leader. Alia wanted to give this dreadful agency a "new image" besides gaining better control over it. For a while, it seemed that his plan had worked. By fall 1989 Stefani encouraged and implemented mild criticism of the *Sigurimi,* a first for

Albania, in an unusual way. A novel titled *Thikat* (Knives), critical of *Sigurimi* agents who looked at every crime as an "opportunity for a promotion," cleared the censors and the first printing was sold out within days after hitting the stands. Its author, Neshat Tozaj, was himself a *Sigurimi* agent, giving his work an authoritative aura.[25] It received an enthusiastic review by Albania's most prominent writer, Ismail Kadare, who predicted that it "will disturb the conscience of many people and in time will prove its emancipating effect."[26] Nevertheless, Alia concentrated his efforts to assure his associates that the changes in the party and government were "not connected in any way with any question concerning the trustworthiness or political position of any comrade; they are dictated solely by the intention of providing new stimuli to the work of the party, the state, and the economy."[27] But the February 1989 changes, like previous cabinet reshuffles that Alia carried out since he assumed power in April 1985, had little impact on the economy; they had a greater impact among the intellectuals who saw them as the beginning of liberalization and confirmation that the events in East-Central Europe had some impact on the Albanian leadership. The privileged youth with TV sets in their homes and access to foreign broadcasts followed with great interest events in East-Central Europe. The mild criticism of *Sigurimi,* the most feared agency, even though it had been orchestrated from above gave ideas to the young people and university students that were probably unthinkable a few months earlier. The state propaganda about the deprivations in the capitalist world was laughed off as a cruel joke. Italian, Greek, and even Yugoslav television programs had already disabused youth of such notions.

PRESSURES FROM ABOVE AND BELOW

For two years, Alia and the communist leadership dismissed *perestroika* and *glasnost'* as irrelevant to Albania's experience. East-Central European communist parties, particularly the Polish and Hungarian, were dismissed as "Khrushchevite revisionist," whose course was predicted "by Enver Hoxha when he broke relations with them." Clinging to orthodoxy, Albanian theoreticians, as late as December 1989, persisted in their "interpretation" that what had collapsed in East-Central Europe with few regrets was not socialism "but ruling revisionist cliques" that Gorbachev and his predecessors had incubated. Foto Çami, an academic who often spoke from both sides of his mouth on political issues, diagnosed the problems in East-Central Europe as being "the outgrowth of expansion of private property . . . class oppression and exploitation in societies that had adopted bourgeois ideology long ago."[28]

Even Alia was assuring his compatriots that Albania would go it alone and on occasion praised the steadfastness of Nicolae Ceauşescu. "We are a small country," he said to a gathering close to the Kosovo border, "but the only country building and developing socialism without asking for anybody's help."[29] He was sure that the change he introduced at the 7th Central Committee plenum would suffice to stem the tide of discontent. The only sign of pressures from below between February and August were two protests: one at the center of Tirana involving students, the other in the Sarandes district involving members of the Greek minority.[30] The students demanded freedom and better living conditions; the Greek farm workers were protesting the brigade leaders' pressures to produce more for the same pay.

As demonstrations go, these two were easily settled. In Tirana, a popular university professor of psychology, Hamid Beqja, and a politburo member who rushed to the scene, persuaded the students to disband; the Greek protest was settled with a few arrests and public humiliation of the ringleaders. Even though small in scale, the protests were significant in another way: they underscored the existence of pressures from below and forced at least parts of the leadership to think about reforms seriously, and other elements to think of the need to crack down harder.

Pressures from below were reflected in splits among the top leaders, and were exacerbated by the events that shook the GDR, Poland, and Hungary. By early summer, the party leadership was visibly split in two groups: a strong pro-Alia component that wanted him to succeed (whatever his goals) and still believed he was carrying out Hoxha's wishes by attacking the "bureaucracy"; and a hard-core Stalinist group (led by Hoxha's widow, and consisting of the Tirana party chief, Piro Kondi, and Vito Kapo, widow of the architect of the Soviet-Albanian break, Hysni Kapo). Rightly or wrongly, this latter group concluded that Alia was deviating from the Hoxha orthodox line and was leading the country into anarchy. All along, looming on the horizon, was the personality of Gorbachev, who was seen on Albanian television shaking hands with Washingtonians and being mobbed in East Germany and exalted in Yugoslavia. The images were too powerful to be ignored, and the party no longer had effective means to stem the inflow of information. The complicating factor that made reforms inevitable were the sociological and political trends that the era of instant communications had sharpened. Those most influenced by the reform were none other than the children of the privileged elites. They had the luxury of television sets in their living rooms and direct access to those who made decisions—their parents, whose word they could hardly believe anymore. Under dual pressures, the Albanian leadership adopted an ingenious approach to reform which is still operative today: they opted to preemptively address, at the cosmetic level, most political demands that were raised in East-Central Europe, including power sharing, but to define their new policies as the product of the "party's wisdom," not the result of *perestroika, glasnost'*, or external pressures. The objective, all along, was a soft landing and maintenance of power by the Albanian Party of Labor, which now had to assume the additional task of developing (and controlling) an acceptable "opposition."

The task of working out the appropriate theses was assigned to Lenka Çuko, a member of the secretariat and the sole woman on the politburo. At the 8th plenum (25-27 September), she put forth the idea of "multiple candidacies for local party and state organs" and "rotation in party posts." Alia endorsed "certain ideas with merit that Comrade Çuko proposed" and added one of his own: i.e., senior posts in the government could be "entrusted to a son or daughter of the people, irrespective of whether he or she is a member of the party."[31] Taken at face value, these changes could be seen as "power sharing"—a central demand in the East-Central European revolutions. But in the Albanian version, it meant very little: the party de facto retained the right to select those nonparty "sons and daughters" to assume governmental posts. Article 3 of the Albanian constitution, assuring the "leading role of the party," was left untouched. And as a firm warning to those who might harbor other ideas of "liberalization" on the ideological front, Alia stated:

> No concessions will be made to the bourgeois ideology in any field, either politics, arts and culture, or in economic relations. There must be no concessions to religious ideology in any of its various forms. We take this stand as convinced atheists, but also in order to protect the unity of a people that over the centuries have suffered from rifts and divisions inspired by churches and mosques.[32]

Adopting a posture of normalcy, the Albanian government routinely congratulated the new leaders who assumed power in rapid succession in Bulgaria, Poland, and East Germany, while the press continued to hammer on the degeneracy of socialism under Gorbachev. By December, the problems of East-Central Europe hit home. Alia's last hope for a European ideological partner, Ceauşescu, was besieged by prodemocracy crowds, and on Christmas Day the macabre scenes of the dictator's and his wife's corpses were seen on Albanian television screens.[33] More ominously, student demonstrations in the northern city of Shkodër turned ugly, with dozens killed.[34] For a while it seemed that the collapse of the Albanian regime was imminent. In the midst of Western pressures for change and East-Central European exaltations over the achievements of the masses, Alia called into session the 9th Central Committee plenum (23 January 1990), supposedly to implement the decisions reached at the previous one. Even that late in the hour, he sounded oblivious to events in East-Central Europe and rejected Soviet calls for "normalization" and reforms. He dismissed "bourgeois press accounts" about demonstrations in his country as "fabrication designed to overthrow the peoples power in Albania and to destroy its independence." Then, in a most unusual public relations stunt, "friends of Albania" on 2 February 1990 bought space in *The New York Times* to reproduce part of Alia's address to the 9th plenum, which "answered" all issues. In that address, he defiantly assured the world "that the Albanian caravan will continue to march forward." But at the same time, Alia commenced the search for a new rationale to remain in power—"he found it in national survival." Masterfully, and taking advantage of what appeared "to have been a carefully planned spontaneous event" in Kosovo that occurred a week after the upheavals in Shkodër, he called upon all Albanians to unite and defend the nation: "When national identity, freedom and independence are at stake, everyone who calls himself an Albanian, wherever he is, will stand up to make any sacrifice and even to lay down his life for the homeland." Western reporters who roamed freely in Yugoslavia showed Albanians beaten by communist police in Kosovo, but could not do the same in Albania. No access was accorded to them to enter Albania but the subject "Albanians demand freedom" was covered for the Western masses via their coverage of the Kosovo issue. The lessons of Madison Avenue are not ignored in Tirana. The focus was elsewhere, while Alia planned his next moves.

Bravado aside, Alia took the pressures from below seriously and the attention given to his country in the West ominously. He dispatched several senior diplomats to "pacify neighbors" and to start the process for normalization of relations with the Soviet Union and the United States. Kosovo was blended into the domestic "reform agenda" and the image of "victim" was firmly established with the help of a prominent Western spokesman, who rose to defend the human rights of Albanians in Yugoslavia, instead of those in Albania! But for the impressionable, Albanians are Albanians; what difference does it make where they live?

RETURN OF THE RUSSIANS

After frantic efforts by Alia to substitute intense Albanian nationalism for Stalinism, three senior diplomats, two of them of Greek descent, were assigned the difficult task of assuring the world that their government was there to stay and that it would decide at its own pace what reforms to introduce and when. Required were normal state-to-state relations with everyone, irrespective of their system, provided Albania was left alone to pursue its independent course toward socialism.

Xenophon Nushi, ambassador to Paris, set the agenda for the immediate course of Soviet-Albanian relations by introducing the issue of Kosovo into any future negotiations with Moscow. The subject was quite familiar to Soviet policy planners. Support for the Kosovo issue became a "litmus test" of relations between Albania and other countries. In his comments, Nushi took note of past relations with Moscow, calmer years, and to make the point as to what Albania will expect in the future. He offered Stalin's and Lenin's contributions to Albanian causes at critical times as examples of "good relations." Lenin's contribution was accidental and essentially consisted of publication of the London Treaty, which envisioned the dismemberment of Albania, and his dispatch to the Balkans of Comintern agents to assist Noli in his grab for power and the liberation of Kosovo. Stalin's contributions, however, spanned the thirties and the postwar period, and Nushi proudly stated that "he will have a place of honor in his county's history." It was a diplomatic way of staking out the Albanian position which rejected interference in internal affairs yet, at the same time, accepted "proper state-to-state relations."

While Nushi was assuring Western newsmen of his government's stability, the senior deputy foreign minister, Sokrat Pliaka, flew to Athens to pacify jittery Greek officials who feared that the Greek minority would bear the brunt of any upheavals in Albania as it did during Noli's "bourgeois revolution," when more than 20,000 were made refugees overnight. On 2 February 1990, Pliaka became the first high-level official to articulate a reversal of a policy of hostility toward the superpowers and to take a serious look into the possibility of joining the EC, participating in a Helsinki II, and adhering to its principles on human rights.[35]

Between February and May 1990, intense negotiations between Moscow and Tirana took place in Sofia, New York, and Paris to smooth the way for the restoration of relations. Similar negotiations have been under way between Washington and Tirana. But while the talks were going on, the Alia regime was pursuing two goals with a sense of urgency: first, to firmly establish Alia as a "militant nationalist"—an ideology with which he is now gradually replacing Stalinism—and second, a frantic effort to ward off the inevitable assault by the worshipers of Hoxha's personality cult.

The achievement of the first goal was rather easy. Since 1981, Tirana has activated all Albanians to pursue Kosovo independence and self-determination. Prominent individuals of Albanian origin with influence in the Western world were routinely invited to Tirana and often seen by senior officials, including Hoxha and Alia. Among them Mother Teresa, an Albanian from Kosovo who was received by Hoxha's widow and the foreign minister. While in Tirana, the Catholic nun visited the "monument of mother Albania, decorated with the flags of Skënderbeg, Albania, and Kosovo"; she did not utter a word about religious persecution. American-Albanian clergymen and personalities with congressional ties made annual pilgrimages to Tirana. The last group, invited for the festivities of national independence, was received by Alia, who thanked them for their work on the Kosovo issue.[36]

The second goal, the neutralization of the Hoxha cult worshipers was more difficult. For almost 30 years, the battle cry for the hard-core Stalinists was "no relations with the superpowers." But conditions had changed. Albania's East-Central European trading partners had little interest in Albanian vegetables, chrome, and copper; the two main suppliers of military hardware (all Soviet-made, incidentally), Bulgaria and East Germany, were now fully behind Gorbachev's reforms.[37] Poland, Hungary, and Czechoslovakia were even farther afield in their pro-Western reformist programs; North Korea, Cuba, and Vietnam could hardly open an arms-supply line to Moscow to keep the Albanian military machine going. Necessity was catching up with principle.

At the 10th Central Committee plenum held on 17 April 1990, Alia formally announced the approval by that body of his recommendation to restore relations with Moscow and Washington. The end of an era had finally come. The practical details for opening embassies were worked out for the most part, and on 31 July 1990 agreement was formally announced.[38]

While negotiations for the restoration of relations were going on, domestically the government proceeded with caution toward liberalization. The 10th Central Committee plenum approved a variety of reforms and granted basic rights, including, for the first time, the right to travel. The parliament was asked to enact ready-made legislative decrees, and Deputy Premier Manush Myftiu was placed in charge of a commission to produce the draft of a new constitution. As evidence of "liberalization," the Ministry of Justice was revived; it had been abolished in 1965 in the wake of Albania's version of a cultural revolution as an "impediment to class struggle." But in July, all hell broke loose. Initially hundreds and later up to 6,000 Albanian students, workers, and former political prisoners sought asylum in Western embassies, demanding to leave the country. After days of procrastination, the Albanian government permitted them to leave. Alia and his colleagues undertook a new offensive to polish their image, but the embassy crisis was used as an opportunity for another governmental change. Again, Western analysts accepted the Alia line and interpreted the purge of "those responsible for the whole affair" a defeat for the Hoxha hard-liners. An analysis of the changes in government positions raised doubts about Alia's sincerity on reforms. The officials who paid the penalty for the embassy fiasco do not seem to fit the mold of the hard core: they were dismissed for failing to foresee and prevent the events, not for being harsh or for causing bloodshed.[39]

The first person to be reassigned (no one was punished or left without another job, except for Myftiu who was retired), and whose removal was heralded as Alia "finally" getting hold of the *Sigurimi,* was Simon Stefani. As mentioned earlier, he was appointed in February 1989 for the same purpose and for a time had permitted limited criticism of that dreadful organization. The second was Lenka Çuko, a member of the Secretariat who first introduced the idea of multiple candidacies for local offices at the 8th Central Committee plenum. The third (retired) was 75-year-old Deputy Premier Manush Myftiu (a former fascist party member who, like Alia and a few others, switched to communism at the right opportunity),[40] who was placed in charge of a commission by the 10th plenum of the Central Committee to enact "reform legislation." And the fourth to be replaced was the minister of defense, Prokop Mura, the only civilian to hold that office. Those who assumed these posts were equally as important as those who had lost them.

The person replacing Stefani, and immediately baptized a "reformer" by Western commentators, was Hekuran Isai. He had held the very same post under Hoxha for seven years and is responsible for one of the country's bloodiest Stalinist purges involving the "followers of Mehmet Shehu and Kadri Hazbiu" (prime minister and minister of interior, respectively). The new minister of defense is General Kiço Mustaqi, an ethnic Greek and a Hoxha protégé with mediocre military training, who had been in charge of the purges to remove "pro-Chinese elements" from the army on Hoxha's orders. The purges ended with the elimination of the minister of defense, Beqir Baluku, and the chief of the general staff, Petrit Dume.[41]

The genius of Alia's response to the pressure for change is that he placed in key posts Hoxha clones to carry out economic, political, and social reforms at his pace, without compromising on the key objective, i.e., perpetuation of the leading role of the party. The question is whether he will be as successful in peddling them as "reformers" domestically as he has been abroad. One way that the Tirana public relations machine has found effective in improving its image is to use Western personalities to generate a positive image. The presence in Tirana and Kosovo of headline-makers, such as Senator Dennis DeConcini, Congressman Tom Lantos, and Senator Paul Sarbanes, has the impact of confirming "normalcy" and "openness." The normalization of relations with Moscow, seen from the domestic perspective, adds to Tirana's claim of vindication of their ideological position and the "correctness" of their foreign policy. Alia feels secure that he has successfully fended off the pressures of East-Central European developments and achieved, with his version of reforms, his basic goals: a soft landing, retention of power by the communist party, exacerbation of nationalist feelings, and successful portrayal of Albania as a "victim of her neighbor's greed," in need of understanding and perhaps protection. His recent speech before the General Assembly of the United Nations underscores Tirana's long-held view that relations with other countries (and that would include the USSR) cannot be based on the principles spawned by the Gorbachev reforms. Alia stated the following:

> In the situation we find ourselves now, we cannot say that the policies and practices produced by the bloc concepts have been overcome. Worse still, the arrogance inspired by the policy of strength, which is reflected in the continuation of attempts at imposing various models, standards and schemes of political or social developments on others has not been overcome, either. Life has shown that pressures to make them compulsory for every country has led to conflicts from which the world is suffering to this date.[42]

SOVIET-ALBANIAN RELATIONS IN THE 1990s

The future of the new rapprochement between Moscow and Tirana will be determined by social, economic, and political developments both in the Soviet Union and Albania. The principles which will guide Albania's policies during the current decade have been enunciated in several statements by the country's leaders since the 10th Central Committee plenum, and reiterated in Alia's 1990 address to the UN General Assembly. In sum, Albanian foreign policy comprises a continuity of goals set by the former Albanian dictator, Enver Hoxha, despite the change in language and approach, which was forced upon the current leadership by the events set in motion by Gorbachev's policies of *glasnost'* and *perestroika*.

In the 1990s, relations with Moscow will be guided by the pragmatic approach that Albania displayed in its opening to the West over the past decades, but without deviation from previous national priorities. The country's new thinking in foreign policy reflects its rejection of "models which have no historical precedent" in Albanian history and aims at retention of its maverick status and underscores its xenophobia. Notwithstanding this newly acquired pragmatism in foreign policy, and to some extent in domestic affairs, Alia seems determined to protect at any cost the role of the party as the ultimate source of authority. The insistence of the regime to retain essentially intact the party's monopoly of power is quite evident, despite what Western analysts have termed as a process of "liberalization." Thus far, Alia seems to have succeeded where other East-Central European communists have failed, i.e., to achieve a soft landing and perpetuate the retention of power by the same ruling elite that has governed the country for three decades.

After growing domestic pressure, street demonstrations and several killings in cold blood on 12 December 1990, the regime permitted establishment of an opposition party, the Democratic Renewal, to contest the forthcoming March elections. Though evidence is substantial that at the leadership level the new party is a communist front, the intelligentsia took it seriously. However, since that time more than 30,000 hungry workers and peasants voted with their feet against the new style pluralism and sought refuge in Greece, Yugoslavia and Italy.[43] Moscow remains skeptical vis à vis the new party (most of the USSR trainees are in the Alia government), while Washington decided to restore diplomatic ties with Tirana, hoping to influence events and keep the Soviets out. However, Tirana's choice between the two superpowers will be determined by their respective position on the Kosovo issue. On that score, Moscow has the interwar experience; Washington has a World War II proven naivete about the Balkans.[44]

In its relations with Moscow, Albania begins with an advantage as compared to other former bloc members. While most of them seek to fashion a relationship which assures them a respectable distance from their former senior partner, Albania has commenced the delicate process to bridge a 30-year gap, without being subjected to interference by or dependence on the Soviet Union. Since the declaration of independence in 1912, Albania's foreign policy has been molded by intense nationalism, economic necessity, and national survival. In contrast to the present, Albania had kept a distance from those neighbors considered a threat to its national integrity. Albania's brief close encounter with Yugoslavia (1945-1948) came rather near to being a national disaster, and the 1927 alliance with Mussolini resulted in de facto annexation in 1939. Relations with Greece, for most of the postwar period, were tense and occasionally outright hostile. The two countries remained in effect in a state of war until 1985.

It is not surprising at all that Albania had sided with Peking in 1961, when relations with Moscow were strained. China was a big power, ideally situated in the backyard of the USSR and thousands of miles away from Albanian shores. When the China-Albania friendship soured in the mid-seventies, the Hoxha clique turned to another emerging power—Western Europe. Within a span of less than ten years, relations with all NATO members (except Great Britain) were restored. In the 1980s, there was little thought given to the restoration of relations with Moscow for two related reasons: the bloc was still pretty firm (despite the Polish events) and party-to-party relations were too constraining for Enver Hoxha, who had been encouraging splinter groups in hopes that his versions of Marxism-Leninism would be vindicated. Tirana was determined not to place itself again within the constraints of an alliance. Alliances were seen by Hoxha and his associates as structures designed to limit sovereignty—a fact that would seriously undermine a cardinal principle of their country's foreign policy.[45] The 1990s provide a different set of circumstances: party-to-party relations are irrelevant, the Warsaw Pact is a meaningless shell, CMEA is out of existence, and whatever is left of "socialist" ideology is in the process of disappearing. Albania, the domino that refuses to fall, is in no hurry to join anything yet, even though the Alia government is on record as wishing to join the CSCE and the European Community.[46]

As was the case during the interwar period, intense nationalism drives contemporary Albanian foreign policy. Albania is an irredentist state with a persuasive cause, i.e., self-determination of the Kosovo Albanians. For this significant and unassimilated Muslim group, the 1912 Albanian declaration of independence remains an unfulfilled dream. Pursuant to this nationalist goal, Albanian foreign policy transcends ideological divisions among Albanians (be they at home or in diaspora) and will markedly shape its national agenda in the 1990s. At every given opportunity since 1912, the Tirana governments (Zogist, fascist, and communist) sought to incorporate Kosovo into the mainland.[47] More importantly, in the interwar period, as mentioned in the first part of this essay, Kosovo was a pivotal instrument in the Comintern's pursuit of a Balkan-wide peasant revolution. There is little doubt that Albanian nationalism will be a driving force in the 1990s as it was in the 1930s, with the Albanians in Yugoslavia as the focal point. The changes occurring in Albania must be evaluated in the context of a history of intense nationalist aspirations, sharpened by the advent of *perestroika* and *glasnost'*. For the Soviet Union, the dilemma is obvious and probably imminent: should it support Albanian self-determination and contribute to the dissolution of the Yugoslav federation or insist on the inviolability of European borders, as prescribed by the Helsinki Accords. Albania has not yet acceded to the latter, seems satisfied with an "observer" status in the CSCE process, and down the road perhaps will participate in "Helsinki II."[48]

A slow process of liberalization had commenced in Albania, prior to Gorbachev's assumption of power, but its pace has been accelerated by his personality and the upheavals in East-Central Europe. With the demise of the hard-line regimes (GDR, Bulgaria, Czechoslovakia, and Romania), Albania lost tenuous ideological partners who had espoused some form of socialism. More importantly, Albania lost trade partners for almost half of her exports, and the rapid development of events made a search for alternatives impossible. It seems that the best option, then, is to join the fashionable trend and "harken to the prewar years." A return to the past might suit Albania perfectly.

Unlike other East-Central European states, Albania had no multiparty system or any sense of pluralism since its foundation, as Alia stated in his New Year's Day address: this concept is "alien to the Albanian experience."[49] The only party the Albanians knew was the communist party, which was created from the various "groups" the Comintern had put together in Kosovo and Albania proper. Although the Albanian government has endorsed the idea of "multiple candidacies" and the acceptance of nonparty people in high government positions, thus far not a single ministry, diplomatic, or military post of significance has gone to nonparty members.

Alia has found a good theoretical alibi for restoration of relations with Moscow, without compromising the party's monopoly on power. He has retained the central elements of "Hoxhaism," i.e., the use of violence to silence opponents, and maintained Hoxha's main objection to restoring relations with Moscow, which, as stated above, was related to his objections to bloc politics and alliances. Blocs, in Hoxha's view, had the capacity of expanding and legitimizing their members' limited sovereignty.[50]

The Soviets facilitated Albania's return by admitting their "error" and by taking most of the blame for past misunderstandings. But at the same time, they have started the process of searching for more relevant experiences in the history of Albanian nationalism to provide the foundation for relations in the 1990s. They can hardly take any credit for supporting Albanian resistance to the Nazis—not a single Red Army soldier set foot in Albania during the war. The interwar period seems to be a safe beginning, but any conclusion on the residues of goodwill, traceable to the Comintern era, must be tempered by the USSR agenda on Yugoslavia. Moreover the Soviets, like many Western observers, are not necessarily sure that the Alia regime can adopt a "heretic" posture and carry on a program of political and economic liberalization which would be persuasive to a young and restless Albanian population. Soviet policy makers are well aware of the implications of having to work with a regime, populated by Hoxha's clones, which has a narrow definition of social reforms in a country without experience in pluralism and democratic institutions. Moscow's determination to pursue relentlessly the restoration of relations has been influenced by several factors of broader strategic concern, which will probably make it necessary for it to ignore the present and future excesses of the Tirana regime.

Reentry into Albania advances Moscow's opportunities to be an influential player in the Balkans. The situation there has reached a stage of heightened ethnic rivalry—with Yugoslavia on the verge of disintegration. Serbia, Montenegro, and Macedonia, with large numbers of ethnic Albanians, are in the process of reestablishing links with Russia. Indeed delegations from all three republics have made their debut in Moscow to make traditional contacts with the RSFSR. For Albania, the Russian tsarist tradition has no meaning, but the Bolshevik/Soviet one does. In other words, Moscow is now in full communication with all the components that will make the Balkans a region of intense ethnic rivalry over the next decade. Given the fact that the Albanian reforms can take a violent turn, one cannot predict what options the Soviets will exercise in a region where subnational groups are in search of distant partners. By December 1990, Alia seemed poised to abandon the cult of Stalin and Hoxha altogether and retain his country's uniqueness during the 1990s: his could be the only state to revert from one form of authoritarianism to another and define the change as democratization. The 31 March 1991 elections heralded in the West as the first "free elections since 1946" reinforce the latter argument.

In this contest the Albanian Party of Labor won 169 seats in the 250-member parliament, defying all predictions and retaining the dubious distinction of a Stalinist clique parading as reformist convert. The main opposition, the Democratic [Renewal] Party, won 75 seats, and a splinter Greek-minority group, *Omonoia,* five. One seat was given to a communist front organization, the Veterans Committee.

Terror and intimidation characterized the electoral process in the countryside.[51] A large number of Western observers, who spent their Easter holiday in the major cities, proclaimed the elections "fair."[52] Even though Alia and several major figures were defeated, they did not resign their government offices. Recognition of the Tirana regime by the United States in the midst of the electoral campaign benefited the ruling clique.⁵³ This gratuitous act by the U.S. government was portrayed by regime propagandists in the Albanian countryside (where 64 percent of the people live) as evidence of Washington's decision to do business with the communists.⁵⁴ It seems that for the foreseeable future, Moscow will maintain a relatively secure base of operations in the Balkans that has a government in Tirana very much resembling the one under Gorbachev. As in the Soviet Union, the police and military are still controlled by the Albanian communist party, whose legitimacy has been enhanced in the West because of its willingness to allow multiparty elections. Even if peaceful transition to a new form of authoritarianism fails in Albania, Moscow is well positioned to benefit even from internal turmoil or broader Balkan upheavals. Russia has indeed returned to the Balkans, with all of its unfinished agendas.

NOTES

1. Nina Smirnova: "The Background to a Rift," *New Times* (Moscow), 21 May 1988, p. 30.
2. In a visit to Sofia during 1984, President Mikhail S. Gorbachev offered to "resolve all issues" with Tirana. The offer was rejected. See *Pravda*, 10 September 1984.
3. The most prominent Albanians of the Comintern operatives included: Lazar Fundo (executed by Hoxha in 1943 as a "revisionist"); Ali Kelmendi (in charge of a Moscow-based Albanian group); and Koci Xoxe, a Vlach, who rose to the number two position in the Albanian party. He was executed in 1948 as a "Titoist." See Sotir Manushi, *Ali Kelmendi: Distinguished Militant of the Albanian Communist Movement* (Tirana: Instituti i Historisë e Partisë, 1960), p. 5.
4. Among the scholars who ignore the Bolshevik and Comintern role in Albanian affairs are Stavro Skendi, *Albania* (New York: Frederick Praeger, 1956); Kemal Vokopola, "Albania," in Vladimir Gsovski and Kazimierz Grzybowski, eds., *Government, Law and Courts in the Soviet Union and Eastern Europe* (London: Stevens and Sons, Ltd., 1959), vols. I & II; Mihali Prifti, *Socialist Albania Since 1944: Domestic and Foreign Developments* (Cambridge: MIT Press, 1978); and Anton Logoreci, *The Albanians: Europe's Forgotten Survivors* (Boulder, Colo.: Westview Press, 1977).
5. Between 1920 and 1924, at least six Comintern-sponsored organizations were active in Albania, Greece, and Kosovo. In all instances, they were pursuing "liberation of Kosovo" under the guise of "Balkan federation." They include *Ora e Maleve* (Hour of the Mountains), *Bashkimi* (Union), *Lidhja Ushtarake* (Military League), *Dora e Kuqe* (Red Hand), *Komiteti*

per Çlirimi e Kosoves (Committee for the Liberation of Kosovo), and Komiteti Nacionale Çlirimtare (National Liberation Committee). For details on the activities of these organizations, see Nikos Argyrocastritis, *Hoi Yioi Ton Misthoforon* (Athens: Petros Petsalnikos Publishing House, 1956), 2 vols., and Stefanaq Pollo, et al., *Historia e Shqipërisë (Vëllimi i Tretë): 1912-1944* (Tirana: Instituti i Historisë, 1984), vol. 3.

6. During a research trip to Moscow (28 July 1990), the author was asked by two senior Soviet scholars for his help to arrange access to Fan Noli's archives, currently under the control of the Albanian Orthodox Church in Boston. "There is a growing interest in the thirties," some of them said.

7. Stefanaq Pollo, et al., *Historia e Shqipërisë* (Tirana: Instituti i Historisë, 1984), vol. 3, pp. 382-420.

8. Among them was Aleks Buda, president of the Albanian Academy of Science and member of the Central Committee of the Albanian Party of Labor. He was a follower of Noli and a Comintern trainee.

9. A critical factor that influenced Noli and other Albanian leaders to become followers of Lenin was the latter's publication of secret tsarist treaties, including the Treaty of London, which envisioned partition of Albania among Greece, Yugoslavia, and Italy. Soviet commentators and Albanian historians religiously refer to Lenin's "good deed." See Stefanaq Pollo, et. al., *Historia e Shqipërisë*, p. 183; also Leonid Reshetnikov and Nina Smirnova: "Sovietsko-Albanskii konflikt: Kak eto bylo," *Kommunist,* no. 9 (July 1990), pp. 107-113.

10. For a list of the organizations, see Note 5. For the early association of Noli with Moscow, see also Nina D. Smirnova: "Albanski 'Krasnyi Episkop' Fan Noli," *Novaia i noveishaia istoria,* no. 3 (1973), pp. 48-60.

11. Joseph Swire, *Albania: the Rise of a Kingdom* (London: William and Norgate, 1929), p. 68.

12. "Shoku Ramiz Alia ne Tropojë," *Zeri i popullit,* 17 September 1989, p. 1.

13. When the Greek Patriarchate refused to ordain him as a priest, because of "character flaws," Noli turned to the Russian Metropolitan Platon of New York, who obliged. See Henry Baerlein, *Under the Acroceraunian Mountains* (London: Leonard Parsons, 1922), p. 77.

14. Kemal Vokopola, "Albania," in Gsovski and Grzybowski, eds., *Government, Law and Courts in the Soviet Union and Eastern Europe,* p. 162; *The New York Times,* 7 October 1927; *The Times* (London), 26 March 1925.

15. Nikolaos A. Stavrou, "Origins of the Albanian Communist Movement," *Hellenic Review of International Relations,* vol. 4 (1984), pp. 73-113.

16. In a conversation with Vladimir Popović in Moscow, Stalin derided the Albanians for their primitiveness. Responding to a comment by Popović that they "are courageous and loyal," Stalin retorted: "They can be as faithful as dogs, but that is a characteristic of primitives." See Vladimir Dedijer, *The Battle Stalin Lost: Memoirs of Yugoslavia, 1948-1953* (New York: Viking Press, 1971), p. 194.

17. William E. Griffith, *Albania and the Sino-Soviet Rift* (Cambridge: MIT Press, 1963), remains the most comprehensive study of this issue.

18. Enver Hoxha: *Titistët* (Tirana: Shtëpia Botuese "8 Nentori," 1982), particularly Chapter VIII, pp. 385-458.
19. During a meeting with Milovan Djilas in January 1948, just months prior to Tito's defection, Stalin told the Yugoslav delegation the following: "The Soviet government has no designs on Albania. Yugoslavia can swallow it up, whenever she likes." See Vladimir Dedijer, op. cit., p. 194.
20. Note verbally presented on 25 November 1961. *Zeri i popullit*, 10 December 1961, p. 1.
21. The Greek prime minister raised the issue during his visit to the United States in June 1990. He stated: "We are determined to defend the rights of the four hundred thousand Greeks now living under oppressive conditions in the country [Albania]." Embassy of Greece, Press and Information Office, Washington, D.C. Address by Constantine Mitsotakis at the National Press Club, 8 June 1990, p. 5.
22. The "legitimacy of Greek claims" in Northern Epirus (southern Albania) was also "acknowledged" by the then Soviet ambassador to Athens, Ivan Sergeev. See *Ethnos,* 25 December 1960, p. 4.
23. Enver Hoxha, "Fjalja me Rastin e Revolucioni i Tetrit," *Zeri i popullit,* 8 November 1961.
24. In June 1988, the politburo issued a decree ordering the transfer of approximately 70,000 cadres from cities to the countryside. See "Vendimi i Brose Politik e PPSh," *Zeri i popullit,* 12 June 1988, p. 1.
25. In a thinly veiled effort to protect himself from the Stalin-Hoxha worshipers, the author stated in a "dear readers," preface that "the novel *Thikat* used as its subject the war of the party and Comrade Enver Hoxha against the hostile activities of the multi-agent Mehmet Shehu and his counter-revolutionary associates." Neshat Tozaj, *Thikak: Roman* (Tirana: Shtëpia Botuese "Naim Frasheri," 1989), p. 3.
26. Ismail Kadare: "Renste Letrire, *Drita,* 15 October 1989, p. 8. In October 1990, Kadare defected to France. See David Binder, "Albanian Writer to Stay in France," *The New York Times,* 26 October 1990, p. A-4.
27. *Zeri i popullit,* 2 February 1989, p. 1.
28. "Fjalja i Shoku Foto Çami ne Gjircaster," *Zeri i popullit,* 19 September 1990, p. 1.
29. "Shoku Ramiz Alia ne Tropojë," *Zeri i popullit,* 17 September 1989, p. 1.
30. For a broader analysis of these two demonstrations, see the author's "Albania: The Domino that Refuses to Fall" in *Mediterranean Quarterly,* vol. I, no. 2 (Spring 1990), pp. 24-39.
31. *Zeri i popullit,* 29 September 1989.
32. See Nikolaos A. Stavrou, "Albania," in Richard F. Staar, ed., *1990 Yearbook on International Communist Affairs* (Stanford: Hoover Institution Press, 1990), pp. 296-308.
33. The author had several opportunities to gauge the prevailing "atmosphere in Tirana" during the East-Central European upheavals. He talked with several senior diplomats serving in the Albanian capital, including Ambassador Spyros Dokianos from Greece.

34. The Western news media (except for ABC, which reported the story with reservations) initially accepted the Albanian version that these rumors were started by the Yugoslavs for self-serving purposes. Almost three months after this writer had provided *The Washington Post* and *The New York Times* with the specifics of the story, the *Post* confirmed the events, but long after the Albanian authorities had taken their toll. See Jonathan Randal, "Hardline Albania's Fear of Falling," *The Washington Post*, 2 April 1990, p. 1.

35. Peter Humphrey, "Albania Ponders Contacts with EC, Superpowers," *The Washington Post*, 17 February 1990, p. A-36. Pliaka's associate, Deputy Foreign Minister Mohammed Kaplani (a Muslim), was dispatched to Ankara where he made a plea for the rights of Muslims in Kosovo. See Nikolaos A. Stavrou, "Albania: Still Stalinist," *The World & I* (June 1990), pp. 28- 31.

36. Several hearings before the "human rights caucus" of the U.S. Congress were held under the chairmanship of Congressman Tom Lantos. The only issue aired before this caucus was that of Kosovo. Albanians from this region were flown over to "testify" about the Serbian oppression. Thus far, not a single Greek refugee from Albania has been invited to testify. Lantos became the first U.S. congressman to visit Tirana in the summer of 1990.

37. In a recent trip to Moscow (25 July-1 August 1990), this writer interviewed a number of Soviet officials who had served in Albania. They all confirmed that trade between Moscow and Tirana continued through the years of diplomatic hiatus "mostly via Bulgaria, and mostly involving military equipment."

38. See "O normalizatsii otnoshenii mezhdu SSSR i Albaniei," *Izvestiia*, 1 August 1990, p. 1.

39. Diplomats on the scene and visitors to Tirana give the number of dead as "above 100" and those wounded much higher. See also AFP (Paris), 5 July 1990; FBIS-EEU (6 July 1990), p.7.

40. The late Stavro Skendi, prominent Albanian historian at Columbia University and Hoxha's colleague at the Korcë lyceum, provides the most accurate biographical information on most of the postwar Albanian leaders. See his *Albania* (New York: Praeger, 1956), pp. 323 and 334, concerning membership of Alia and Myftiu in the fascist movement.

41. See Nikolaos A. Stavrou, "The Political Role of the Albanian Military," *Intellect Magazine* (July-August 1975), pp. 18-21.

42. People's Republic of Albania, Mission to the United Nations, "Statement by H. E. Ramiz Alia at the 45th Session of the General Assembly of the United Nations" (New York, 28 September 1990), p. 5.

43. During 2-10 January 1991 the author visited five refugee camps, containing approximately 6,000 refugees. All of those questioned, about their views on the new party, almost unanimously dismissed it as a front. A month after the author's visit, the outflow of refugees resumed in the direction of Italy.

44. Relations with Washington were formally restored on 15 March 1991. See "U.S. and Albanians Re-establish Diplomatic Ties After 52 Years," *The New York Times,* 16 March 1991, p. 3.
45. The late Enver Hoxha seemed obsessed with threats to his survival from blocs and superpowers. Two volumes on the subject attest these fears, which bordered on paranoia: *Superfuqitë, 1955-1984: Nga Dritari Politik* (Tirana: Shtëpia Botuese "8 Nentori," 1986) and *Rreziku Anglo-Amerikan për Shqipërinë: Kujtime* (Tirana: Shtëpia Botuese "8 Nentori," 1982).
46. Michael Parks, "Albania Comes In from the Cold" *The Los Angeles Times,* 4 August 1990, p. A-3.
47. See Dimitris Mihalopoulos, *Scheseis Elladhos-Alvanias* (Athens: Paratiritis, 1986), p. 162. On 2 April 1943 the Albanian communist party and Balli Kombëtar (National Front, which later collaborated with the Germans) signed an agreement to coordinate their resistance, essentially based on the communist party's acceptance that they would jointly pursue the liberation of Kosovo and its incorporation into Albania after the war. The agreement was torpedoed by Svetozar Vukmanovič-Tempo, coordinator of communist resistance in the Balkans on behalf of Tito, who chided the Albanians for their "chauvinist deviation." Interview with the author, 3 December 1989. See also Vukmanovič-Tempo, *The Struggle for the Balkans* (London: Merlin Press, 1990), p. 74.
48. Peter Humphrey, "Albania Ponders Contacts With EC, Superpowers," *The Washington Post,* 11 February 1990, p. A-30.
49. Quoted by Nikolaos A. Stavrou: "Albania: The Domino that Refuses to Fall," *Mediterranean Quarterly,* vol. I, no. 2 (Spring 1990), p. 40.
50. The demise of blocs was used as a justification for the restoration of relations in the first official commentary on the subject. See "Nje Hap me Rendesi," *Zeri i popullit,* 2 August 1990, p. 2.
51. Blaine Harden, "3 Die as Vote Protesters, Police Clash in Albania," *The Washington Post,* 3 April 1991, p. A-20.
52. Blaine Harden, "Visitors Too Quick to Approve Albanian Vote," *The Washington Post,* 6 April 1991, p. A-18.
53. U.S. Department of State, "Memorandum of Understanding Between the United States and Albania" (Washington, D.C.: Bureau of Public Affairs, 15 March 1991).
54. U.S. Department of State officials claimed that the opposition party, too, favored recognition prior to the elections. That, however, does not alter the fact that the principal beneficiary was Ramiz Alia.

12

The Future of Romanian-Soviet Relations in the Post-Ceauşescu Era

Robert R. King

For the past 30 years Romania's principal claim to international attention was its autonomy from the Soviet Union. While they remained within the Soviet orbit as a member of the Warsaw Pact and the Council for Mutual Economic Assistance (CMEA), its leaders frequently made a point of emphasizing their differences with the USSR. Romania pressed against the limits of Soviet tolerance and occasionally provoked an angry Soviet reaction, but it managed to avoid Soviet military intervention while at the same time continuing its foreign policy autonomy.

The development of differences between the communist parties of the Soviet Union and China in the early 1960s provided the Romanian Communist Party (RCP) the opportunity to expand its autonomy from the USSR in interparty affairs. This reached a high point in the April 1964 Statement of the RCP Central Committee, which asserted the sovereignty and independence of each party and affirmed the principle of noninterference in the internal affairs of other parties.

These policies were initiated under the leadership of Gheorghe Gheorghiu-Dej, RCP leader from 1944 until his death in 1965, but they were continued and expanded by his successor, Nicolae Ceauşescu, who led the country from 1965 until his violent death in December 1989. The apex of autonomy came during 1967-1968 when Romania continued diplomatic relations with Israel while the rest of the Warsaw Pact nations severed their diplomatic ties, established diplomatic relations with West Germany before the Soviet Union gave *Ostpolitik* its imprimatur, and moved closer to the nonaligned nations. Its foreign minister's election as president of the United Nations General Assembly was an important symbol of Romania's increased international status.

Ceauşescu's impassioned denunciation of the Soviet-led invasion of Czechoslovakia in August 1968 marked both the pinnacle of Romanian defiance of the Soviet Union and dramatically emphasized the limits of deviance. Although Ceauşescu continued to pursue an international policy with a high degree of autonomy from the USSR, he carefully avoided pushing that policy to the point of provoking Soviet military intervention.

This foreign policy gave Romania increased international status and, at least initially, concrete economic benefits. Particularly during the 1960s, when autonomy from the Soviet Union was initially undertaken, Romania was courted by the United States and its NATO allies in an effort to fragment the Soviet bloc. In 1967, when Romania became the first East European country to establish full diplomatic relations with West Germany despite clear disapproval by the Soviet Union and East Germany, it received substantial hard-currency loans and grants from the Bonn government. As a reward for its autonomy from the Soviet Union, the United States gave it Most Favored Nation (MFN) trade status at a time when the Soviet Union and all other East European states except Poland were pointedly denied this benefit.

Foreign policy autonomy from the Soviet Union was a key factor in winning popular support and a degree of legitimacy for Ceauşescu and the RCP. There is a historic anti-Russian element of Romanian nationalism, and a foreign policy that deviates from that of the Soviet Union struck a responsive chord among Romanians. Periodic confrontations with the Soviet Union were provoked when the party needed to bolster its legitimacy or rally the population. After Ceauşescu's popularity peaked with his passionate denunciation of the Soviet-led invasion of Czechoslovakia in August 1968, foreign policy autonomy declined in importance as a means of establishing the regime's authority. Human rights abuses multiplied, and Ceauşescu increasingly relied on the brutality of the *Securitate* and nepotism to rule. Romania's relationship with the USSR, however, continued to be a significant element in legitimating Ceauşescu's rule.[1]

RELATIONS WITH THE USSR AT THE CLOSE OF THE CEAUŞESCU ERA

The ascendancy of Mikhail S. Gorbachev in the Soviet Union did not alter Romania's policy of pursuing its separate path in foreign policy, but as the Gorbachev reforms gained momentum in the USSR and elsewhere in Eastern Europe, the Romanian independent line made an abrupt about-face. Before 1985, Romanian policy focused on the right of every party independently to pursue its own sovereign interest. As reform in Hungary, Poland, and the Soviet Union began to question and then eliminate the communist monopoly of power and the underpinnings of the centrally planned economies, Ceauşescu began to call for enforced orthodoxy among the Warsaw Pact countries.

More than any other member of the Warsaw Pact, Romania openly criticized and vigorously opposed the reforms Gorbachev was seeking to implement in the Soviet Union and foster in Eastern Europe. Romanian media reports and official comments on *glasnost'* and *perestroika* were hostile. The personal animosity between Ceauşescu and Gorbachev was obvious. Ceauşescu was the last of the East European leaders to visit Moscow after Gorbachev's selection as party leader, and Romania was the last of the East European countries to be visited by the new Soviet leader after his installation. The visit to Bucharest was noticeably cold. In the Soviet leader's presence, Ceauşescu reiterated his opposition to reform, and Gorbachev indirectly criticized Romanian domestic policies as Ceauşescu yawned and looked pointedly at his watch.[2]

The last few years of Ceauşescu's rule must have been extremely frustrating for him. More than any other communist leader, he considered himself an international statesman. During his early years as Romanian leader, he cultivated a wide range of international contacts and prided himself on being able to talk with major world leaders on all sides of controversial issues. It was a key element of Romanian policy to develop a broad spectrum of contacts as a means of bolstering the country's autonomy from the Soviet Union. During Ceauşescu's final years, however, all this disappeared and he faced increasing international isolation because of domestic repression, human rights abuses, and denial of rights to Hungarians and other ethnic minorities in Romania.

Ceauşescu was an embarrassment to the Soviet Union and the reform-minded leaders of Eastern Europe; Western Europe and the United States shunned him; and Third World leaders saw little advantage in cultivating ties with Romania. In little over a decade, Ceaușescu went from being a guest welcomed in major world capitals for his independence from the Soviet Union to an isolated despot whose international contacts were limited to the antireform states of Eastern Europe and other international outcasts such as China, North Korea, and Iran.

Gorbachev's leadership of the reform forces intensified the strain inherent in Soviet-Romanian relations. The RCP reiterated its firm rejection of the prerogative of any other communist party, including that of the USSR, to prescribe reforms for Romania.³ From the Romanian perspective, however, the Soviet Union was not the principal villain in encouraging reform. Hungary and Poland were plunging ahead at a much faster pace even than the USSR, and Hungary, in particular, was much closer geographically and psychologically, so that the contagion of reform was more dangerous from Budapest than Moscow.

As Romanian paranoia about reform in Hungary, Poland, and the Soviet Union increased, Romania's ties improved with those communist states in Eastern Europe which opposed reform—East Germany, Czechoslovakia, and Bulgaria. In the past these were the states which had the most distant relationship with Romania because of their consistent subservience to conservative Soviet policies, particularly in international affairs.

Ceaușescu's vehement opposition to reform, which became a dominant element in Romanian foreign and domestic policy, even led the regime to adopt positions that were dangerously close to endorsing the Brezhnev Doctrine—a major departure in Romanian foreign policy. Just as Soviet leaders were in the process of abandoning the Brezhnev Doctrine, which had been enunciated to justify Soviet intervention in Czechoslovakia in 1968, Romanians began to sound the antireform alarm in terms that would justify intervention. This was a total reversal of the fundamental Romanian position propounded since the early 1960s opposing intervention by the Soviet Union or any other state in the internal affairs of other countries.⁴

The 14th RCP Congress in November 1989 demonstrated Ceaușescu's total opposition to the reforms that were sweeping Eastern Europe and his complete unwillingness to acknowledge reality. The congress convened in a Valhalla-like atmosphere: Poland had appointed a noncommunist prime minister; the Berlin Wall had collapsed a few days before, crushing the East German communist party; the velvet revolution brought an end to the communist hold on power in Czechoslovakia during the RCP congress; and just three weeks later Ceaușescu and his regime were toppled in a bloody, violent revolution. Nevertheless, in his marathon speech to the congress, Ceaușescu repeated 16 times that Romania had reached "new heights of progress and civilization" and six times affirmed that the country was headed for the "golden dream" of communism.[5] The Soviets quietly sent a low-level delegation.

RELATIONS WITH MOSCOW AFTER THE REVOLUTION

As the Romanian dictatorship began to unravel in late December 1989, Ceaușescu made a vain effort in his last public appearance to rally Romanian nationalism to the defense of the regime by playing the anti-Russian card one last time. His final speech in Republic Square, during which it became obvious to the live television and radio audience that his grip on power was slipping, he once more referred to "foreign conspirators" who were attempting to undermine Romanian "socialism." The attempt to mobilize the population against this imagined Soviet interference, however, did not work this time.[6]

The Soviet attitude toward the Romanian revolution did not differ substantially from the reaction of most other nations around the world. Official Soviet commentaries expressed regret at the violence and loss of life, and Soviet government officials offered medical and other emergency assistance.

At the height of fighting in Bucharest, when the threat of *Securitate* resistance seemed the strongest, the United States government indicated it might be useful for Soviet military forces to help bring the *Securitate* under control. There is no indication, however, that the USSR ever seriously contemplated military intervention. Soviet forces would have faced difficulties in deploying to restore order since there were no Soviet troops stationed in the country. Furthermore, this use of the military would be the exact opposite of the message the Soviets were then trying to convey to the world and to their allies in the Warsaw Pact. They had just publicly renounced the Brezhnev Doctrine, which justified intervening to maintain socialism in Eastern Europe. At that point it was going too far to expect Soviet intervention to overthrow a communist regime, even when it was of the vicious and repressive Ceaușescu variety.

Since the Romanian revolution, neither Romania nor the USSR have been in a position to give much attention to developing their mutual relations. The Soviet Union has been faced with severe domestic economic and political problems. The disintegration of its economy has created serious market shortages of many basic commodities, and the need to undertake a comprehensive economic restructuring has provoked major political controversy. At the same time, Moscow has had to deal with an upheaval of nationalist tensions, and the acceleration of centrifugal ethnic forces. Meanwhile, the time and effort that can be devoted to international issues has been focused on critical ones—German reunification, arms control negotiations with the United States, development of closer economic and political relations with Western Europe, and more recently the dangerous crisis in the Persian Gulf. In the context of Soviet domestic and international problems, relations with Romania are not now a high priority, and it is unlikely that ties with Bucharest will be given much high-level attention by Moscow for some time.

The same is true on the Romanian side as well. The National Salvation Front (NSF) government was initially preoccupied with establishing its authority in the face of entrenched *Securitate* opposition, holding elections to give legitimacy to its government, and getting the faltering economy functioning again. In the face of these overriding domestic considerations, relations with the USSR have not assumed top priority. Clearly, however, Romania's concern with Soviet relations is—and will remain—of much greater interest than Moscow's interest in Bucharest.

TRADE AND ECONOMIC TIES

For now—and for the foreseeable future—the principal concern in Romanian-Soviet relations will be economic, and here, in particular, the Romanian interest and concern is much greater than that of the Soviet Union.

As Romania began to assert its independence vis-à-vis the Soviet Union in the early 1960s, the country also began an effort to diversify its foreign trade and reduce its economic dependence on the Soviet Union. As the figures in Table 2 show, Romania reduced its Soviet trade from 41 to 17 percent through 1980. Until 1986 the trend reversed itself, only to drop again the following year. Romania is dependent on the Soviet Union for significant quantities of raw materials, as well as manufactured products.

The Soviet Union remains an important source of crude oil for Romania. Domestic oil fields continue to supply a significant part of the country's energy needs, but that proportion has been declining over the past decade and will continue to drop. Of all the East-Central European countries, Romania receives the smallest amount of crude oil and refined oil products from the USSR. (In 1989 it imported about 20 percent of its oil imports from the USSR.)[7] The cost is now essentially the world market price, and, thus, there is no price advantage for Romania in purchasing Soviet oil. Long-term supply and delivery relationships have been established, however, and it would be disruptive to seek supplies elsewhere.

TABLE 2

Trade with the Soviet Union as a Percentage of Total Romanian Trade

Year	Percentage
1960	41
1965	38
1970	26
1975	18
1980	17
1984	21
1985	22
1986	38
1987	28

Note: Romanian foreign trade data for recent years are incomplete, and the accuracy of some of the more recent figures is unreliable.
Source: Central Intelligence Agency, *1990 Handbook of Economic Statistics* (Washington, D.C., Directorate of Intelligence, September 1990), CPAS 90-10001, Table 142, p. 171.

As the USSR economy faces disruption as it undergoes market restructuring, economic ties with Romania are likely to suffer as well. The Romanian economy is experiencing similar restructuring, and it will be negatively impacted by Soviet supply disruptions. Economic frictions between the two countries will likely be a major source of problems in relations between the two countries in the future.

THE UNIQUE PROBLEM OF SOVIET MOLDAVIA

One issue which is likely to emerge as one of greater importance in future Soviet-Romanian relations than it has since the end of World War II is the disputed territory of Bessarabia or Soviet Moldavia. The new importance of this issue is largely due to the changes which have taken place recently in both countries as both have moved toward greater openness and pluralism.

Bessarabia, which makes up the bulk of the Soviet Socialist Republic of Moldavia, is the territory that lies between the Prut and Dniester rivers. Turkish until 1812, when the area was added to the Russian empire, it became part of Romania in 1918 when Russia was convulsed with revolution. The Soviet Union never accepted that change of ownership, and in 1940 under terms of the infamous Molotov-Ribbentrop Pact, Soviet troops took it back.[8] Romania joined Hitler's armies in the attack on the Soviet Union in 1941 in

TABLE 3

Ethnic Composition of the Population of the Moldavian Soviet Socialist Republic

Ethnic Group	Number	Percentage
Moldavians	2,797,749	64.5
Ukrainians	600,366	13.9
Russians	562,069	13.0
Gagauzi	153,458	3.5
Bulgarians	88,419	2.0
Jews	65,672	1.5
Others	67,627	1.6
Total	4,335,360	100.0

Source: "Nas 285,761,976 chelovek...," *Soiuz*, no. 32 (August 1990), p. 3; weekly supplement to *Izvestiia*.

order to retake the disputed territory, but the Soviets again occupied it in 1944, when they drove out Nazi and Romanian troops. Since World War II, the Soviets have been in possession of the territory. Shortly after retaking the area for the last time, Moscow established the Moldavian Soviet Socialist Republic as a full republic of the USSR. The population of Moldavia is ethnically mixed. Just under two thirds are "Moldavian," with smaller numbers of Ukrainians, Russians, Gagauzi, and others. The fact that one-quarter of the population of Soviet Moldavia is composed of Ukrainians and Russians further complicates the issue.[9] While the Romanians consider the Moldavians to be Romanians, in the past the Soviets have emphasized that they are Moldavians, a separate and distinct nationality.[10] The Moldavians speak Romanian, although the Soviets call the language Moldavian. Until 1989 the official alphabet was Cyrillic, while the Romanians write their language in the Latin alphabet.

Under Ceauşescu veiled Romanian claims to Bessarabia were periodically raised as a means of rallying Romanian nationalism or irritating the Soviet Union,[11] but Ceauşescu's repressive, austere regime held little attraction for the Moldavians. The Soviet Union has made clear its opposition to any changes in boundaries, and in the past there was little serious consideration of altering frontiers.

The recent national assertiveness of Soviet nationalities in Lithuania, Latvia, Estonia, Armenia, Georgia, Azerbaijan, and elsewhere, however, has raised new questions about Soviet Moldavia, particularly when coupled with the fall of Ceauşescu and the new government in Bucharest. In 1988 Moldavians held mass demonstrations to demand that Moldavian/Romanian be made the official language of the republic, and that it be written in the Latin script. In August 1989, Soviet authorities finally agreed to these demands. A reflection of the complex ethnic problems in the Moldavian Republic came in October-November 1990 when the Gagauzi minority opposed the increasing assertiveness of the Moldavian/Romanian majority, and ethnic Russians came to the aid of the Gagauzi. Moldavian militants mobilized to prevent Gagauzi separatism and to reinforce their demands for greater ethnic recognition.[12]

Since Ceauşescu's fall, there have been new signs of nationalist stirrings. The leader of the Moldavian Popular Front, a mass movement pressing for greater Moldavian autonomy, reported crowds chanting "reunification" at a nationalist rally in Soviet Moldavia. The same reaction has been observed by journalists in Romanian territories adjacent to the Soviet border. Communication between peoples on both sides of the border has been easier since the overthrow of Ceauşescu. Soviet authorities began removing barbed-wire fences along the frontier with Romania and have relaxed restrictions to permit people in frontier regions to move back and forth across the border, and Romanian authorities have likewise allowed greater contacts.[13]

Under conditions of pluralism and greater openness, the question of Bessarabia's rejoining Romania is an issue that lurks just beneath the surface. On the one hand, greater cultural ties now being permitted will bring the Romanians in Soviet Moldavia closer to those living in Romania. On the other hand, the Soviet government is reluctant to see any territories separated from the USSR because of the possible domino effect upon other nationalities, which make up over half the Soviet population.

A related question, which further complicates any Romanian effort to strengthen ties with Soviet Moldavia, involves Transylvania. The western third of Romania, known historically as Transylvania, was a part of Hungary until 1918 when it was annexed to Romania. The region still has a substantial Hungarian minority population of as many as 2 million, one of the largest ethnic minorities in Europe. Transylvania has long been a source of tension and discord between Romania and Hungary. RCP policy toward the Hungarian minority after 1958 sought to force assimilation through reducing and eliminating Hungarian language and cultural institutions.[14] Initially after the overthrow of Ceauşescu, which the Hungarian minority clearly supported, there were indications of improved conditions for Hungarians and better relations between Hungarians and Romanians. An outbreak of violence in

March 1990 against ethnic Hungarians, however, which resulted in the death of eight and the injury of some 365 others again raised questions about the success of reconciliation efforts.[15]

The Transylvania question, which is an important domestic and international concern to Hungary, acts as a deterrent to precipitous or aggressive action by Romania vis-à-vis Moldavia. If borders can be changed with Soviet Moldavia, there is justification for changing them in the west with Hungary. Good cultural ties with Soviet Moldavia ought to be balanced with equally good cultural links between Hungarians in Hungary and those living in Transylvania.

The Transylvania issue is probably the principal reason Romania has not advanced territorial claims on Moldavia. Despite Ceauşescu's periodic tweaking of the Soviet Union with historical claims to Bessarabia, he never suggested changes in borders, knowing full well that if he opened that Pandora's box, the Hungarians—with Soviet support—would raise the question of Romania's border with Hungary.

The new post-Ceauşescu Romanian leadership seems to have taken that same cautious approach of not questioning borders. Within a few days of Ceauşescu's death, Silviu Brucan, one of the NSF leaders and spokesmen, reaffirmed that for the NSF "there is no Bessarabian problem" because the territory is "the Moldavian Soviet Socialist Republic," although he expressed the belief in greater contacts between Romania and Moldavia.[16] When Soviet Foreign Minister Eduard Shevardnadze visited Bucharest shortly after the NSF government took power, he encouraged opening the Soviet border with Romania, but noted that "existing treaties rule out changing the Soviet borders."[17] On 26 January 1990, when the new Romanian ambassador presented his credentials in Moscow, he reiterated that Romania was fully committed to existing borders in Europe.[18]

The new Romanian president, Ion Iliescu, has taken that same position. In an election speech in Turnu-Severin, he called the Soviet seizure of Bessarabia "a historical injustice," but added that redrawing Romania's present borders was not in the country's best interest.[19] In a key speech at the first celebration of the new Romanian national day on 1 December, Iliescu could not avoid mentioning Bessarabia since the day marks the date in 1918 when both Bessarabia and Transylvania were united with older Romanian lands. He said that "history will find a way of correcting the injustice of Romania's loss of its former territories," but he did not call for changing borders.[20]

Because of popular Romanian nationalist sentiment for the reunion of Bessarabia with Romania, the government has been caught on the horns of a dilemma, seeking to rally and manipulate Romanian nationalism to strengthen its position among the Romanian masses, but at the same time balancing that with the urgent need to avoid antagonizing the Soviet Union. The result has been public statements strangely reminiscent of Ceaușescu's carefully measured manipulation of the issue.

The rise of national sentiment in Soviet Moldavia and the rise of sentiment for reunion on the Romanian side of the border, however, may make it difficult for foreign ministry officials in Moscow and Bucharest to keep this emotional issue from becoming an explosive element in future Soviet-Romanian relations.

THE FUTURE OF SOVIET-ROMANIAN RELATIONS

Making projections about the future course of Romanian-Soviet relations in view of the present volatile and uncertain domestic conditions in both countries is a hazardous undertaking. If this discussion, however, focuses on the range of future possibilities and emphasizes the most likely probabilities, rather than relying on specific assumptions about either country, projections about future relations make sense. But there are a number of caveats which should be kept in mind. As Sir Francis Bacon observed, if we begin with certainties, we end in doubts; but if we are content to begin with doubts we can end in certainties—or at least we can end with reasonable probabilities.

The dynamics of domestic policy is the key element in determining the future course of foreign policy in any country. Since both the Soviet Union and Romania are undergoing a radical and unpredictable transformation of their domestic economic, political, and social systems, the key ingredient on both sides of the international boundary is subject to substantial change and uncertainty. Before drawing any conclusions about the future of Soviet-Romanian relations, it is important to make explicit my assumptions about the range of probable domestic transformation that is likely to occur in both countries over the next decade.

The new Romanian leadership faces serious internal problems dealing with the unresolved conflict between the popular anticommunist masses, who rose against the old regime, and the new leadership, which is essentially an administration of former communists who were out of favor with Ceaușescu or were young enough to hold lower level positions in the previous regime and who staged the successful *coup d'état* against Ceaușescu's leadership. The overwhelming vote for the National Salvation Front government in the relatively free elections of April 1990 does not accurately reflect the reality that the country is deeply divided and the new government does not have the trust of its citizens. The large number and frequency of popular demonstrations against government policies that have taken place throughout the country since the overthrow of Ceauşescu are a clear indication of popular dissatisfaction and disaffection. There is general agreement that the first priority of the new government must be the restructuring of the country's economic system as well as the transformation of its political structures. Thus, for the Romanian government, the highest priority and greatest attention for some time will be given to domestic issues.

The same is true for the Soviet Union. The most important effect of the domestic turmoil that will affect the USSR during the next few years is that the Soviet political leaders will have little time or energy to devote to foreign policy questions that are not of primary importance. Soviet leaders will be preoccupied with their own political survival, as they grapple with enormously complex domestic economic and political issues. The advocates of radical reform and restructuring who were unleashed under Mikhail Gorbachev's early leadership will continue for some time to compete with conservative party and military elites for control in the USSR. The leadership that emerges from this clash of alternatives in the struggle for power and for public support will have to deal with the central question of the future relationships among the constituent Soviet republics and nationalities. Whatever form the USSR takes over the next decade, the effort to deal with these questions will leave the Soviet leaders little time for issues low in the hierarchy of their concerns. Foreign affairs will not rank high, and even within that sphere, relations with Romania will be well down the list.

Soviet security concerns will continue to be the major factor in relations with Romania because of its important strategic location on the USSR's southeastern border. The area is traditionally unstable. The disintegration, or at least significant weakening of central authority in Yugoslavia and the turbulence of the nearby Middle East give Romania greater importance than Poland, Czechoslovakia, or Hungary which all border on more stable areas. Furthermore, since the Moldavian Soviet Socialist Republic (SSR) borders on Romania and this republic has been one of the constituent republics most opposed to Moscow, Romania assumes a special significance in Soviet domestic considerations.

In view of its domestic preoccupation, the USSR priority in relations with Romania will be to assure a friendly regime on its southeastern border. The new Romanian leadership has already shown considerable sensitivity to this Soviet interest, and a conscientious effort has been made on a number of occasions to reassure Moscow. In addition to assuring the Soviet leaders that Romania harbors no claims against Moldavia, when USSR troops took strong military action in the Baltic Republics during January 1991, official Romanian reaction was the mildest and most circumspect among all former Warsaw Pact countries. Furthermore, the government-dominated Romanian media were particularly guarded in their reporting on those events. Any government that comes to power in Bucharest will make a calculated effort to maintain good relations with Moscow, and it will be sensitive and cautious to avoid giving any offense.

Moldavia is the one critical issue that, under present conditions, neither government can fully control, and it is the one issue that could produce serious tension during the foreseeable future in Soviet-Romanian relations. The territory annexed by the Soviet Union in 1944 includes almost all of the current Moldavian SSR, but it also includes the Chernovtsy *oblast'* and part of the Odessa *oblast'*, both of which are parts of the Ukrainian SSR. Furthermore, Ukrainians are the second largest ethnic group within the Moldavian SSR. This suggests that Ukrainian nationalism, as well as resurgent Moldavian nationalism, could become enmeshed in the question of Moldavia.

The Moldavian problem is made more troublesome by the fact that the central Soviet government is having increased difficulty in maintaining control of some of its peripheral republics, and Moldavia—as well as the three Baltic Republics and Georgia—has been one of the most unruly to govern. Moldavian nationalism has intensified, and forces favoring reform and democracy have been linked with national sentiment. Until the Soviet government is able to reform the union on some acceptable basis and then win the support of the peripheral republics, containing Moldavia will continue to be a problem for officials in Moscow. Even if this does happen—and it will take an extended period of time until it will—Soviet authority will not approach the degree of control it exercised over Moldavia prior to 1989.

Controlling Romanian nationalism in order to avoid spontaneous popular conflict with the Soviet Union over Moldavia will be equally difficult. Although, the post-Ceauşescu Romanian government has been most anxious to avoid antagonizing the Soviet Union over this issue, it does not have the degree of control over its population necessary to prevent a minor incident from escalating. Whereas Ceauşescu could tweak the Soviets by asserting a historical claim to Bessarabia and then be certain that the issue was kept under control so that it did not intensify further, the government of Ion Iliescu and Petre Roman does not have that kind of control over the population or even over some sections of the news media. For the foreseeable future, any Romanian government will have trouble containing a crisis. Furthermore, the NSF government has fostered Romanian nationalism and positioned itself as the champion of Romanian national interests in order to gain and maintain its popular support. This has unleashed forces the government cannot fully control. While it can diplomatically reassure the Soviets that it does not seek border changes with Moldavia, it cannot control popular demonstrations supporting reunification of the territory with Romania. Furthermore, to maintain its position as the champion of the Romanian nation, the NSF government cannot go too far in renouncing or minimizing those national claims.

It is very likely that the issue of Moldavia will exacerbate tensions between the USSR and Romania in the future. How far those strains escalate will depend on domestic conditions in the two countries at the time problems begin. If the pendulum of central authority in the Soviet Union is swinging toward the hardline forces favoring the reassertion of central control, it is quite conceivable that tough military action could be taken to reaffirm the Soviet claim to the territory. Under such conditions, Soviet-provoked border clashes with Romania are certainly a possibility. Taking strong action could be an occasion for hard-line forces to reassert their authority and, under the right conditions, Moldavia could provide an opportunity used to assert control.

Under most conditions, the Romanian government—either the NSF or a successor regime—would not seek to provoke such a confrontation, and if one developed, it would seek actively to defuse tensions. The imbalance in military forces between Romania and the Soviet Union is so great that no responsible Romanian political leader could incite such action. It is possible that an incident could inflame Romanian nationalism, however, and this would make it difficult for the Romanian government to maintain control.

There are alternative scenarios that could develop under which the Romanian government could provoke a Moldavian crisis in an effort to maintain domestic control or as a radical step to further its own domestic agenda in the face of serious internal challenge. This would occur only if there were a grave domestic crisis, however, because of the serious potential consequences. Romanian political leaders are well aware that King Carol was forced to abdicate in 1941, when Romania lost northern Transylvania to Hungary and Bessarabia to the Soviet Union. Those leaders who precipitate a crisis or who fail to mollify the USSR could find themselves quickly out of office.

A return of rampant popular anti-Russian sentiment and an anti-Soviet foreign policy, which marked Romania in the 1920s and 1930s, is not likely. The memory of USSR-imposed communism is still fresh in the minds of the Romanian people. Despite the relative decline in Soviet military capabilities, because of domestic instability and preoccupation, the military asymmetry between the USSR army and the Romanian army is evident to all. No one in Romania will want to provoke another period of Soviet domination.

The basis for economic collaboration, technological cooperation, and trade between Romania and the USSR has shifted as a result of changes in the Soviet Union. Economic relations no longer have the political dimension they had in the past. When Romania as a member of the Warsaw Pact pursued its autonomy in foreign policy, economic ties with the USSR were an important instrument for Moscow to maintain its links with Bucharest. These economic ties gave Moscow a source of leverage and influence over Bucharest. Now that the political grounds for economic relations are no longer valid, trade and cooperation must stand on their own merits.

The severe economic dislocations of the past year have made that more difficult. In both countries economic inefficiency, uncertainty, and disruption have made foreign economic relations more difficult, and that will continue into the foreseeable future. With trade now moving toward exclusively hard currency transactions at world prices, both countries will find it more difficult to expand trade. Both economies are sputtering. Essential economic reform will be slow and painful and, as a result, trade between the two will decline in the short run and then stagnate for a period before conditions are again suitable for expansion. As the economies recover, trade will expand, but the process will be a slow one, and it is unlikely that there will be much growth until the end of the decade. For both countries technological cooperation will focus on Western Europe and the United States, and neither Romania nor the USSR will be in a position to provide the other with needed technology.

Relations with the Soviet Union are a much higher priority for Bucharest than vice versa. The USSR is a global power, although its influence is significantly diminished from what it was only a few years ago. The Soviet Union is still a world-wide player—it can influence the outcome of issues that affect the global international environment, such as European security, the Middle East, relations with the United States and China, and arms control.

Romania, on the other hand, is a regional power. Under Ceauşescu, particularly during the decade beginning in 1964, Romania's importance in the international sphere was significantly greater because of its disruptive role in the Warsaw Pact, its status at the United Nations, and its efforts with the nonaligned countries. This is no longer true. The collapse of Soviet control in Central and Eastern Europe leaves Romania as simply one of several medium-sized states with regional capabilities and regional influence in the Balkans.

Because of its long common border with the USSR and the differences over Moldavia, Romania has a major interest in the Soviet Union. Any government of the USSR will have a major impact upon Romania. The same is not true of Romania. Whatever the direction in the evolution of its political, economic, and social system, Romania will continue to have minimal influence over the USSR. That imbalance will continue, and Bucharest's relations with Moscow will be significantly more important for Romania than for the Soviet Union.

NOTES

1. Romania's autonomous foreign policy during the period 1960-1989 has been the subject of a number of descriptive and analytical works. A discussion of that policy and the reasons for it are beyond the scope of this paper. The following deal with this period in considerable detail: R. L. Braham, "Rumania on to the Separate Path," *Problems of Communism* 13, no. 2 (May-June 1964): 14-24; J. F. Brown, "Rumania Steps Out of Line," *Survey*, no. 49 (October 1963): 19-34; R. V. Burks, "The Rumanian National Deviation: An Accounting," in Kurt London, ed., *Eastern Europe in Transition* (Baltimore, Md.: The Johns Hopkins University Press, 1966); Robert Farlow, "Romanian Foreign Policy: A Case of Partial Alignment," *Problems of Communism* 20, no. 6 (November-December 1971): 54-63; Stephen Fischer-Galati, *The New Rumania: From People's Democracy to Socialist Republic* (Cambridge, Mass.: MIT Press, 1967); David Floyd, *Rumania: Russia's Dissident Ally* (New York: Praeger, 1965); Graeme J. Gill, "Rumania's Background to Autonomy," *Problems of Communism* 15, no. 1 (January-February 1966): 16-28; and Kenneth Jowitt, *Revolutionary Breakthroughs and National Development: The Case of Romania, 1944-65* (Berkeley and Los Angeles: University of California Press, 1971), pp. 198-272. For the author's own analysis of Romania's autonomous foreign policy, see *History of the Romanian Communist Party* (Stanford, Calif.: Hoover Institution Press, 1980), pp. 135-149; "Autonomy and Detente: The Problems of Rumanian Foreign Policy," *Survey*, no. 91-92 (Spring-Summer 1974): 105-120; "Romania's Struggle for an Autonomous Foreign Policy," *The World Today* 35, no. 8 (July 1979): 340-348, and "Romania: Projections," in Richard F. Staar, ed., *United States-East European Relations in the 1990s* (New York: Crane Russak, 1989), pp. 193-201.
2. The Soviet photograph of the two leaders meeting in Bucharest—unlike the usual bear hug embrace or the fraternal kiss—showed both grim-faced and unsmiling. *Pravda* (Moscow), 26 May 1987, p. 1.
3. See, for example, a commentary on the Warsaw Pact summit at Bucharest in July of 1989 which strongly criticized attempts by "certain participants" to give some countries, including Romania, "advice" and "recommenda-

tions" that they should renounce "the basic principles of socialism" and reintroduce private property and Western-style democracy. *România Liberă*, 10 July 1989, p. 1. See also the commentary in ibid., 17 January 1989, p. 30.
4. An indication of the high-level support for this shift was an article by Lt. Gen. Ilie Ceauşescu, brother of party leader Nicolae Ceauşescu, in which he compared historical struggles to preserve Romania's territorial integrity with the contemporary RCP struggle against Hungary's efforts to call attention to Romanian human rights violations in the international arena. Lt. Gen. Ceauşescu observed: "The overtly revisionist, revanchist attitudes displayed by the neighboring state [Hungary] in its relations with Romania cease to be a problem that interests the Budapest government alone." Lupta Întregului Popor, no. 2 (1989): 22-28. See Radio Free Europe, RAD Background Report, no. 86 (17 May 1989).

   Similar arguments that would support intervention to quell reform were voiced in the RCP daily *Scînteia* (20 August 1989) when a noncommunist prime minister was nominated in Poland: developments in Poland placed "in jeopardy the interests of socialism, including those of the Warsaw Pact." Polish news media reported that things went even farther. The RCP leadership reportedly held an urgent meeting on Tadeusz Mazowiecki's nomination to be prime minister, and the Polish ambassador in Bucharest was called in by the RCP Central Committee secretary for international relations, Ion Stoian, who read a statement on behalf of Ceauşescu informing the Poles that the RCP and Romania, "as a socialist country," could not consider the Polish developments "as Poland's purely internal affair." *Gazeta wyborcza* (Warsaw), 29 September 1989, p. 6.
5. *Scînteia*, 21 November 1989, pp. 1 ff.
6. Ceauşescu's speech was broadcast live by Radio Bucharest and Bucharest Television, 21 December 1989.
7. *Adevărul*, 1 October 1990; *Azi*, 3 October 1990; and PlanEcon Report, 15 June 1990. See also Marvin Jackson, "The Impact of the Gulf Crisis on the Economies of Eastern Europe," *Radio Free Europe: Report on Eastern Europe* 1, no. 35 (31 August 1990): 40-45.
8. For a discussion of the background on Bessarabia, see *Facts and Comments Concerning Bessarabia, 1812-1940* (London: G. Allen and Unwin, 1941); and Charles Upson Clark, *Bessarabia: Russia and Roumania on the Black Sea* (New York: Dodd, Mead and Co., 1927).
9. Data from the 1989 Soviet census suggests a substantial outmigration from Soviet Moldavia of 56,000 people between 1979 and 1989. It is likely that this migration consists primarily of Ukrainians and Russians seeking better opportunities in Ukraine or elsewhere in the Soviet Union, rather than Moldavians leaving the republic. For Moldavians, opportunities and interests would be more limited because of the language and cultural differences. In the long run this may contribute to greater ethnic homogeneity. See Ann Sheehy, "1989 Census Data on Internal Migration in the USSR," *Radio Liberty: Report on the USSR* 1, no. 45 (10 November 1989): 7-9.

10. For a summary of the historical background of Bessarabia and a discussion of Moldavian ethnicity, see Robert R. King, *Minorities Under Communism: Nationalities as a Source of Tension among Balkan Communist States* (Cambridge, Mass.: Harvard University Press, 1973), pp. 31-35 and 91-108.
11. For a discussion of these Romanian historical claims, see King, *Minorities Under Communism*, pp. 220-241, and Robert R. King, "Verschärfter Disput um Bessarabien: Zur Auseinandersetzung zwischen rumänischen und sowjetischen Historikern," *Osteuropa*, 26, no. 12 (December 1976): 1079-1087 and A670-A676.

   On the eve of his overthrow in December 1989, Ceaușescu raised the Bessarabian issue in his speech to the 14th RCP Congress. He insisted that all agreements concluded in the past with Nazi Germany be condemned and annulled. (The full text of the Ceaușescu speech was published in *Scînteia*, 21 November 1989, pp. 1 ff.) This was clearly interpreted by Romanians and Soviets alike as a demand for repudiation of the Molotov-Ribbentrop Pact, which included the provision that Bessarabia should be Soviet. A commentator from the official news agency TASS responded "to Western media interpretations" of Ceaușescu's remarks that "no serious or responsible politician" could question postwar borders, "including the Soviet border with Romania." (TASS and Radio Moscow, 23 November 1989; FBIS-SOV [24 November 1989], p. 49.)
12. On the ethnic violence in Moldavia in October-November 1990, see the articles by Francis X. Clines in *The New York Times:* "6 Killed in Ethnic Violence in Moldavia," 3 November 1990, p. A-7; "Moldavia Averts Ethnic Violence," 1 November 1990, p. A-7; and "In Soviet Union, Dizzying Disunion," 26 October 1990, p. A-6; and the articles by Michael Dobbs in the *The Washington Post*: "6 Killed in Soviet Moldavia; Russians, Pro-Romanian Nationalists Clash in Border Republic," 3 November 1990, p. A-13, and "Soviet Moldavia Declares Emergency as Turks Rebel; Gagauz Minority Tries to Elect Its Assembly," 27 October 1990, p. A-19.
13. See Michael Dobbs, "Moldavian Reunification with Romania Is Back on Soviet Political Agenda," *The Washington Post*, 16 January 1990, p. A-16; and Mihai Carp, "Cultural Ties between Romania and Soviet Moldavia," *RFE: Report on Eastern Europe* 1, no. 30 (27 July 1990): 42-44.
14. King, *Minorities Under Communism*, pp. 76-90 and 146-169.
15. On Hungarians in Transylvania since the overthrow of Ceaușescu, see Judith Pataki, "Free Hungarians in a Free Romania: Dream or Reality?" *RFE: Report on Eastern Europe* 1, no. 8 (23 February 1990), and "Special Report: Transylvania," RFE/RL, *Soviet/East European Report* 7, no. 24 (1 April 1990): 1-4.
16. Reuters News Agency (Bucharest), 4 January 1990; TASS (Bucharest), 4 January 1990.
17. Associated Press (Bucharest), 6 January 1990.
18. Moscow Television, 26 January 1990, 9:48 p.m. Cited in Mihai Sturdza, "Changes in the International Status of Bessarabia," *RFE/RL: Report on Eastern Europe* 1, no. 25 (25 May 1990): 51-52.

19. Rompres, 4 May 1990; *Adevărul*, 5 May 1990.
20. Rompres, 1 December 1990; *Adevărul*, 2 December 1990.

INDEX

Academy of Sciences, Czechoslovakia, 148
ACDA, *see* U.S. Arms Control and Disarmament Agency
Action Program, KSC, 152
Afghanistan, Soviet troop withdrawal from, 107, 109
Afghanistan, socialist fatherland defense, 25
 and USSR, 17, 18
Albania, 204, 205
 cautious liberalizations in, 10, 216, 221
 and diplomatic relations with superpowers, 203
 independent communist party of, 23, 24
 and Kosovo, 207
 lag in pluralism, 5
 mass flight from, 10, 216-17, 219
 nationalism of, 207
 self-determination of, 207
 student rebellions in, 211, 212
Albanian communism, 10, 203, 204, 205
Albanian Party of Labor (APL), 10, 209
 elections victory of, 222
 leading role of, 213
 9th congress of, 209
 problems of, 203
Albanian regime, U.S. recognition of, 222-3
Albanian-Soviet relations
 complications in, 221-2
 pragmatism of, 219
 prospects of, 218-223
 rift in, 204-5, 207-9
Albania-Peking (China/Beijing) relations, 220
Alia, Ramiz, 219, 221-2
 cabinet change by, 210, 211
 and East-Central Europan changes, 218
 and Hoxha policies, 210, 212, 211, 216, 217-218, 221
 as militant nationalist, 216
 1990 speech to U.N. General Assembly, 218
 report to 9th Congress of Albanian Party of Labor, 209
Alksnis, Colonel V. I., 9
Alliance of Democratic Forces, 114
Alliance of Reform Forces, 111, 117
Alpine-Adriatic Cooperation, 169
Andropov, Iurii V., 33, 106, 174
 and Zhivkov, 190
Antall, Jozsef, 168, 171, 172
anti-communist sentiments
 in East-Central Europe, 27
 in Czechoslovakia, 152-3
 in Romania, 239-40
anti-Russian coalition, 76
anti-Russian tradition, Bulgaria, 188
anti-Soviet feelings
 in Bulgaria, 188, 195, 196
 in Romania, 239-40, 243-3
APL, *see* Albanian Party of Labor
Argumenty i fakty, 99
arms race, 25
arms reduction, 27
"asymmetric convergence," 176, 178
"Atlantic to the Urals" (ATTU) region, 60
ATTU, *see* Atlantic to the Urals

Baker, James, 60, 89,
Balcerowicz, Leszek, 19, 135
"Balkanization," of the USSR, 197
Balkan security efforts, 73

Index

Baltic states, crackdown in, 140
   Czech concern of, 157, 161
   Hungarian concern of, 172
   Romanian reaction to, 241
Baltic states, Soviet dilemma of, 17, 129
"Baltic to Bosporus" corridor
   changes in, 75, 76
Baluku, Beqir, 217
BCP, *see* Bulgarian Communist Party
Belgrade Declaration (March 1988), 26, 105, 107
Beqja, Hamid, 212
Beria, Lavrentii, P., 23
Berlin Wall, fall of, 30, 86-7, 95, 103, 103, 126, 166, 232
Bessarabia, 235, 238-9
   and Romanian nationalism, 236
Bielecki, Krzysztof, 135
bilateral relations, USSR, with Eastern Europe, 128
Blagoev, Dimitur, 188
Blechman, Zbigniew, 69
Bolshevik revolution, 165
Bolsheviks, in the Balkans, 205
Bondarenko, A. P., 91
Brandt, Willy, 87
Braun, Andreas, 61
Brezhnev Doctrine, 1, 43, 176, 232
   renunciation of, 105, 109, 113, 177, 233
Brezhnev era, 21, 22, 105
Brezhnev, Leonid I., 3, 17, 26, 33, 106, 109
   and "common European House" interpretation, 174
   and independent communist party conflicts, 24
   and invasion of Poland, 131
   September 1971 Belgrade visit of, 105
   socialist commonwealth of, 19
Brucan, Silviu, 238
BSP, *see* Bulgarian Socialist Party
Bucharest agreement (1958), 47
Bucharest conference (1960), 208
Bulgaria, 2
   environmental protests in, 30
   military force reduction in, 70
   name changes in, 196
   as "sixteenth republic," 187-88
   as USSR ally, 187, 188
   and the West, 196, 197
Bulgarian Communist Party (BCP), 3, 30
   14th Congress (Jan., Feb., 1990), 193
   and party name change, 193
Bulgarian communist regime, 188
Bulgarian goods
   quality of, 190
Bulgarian People's Army (BPA), 70
Bulgarian-Russian peoples, 188
Bulgarian Socialist Party (BSP), 3, 74
   Congress (Nov. 1990), 194
   loss of influence by, 194, 195
   progress of, 10
Bulgarian-Greek linkage, 74
Bulgarian-Soviet relations, 188
   in post-Brezhnev era, 190-192
   prospects of, 196, 197
   support of industrial projects in, 188
   trade agreement in, 49
Bunce, Valerie, 25
Bundeswehr Akademie, 72
Bundeswehr, 93, 94, 97
   limiting of, 94
Burgas petrochemical complex, 188
Bush, George, 117
Bush-Gorbachev summit (June 1990), 93
   Camp David meeting with Kohl, 89-90
   and NATO defense emphasis, 93

Calfa, Marian, 40-1, 153
   and Soviet oil deliveries, 161
   USSR trade importance of, 156
Cami, Foto, 209, 211-12
Carcani, Adil, 210
Carol, (King of Romania), 242
Castro, Fidel, 106
Catholic Church, Poland, 133, 134
Ceausescu family
   and the military revolt, 30
Ceausescu, Nicolae, 2, 229, 237
   and Albania, 212, 213
   and changes in Hungary, 175

"embarrassment to socialism," 176, 231-32
  and Gorbachev, 181, 231
  last speech of, 233
  legacy of, 239-40
  overthrow of, 126
  as statesman, 231-2
Center Alliance (Poland), 135
Central European culture, 27
Cernnii Episkop, *see* Noli, Bishop Fan S.
CFE, *see* Conventional Armed Forces in Europe
change
  as condition of stability, 181-2
  Hungary's role in, 181-2
  USSR need of, 182
  dangers of, 182
  hardliner criticism of, 182
changes in East-Central Europe, 3, 33
  in Czechoslovakia
  influence on Albania of, 203, 211, 212
  irreversibility of, 159
  and pluralism, 204
  and USSR, 4-5, 103,175
  in Yugoslavia, 103
Charter 77, 72, 77
Chebrikov, Viktor M., 108
Chernenko, Konstantin U., 33, 106, 174, 190
Chernobyl disaster, in Bulgaria, 192
Chervov, Colonel General N. F., 7-8
China, independent communist party of, 23, 24
Christian Democrats (GDR), 92
civic activity, Poland, 132
civic culture, maturity of, 182-83
Civic Forum (Czechoslovakia), 72
  and the USSR, 9
Civic Forum/Public Against Violence, 151-2
  governing principles of, 161-162
  dangers to, 162
Civic Movement-Democratic Action, Solidarity faction, 135
civil society, 11

CMEA, *see* Council of Mutual Economic Assistance
collective leadership, Yugoslavia, 105
Comintern
  influence in Albania, 205, 206, 207
  and the Balkans, 220, 221
Committee for the Liberation of Kosovo, 206
"Common European Home," 26-33, 176
  and arms reduction, 26
  and economic revitalization, 26
  and European Community, 177
  and European security, 113
  interpretations of, 174, 175
  and perestroika, 28
  power of, 178
  tenets of, 174-5
"Common European House," *see* "Common European Home"
communism, collapse of, 2, 28-33
  results of, 11
  significance of, 204
  and Soviet military power, 28
communist economies, shortcomings of, 126
communist leaders, Albanian, 205, 209, 212
communist movement, Albania, 23
  reasons for, 205, 206-7
communist parties, East-Central European, 3, 24
communist parties, German,
  early 1991 Berlin meeting of, 3
communist parties, independent nationalist, 23, 24
communist parties, East-Central European, 22, 24
Communist Party of Czechoslovakia (KSC), 2, 4, 152
  Action Program of, 152
  assets seizure of, 153
  and CPSU relations, 152
  1969 "normalization" of, 148
  old politicians of, 149
  and the Slovak Communist Party (KSS), 152
Communist Party of Romania,

Index

and National Salvation Front (NSF), 4
Communist Party of the Soviet Union (CPSU), 2-3
　leading role renunciation of, 30
　multi-national composition of, 21, 24
　28th Congress of, 31, 94
communist system, disappearance of, 97-8
communists, Greek, 209
compensation to USSR, German, 94-95, 97
Comprehensive Treaty (13 September 1990), Germany-USSR, 95, 96, 99
Conference on Security and Cooperation in Europe (CSCE),
　and Albania, 220, 221
　and the Baltic states crackdown, 172
　Conflict Prevention Center in Vienna of, 19-20
　and Gorbachev's aims, 29
　Helsinki (1989) meeting, 29
　Nov. 1990 meeting of, 19, 72
　Office for Free Elections in Warsaw of, 19
　role of, 92-93, 96, 98, 99, 154
　secretariat in Prague of, 19, 72
conflict potentials, East-Central Europe, 63-6
"consolidated pluralism," Poland, 130
Constitution, Bulgarian, 188
Conventional Armed Forces in Europe (CFE) treaty (1990), 7, 20, 59, 60, 68
　and WTO, 60
　and NATO, 60
convertible currency, Czechoslovakia, 161
Council for Mutual Economic Assistance (CMEA), 24, 138, 177, 178
　and Albania, 204
　bureaucracy, 40, 41
　and Common European Home, 26
　contract of, 43-48
　effectiveness of, 38-39, 40, 155
　end of, 6, 42, 97-8, 140, 157, 178, 179
　establishment of, 22, 37
　obligatory quotas of, 41
　replacement of, 153, 54
　and world market oil prices, 176-7

Council for Mutual Economic Assistance, structure
　and pricing system, 46-7, 48, 49
　and market economy, 41, 42, 50
Council for Mutual Economic Assistance trade, 172, 173
　and the USSR, 41-42, 46, 48
　shift in pattern, 44, 45-46, 50
Council of Europe (CE), 1, 10,
　addresses to: Gorbachev (1989), 1; Havel (1990), 18
　as CSCE representative, 72-73
　Hungarian membership of, 183
Council on Foreign Relations, 171
CPSU, *see* Communist Party of the Soviet Union
Craxi, Bettino, 177
Croatian separatism, 9, 105
CSCE, *see* Conference on Security and Cooperation in Europe
Cuko, Lenka, 213, 217
cultural resistance, East-Central Europe, 23
currency,
　CMEA, 47, 49, 50
　Czechoslovak, 161
　Polish, 135-6
Czech and Slovak Federative Republic, 150
Czech-Soviet relations, change in, 148-9
Czechoslovak 1968 invasion, 9, 105, 147
　repudiation of, 147-8
　Romania's condemnation of, 230
Czechoslovakia, 2
　Council of Europe membership of, 5, 73
　cut in military forces, 68
　defense/security policy, 154, 155
　demonstrations in, 30
　independent communist stance of, 24
Czechoslovakia, First Republic, 147
Czechoslovakia, renamed, 150
Czechoslovkia-Hungary-Poland Group, 169
Czechoslovak People's Army, renamed Czechoslovak Army, 153
Czechoslovak-Soviet economic relations, 155-56

Index

Czechoslovak-Soviet relations, from 1989, 150-2

Dashichev, Viacheslav, 91, 94
Davydov, Yurii, 91
"Declaration of Principles," 109, 113
DeConcini, Senator Dennis, 117, 218
deficits, East-Central Europe, 51-2
Demichev, Petr N., 108
Democratic Forum, 166, 167
democratic processes, Poland, 134
Democratic Renewal, Albania, 10, 219
democratization, East-Central Europe, 59
 and the USSR, 11
 as a reform tool, 127
 and perestroika, 128
destalinization, Albania, 208
destalinization, Bulgaria, 191
Dienstbier, Jiri, 9, 151, 154
Dimitrov, Georgi, 187, 188, 196, 206,
diplomatic relations, Albanian, 210
 with superpowers, 216, 219
Discussion Clubs for the Support of Glasnost' and Prestroika, 192, 194
distribution problems, food, and CPSU management, 32
Dlouhy, Vladimir, 54
Dobrovsky, Lubos, 72
domestic agenda, Bulgarian, 195
domestic policies, Romania, 239, 240
domestic problems, USSR, 157, 239, 240
draft union treaty, USSR, 115
Dubcek, Alexander, 148, 180
Dume, Petrit, 217
Dzasokhov, Aleksandr, 110
Dzhurov, Dobri, 193, 194

East-Central Europe, 75
 as bridge to USSR, 19
 as postcommunist models, 19
 "threat-rich" environment of, 62
East-Central European changes
 Romanian opposition to, 232
East-Central European confederation,
 and Soviet republics, 170

East-Central European economy, 38
 and USSR, 50, 51, 52, 54
"East-Central European Union," 169
East Germany, 2
 reunification vote of, 19
 transition rate of, 5; *see also* GDR, German Democratic Republic
Eastern Orthodox Church, 188
EC, *see* European Community
Ecoglasnost', 192, 194
economic crisis, Soviet, 32, 43-45, 46;
 see also domestic crisis
economic problems
 Albania, 210
 Bulgaria, 196
 Hungary, 172-174
economic reform plan, Poland, 134, 135-6
economic subsidies, Soviet, 26
economic transformation, difficulties of, 178
EDA. *see* United Democratic Left
education, Bulgarian, 188
Efimov, General A. N. 108
"elder brother" myth of, 22, 24
election,
 Albania, 219, 222-3
 Greece, 208
 Romania, 234
 Hungary, 165, 2
 Poland, 2, 133
 East Germany, 2, 89
electoral reforms, Poland, 133
employment, 52-53
energy, 172-173
 Hungarian need for, 171, 172
 Czechoslovak need for, 156
energy supply, Soviet, and CMEA trade, 42
environmental problem, Czechoslovakia, 156
ethnic diversity, 183
ethnic minorities, 169, 180-1, 182
 Czechoslovakian, 160
 Greek, 208, 209, 212
 Hungarian, 171, 179, 231, 237-8
 Polish, 140

in Romania, 231
in USSR, 233
ethnic minorities, Bulgarian, 196-7
in Macedonia, 196
in Ukraine, 197
in Moldavia, 197
ethnic rivalries, in the Balkans, 222
Euro-communist victory, 105
European Bank for Reconstruction and Development, 20
USSR membership of, 97
European Community, 173, 174
and German plea for Soviet aid, 97
Hungarian ties to, 167, 169, 173, 174
and Yugoslav unity, 116-117, 118
neutrality of, 177
and Single Europe Act, 177
European Community membership, 5, 182
and Albania, 220, 215
preparations for, 18
and Hungary, 162, 166, 183
Polish, 141
prospects of, 6
European Economic Space, 183
European Free Trade Association, 183
European mutual security system, 20
European Parliament, 175
Evtushenko, Evgenyi, 19

Falin, V. M., 3, 91
and communist ideals, 4
Federal Republic of Germany
reunification cost for, 8-9
"Finland-like," states, 4
Soviet hopes for, 129
"Friends of Albania," 214
Firiubin, Nikolai, 208
force, renunciation of, 1
foreign policy, Albania, 219
and China, 220
and Western Europe
foreign policy, Hungary, 169, 170
EC country cooperation goals of, 169
foreign policy, Romania, 230
foreign policy, Soviet, in Afghanistan, 29
Four Power meeting, 88-89

Free Democratic Party (FDP), GDR, 92
French Revolution, 12
"from Brest to Brest" plan, 27, 32
Fur, Lajos, 74

G-7 meeting (1 July 1990), Houston, 97
GATT, *see* General Agreement on Tariffs and Trade
Gazeta wyborcza, 71
GDR. *see* German Democratic Republic
General Agreement on Tariffs and Trade (GATT), 53
general strike, USSR, 116
Genscher Plan, 93, 94
Genscher, Hans-Dietrich, 89, 96
visit to Zheleznovodsk (16-17 July, 1990), 94
Georgia, Republic of, declaration of independence, 115
Gerasimov, Gennadii I., 175, 176
Geremek, Bronislaw, 67
German compensations, 94-95
loans to USSR, 95
German Democratic Republic (GDR), 29, 97
cost of rebuilding, 8
dependence on Soviet oil of, 84
disappearance of, 37, 83, 140
importance to USSR of, 84, 85
mass demonstrations in, 30, 86, 87
mass flights from, 86-87
parliamentary elections, 92
German diplomacy, and Soviet policy reversal, 96-97
German revolutionary process, and USSR, 86-87
German unification, 95, 126
acceptance of, 85-88
process of, 88-94
swiftness of, 83
three stages of, 85-86
German-Soviet relations, 94, 96, 97
prospects for, 98-9
public support of, 99
Germany, united, 98
army reduction offer of, 93

Index

and Gorbachev, 84
NATO membership of, 85, 86
and Volga Germans, 98-9
and workers' role in , 3
Gheorghiu-Dej, Gheorghe, 229
glasnost',
  and Albania, 210
  and Bulgaria, 190
  influence on society of, 192
  as reform tool, 127
  Soviet radicalization of, 113
Gorbachev, Mikhail S., 1, 22, 118, 137, 141, 209, 213, 240
  and the Baltic dilemma, 17-18, 20, 32, 96
  Brezhnev Doctrine renunciation of, 113
  and Bulgarian economic performance, 190
  and critics, 24, 75, 91-2, 94, 116, 212, 231-4
  and CMEA, 41, 48
  and a Common European Home, 28-29
  domestic agenda priority of, 26, 83, 96 115-16
  and East-Central European change, 175-6, 181
  and the 500-day plan, 104
  and the use of force, 26, 84
  and foreign policy "new thinking" of, 26, 62, 109
  and Germany, 83, 84, 85, 93, 94, 96
  and intracommunist relations, 113
  and national sovereignty , 29, 149,57, 158
  Nobel Peace Prize of, 28
  and preservation of the Soviet Union, 115
  and Solidarity, 29
  trial and error policy of, 38, 158
  and the West, 32, 177-8
  and Yugoslavia, 106, 107-9, 111, 112, 113
Gorbachev Doctrine, 2
Gorbachev reforms, 33, 38, 127-129, 204
  and Romanian opposition, 231-4
  support of, 125
Gorbachev speeches: Strasbourg (6 July 1989), to Council of Europe, 1, 27; to the 10th Congress of PUWP (30 June 1986), 131; Helsinki (1989), 2

Gorbachev visits: in Berlin (7-8 October 1989), 86; to the U.S. (1987), 210; to Yugoslavia (1990), 108
Grand National Assembly, Bulgaria, 196
Greek-Soviet rapprochement, 208
Grekov, L. I., 190
Grosz, Karoly, 1
Gypsies, 181
Gysi, Gregor, 3, 30

Havel, Vaclav, 6, 18, 30, 126, 150
  on Central European role, 18
  and Czech Army, 161
  Hungarian support of, 180
  political effectiveness of, 150-1
  and security system, 154
  U.S. (February 1990) visit of, 151
  and USSR aid, 151
  on WTO, 71
Havel-Dienstbier policy approach, 162
Hazbiu, Kadri, 217
Helsinki Accord, 18, 126, 182, 210, 215
Helsinki II, and Albanian participation, 215
Hitler-Stalin Agreement (1939), 99
Honecker, Erich
  and changes in Hungary, 175
  fall of, 2, 30, 86, 166
  Gorbachev criticism of, 176, 181
  state visit to Bonn of, 85
Hoxha clique, 216, 220
  in Albanian government, 217-8
Hoxha, Enver
  and East-Central European rebellions, 211
  rejection of USSR overtures by, 209
  and Soviet-Yugoslav rapprochement, 208
Hoxha, Nexhmije, 212
HSWP, *see* Hungarian Socialist Workers' Party
human rights abuses, Romania, 230, 231
Hungarian Communist Party, 30
Hungarian EC membership, 5, 177
Hungarian minorities
  in Romania, 231, 237
  in the USSR, 181

Index

Hungarian Socialist Workers' Party (HSWP), 1, 3
  demise of, 166
  and free elections, 174-5
Hungarian-Soviet relations, 165
  cooperation possibilities, 166, 170
  prospects for, 178-179
Hungary, 2
  agricultural success of, 10
  Council of Europe membership of, 72-73
  cut in military force, 68
  as East-West bridge, 166
  economic transformation of, 9-10
  European Community membership, 5
  free 1990 election, 30
  Gorbachev's approach to, 174
  as model for USSR transition, 167, 183
  and Soviet republics relations, 182
Husak regime, 158
Husak, Gustav, 3
  and changes in Hungary, 175
  and prestroika, 148-9
  Gorbachev criticism of, 176, 181

Iakovlev, Aleksandr N., 3
  and support for Hungary, 175
Ianaev, Gennadii I., 118
Iazov, Dmitrii T., 108-9
IECO, *see* International Economic Cooperation Organization
Ignatenko, Vitalii, 7
Iliescu, Ion, 241
Ilinden, 64
IMEMO, *see* Institute on the World Economy and International Relations
IMF, *see* International Monetary Fund
Independent Students' Society, 195
industrial development, Czechoslovakia, 155, 156
Institute of Fiance (Poland), 7
Institute of Industrial Economics (Hungary), 7
Institute of International Economic and Political Research (USSR Academy of Sciences), 7

Institute of International Relations (Sweden), 7
Institute of World Economics (Romania), 7
Institute on the World Economy and International Relations (IMEMO), 170
intellectuals, 11
intelligentsia, Russian, 23
interethnic conflict, Yugoslavian, 112
international communist movement, 23
International Economic Cooperation Organization (IECO), 6
International Military Education and Training Program, 72
International Monetary Fund (IMF)
  assistance to Hungary, 10, 46
  USSR membership of, 97
international security structure, 92
Iron Curtain, 166
Isai, Hekuran, 217
Ivashko, V. A., 4
Izvestiia, 71, 205

Jarai Zsigmond, 41
Jakes, Milos, 2, 158
Jaruzelski government, 60-69, 131, 132, 133
Jaruzelski, General Wojciech, 135
  and election results,, 28, 133
Jeszenszky, Geza, 172, 180
  on Pentagonale, 73
  and USSR relations, 170, 177
John Paul II (Pope), 19
Jovic, Borisaw, 116, 117
Juan Carlos, 195

Karpati, Ferenc, 68
Kadar, Bela, 168
Kadar, Janos, 166, 172
Kadare, Ismail, 211
Kadijevic, Veljko, 112
Kanis, Pavol, 4
Kapo, Hysni, 212
Kapo, Vito, 212
Karavelov, Liuben, 188

Index

Katushev, Konstantin F., 168
Katyn Forest massacre, 137
Khasbulatov, Ruslan I., 115, 182
"Khrushchev doctrine," 209
Khrushchev, Nikita S., 3, 33, 187, 205
   and Albanian-Soviet rift, 204
   and independent communist party conflicts, 24
   and Mao Tse-tung clash, 207
   and Tito, 105
   in Yugoslavia, 208
Kun, Bela, 165
Kiszczak, Czeslaw, 133, 134
Kiuchkov, Liubomir, 3
Klaus, Vaclav, 151-52
Kohl, Helmut, 85, 138
   and currency union, 89
   moderating effect of, 96
   Moscow (Feb. 1990) visit of, 88
   ten-point program of, 87
   Zheleznovodsk visit (16-17 July, 1990) of, 94
Koivisto, Mauno, 29
Kolodziejczyk, Piotr, 69-70
Komorowski, Bronislaw, 71
Kondi, Piro, 212
KOR, *see* Workers' Defense Committee
Kosovo
   and Albanian nationalism, 205, 206, 214, 215, 216, 220
   and the Western media, 214
Kostov, Traicho, 188
Kremikovtsi metalurgical combine,
Krenz, Egon, 30, 86
Kuczynski, Waldemar, 41
Kulikov, Marshal Viktor G.,
   and invasion of Poland, 131
Kundera, Milan, 22, 27
Kusin, Vladimir, 139-40
Kuwait, invasion of, 173
Kvitsinskii, Iu. A., 4-5

Lalumiere, Catherine
   and Romania's CE membership, 10, 73
land reform, 10
Langos, Jan, 9

Lantos, Congressman Tom, 218
LCY, *see* League of Communists of Yugoslavia
League of Communists for Democratic Renewal, Slovene, 111
League of Communists of Yugoslavia, 9
   boycott of, 103
   insignificance of, 111
   Congress, 12th, 1982, 107
League of Communists, Slovene, 111
League of Nations, 92-3
Lenin, V.I., 208, 215
Ligachev, Egor, 91
Lilov, Alexander, 193, 194
Lithuanian declaration of independence, 111
Lomakin, Viktor P., 150
Lukanov, Andrei, 40, 74, 193, 194
Lysenko, Trofim D., 23

Main Political Administration (of the USSR military), 24
Mamula, Branko, 108-9
Maritsa-Iztok energy-industrial complex, 188
market competition, East-Central European, 52
Markov, Dmitrii, 170
Markovic, Ante, 109, 113, 117
   and Alliance of Democratic Forces, 111, 114
Marshall Plan, 104
martial law, Poland, 28
Masaryk, Tomas G., 150
mass flight, Albania, 216-17, 219
Mavromates, Stylianos S., pseud.; *see* Noli, Bishop Fan S.
Mazowiecki government, 134
Mazowiecki, Tadeusz, 28, 134, 137
   intellectuals support of, 135
   problems of, 134-35
   on Red Army withdrawal, 71
media impact, Albania, 212-3
Mikhailov, Stoyan, 191
Mikulic, Branko, 107
military forces, East European/Soviet, cuts in, 68-70, 160-1

military security effort, 74-75
military security guarantee, Soviet, 25
Milosevic, Slobodan, 64, 114, 116, 117
Milosz, Czeslaw, 27
miners' strike, USSR, 116
ministry of justice, restoration of, Albania, 216
Mitrovic, Aleksandar, 109, 110
Mladenov, Petur, 193, 194
Modrow, Hans, 86, 87
  and GDR riots, 86
  and Kohl (December 1989) visit in Leipzig, 87
  Moscow visit of, 88
Mohorita, Vasil, 152, 153
Moldavia, 242, 243
  ethnic background of, 235, 236-7
Molotov-Ribbentrop agreement, 170, 235
Moscow conference (1960), 208
Mother Teresa, 216
Movement for Soviet-Bulgarian Friendship, 187
Mozhaiskov, O., 47
MPA, see Main Political Administration
multinational states, 182-3
multiparty elections, Albania, 10
"multiple candidacy," Albania, 221
Mura, Propkop, 217
Musataqi, Kico, 217
Musatov, V. L., 4
Mussolini, Benito, 219-20
Myftiu, Manush, 217
  and draft constitution, 216

Nagy, Imre, 165, 166, 170
NAM, see nonaligned movement
Nastase, Adrian, 73
National Salvation Front (NSF) Romania, 2, 30
  and CPSU Friendship and Cooperation Treaty, 10
  deceptive representation of, 239-40
  preoccupation of, 234
  and Romanian nationalism, 241-2
national security policy, East-Central Europe, 66-68

national self-determination, East-Central Europe, 29, 30
national/ethnic problems, in East-Central Europe, 111, 180, 181
  anti-Soviet sentiments, 24, 230
nationalism
  Albanian, 205-6, 220-1
  anti-Russian elements of, 230
  anti-Soviet, 24
  Romania, 233, 241-3
  in the Soviet Republics, 23, 233-4, 236-37, 239
NATO, see North Atlantic Treaty Organization
Nemeth, Miklos, 40, 68, 167
"new Soviet man," 20
"new thinking," 21, 26, 62, 103, 126
  and Bulgaria, 190, 192
  on Germany, 84
  importance of, 157
  on national security, 62
  in Poland, 137
New York Times, 214
Nixon, Richard M., 116
Nobel Peace Prize, for M. S. Gorbachev, 28
Noli, Bishop Fan S. (a.k.a. Stylianos S. Mavromates), 215
  Leninist coup of, 206
  and the Comintern, 206
  goals of, 207
nomenklatura, demise of, 127
nonaligned movement (NAM), 105, 106, 108 Harare summit of, 108
  "natural alliances" 107
  summit of NAM leaders, 106
North Atlantic Treaty Organization (NATO)
  allied modification plan of, 92, 93
  and a Common European Home, 26
  and conventional armed forces treaty, 7
  and German unification, 88 90
  Hungarian ambassador to, 169
  and Soviet military security guarantee, 25
  and WTO, 7
NSF, see National Salvation Front

Index

Nushi, Xenophon, 215

Obligatory quotas, CMEA, 41
Oder-Neisse frontier issue, 63, 67, 89-90, 138
officers' corps, replacement of, 71-72
oil prices, Soviet, 45, 47, 50, 51, 177, 234
    and East-Central European economies, 52, 53
    and political stability, 52
"oil shock," 45, 47
Olympics boycott, 190
Omonoia, 222
OPEC, *see* Organization of Petroleum Exporting Countries
opposition parties, Bulgaria, 193-4
Organization of Petroleum Exporting Countries (OPEC), 47
Orthodox Church, 206, 207

Papandreou, Andreas, 74, 208-9
parliamentary elections
    Poland (9 June 1989), 137
    Czechoslovakia (June 1990), 150
    East Germany (March 1990), 92
Party of Democratic Socialism (East Germany, PDS), 3, 87, 92
Party of Social Democracy of the Republic of Poland, 134
party system, Czechoslovakia, 152
party-to-party relations, 157
PASOK, 74
Patriotic Movement for National Revival (PRON), 130
Pavlov, Valentin S., 103
PDS, *see* Party of Democratic Socialism (East Germany)
peaceful coexistence," 105
Peking-Tirana axis, 208
Pentagonale, 73, 169
perestroika, 17, 28, 32, 33
    and Bulgaria, 190, 191
    in Czechoslovakia, 148-9
    and divided Germany, 83, 85
    Soviet radicalization of, 113
Persian Gulf crisis, 114, 115
    effects of, 38
PlanEcon estimate, 46
Planinc, Milka, 107, 109
Pliaka, Sokrat, 215-16
pluralism in East-Central Europe, 5, 126
Podkrepa, 194
Pogled, 190
Poland, 2, 126, 130
    defense spending consideration of, 69
    development, 9, 139
    and EC membership, 5
    economy, 9, 129, 139, 141
    dependence on the USSR of, 141
    independent stance of, 126, 129
    martial law, 130, 131
    military force cuts of, 68-69
policy changes,
    Czechoslovakia, 158-9
    USSR, 158-9
Polish foreign policy
    assertion of independence of, 129, 137
    with Czechoslovakia and Hungary, 138-9
    and WTO membership, 131, 137
Polish-Soviet relations, 136-7
    bases of, 138, 139, 140,
    prospects of, 140-1
Polish United Workers' Party (PUWP), 130, 140
    challenges to, 131
    defeat of, 133, 134, 137
    "pluralism resolution" of, 132
    renaming of, 134
politburo, Czechoslovak
    resignation of, 150
political prisoners, Poland, 131
political prospects, East-Central Europe, 53
political system, Hungary, 166-7
political transition, 53-54
Pomaks, 64
Popov Gavril, 31-2
Popov, Dimitur, 194
Portugalov, Nikolai, 91
post-communist models, 19, 20
post-hegemonic Europe, 62
Potsdam Agreement (1945), 87

Pozsgay, Imre, 30
Prague demonstration, 1989, 9
Prague Spring (1968), 147,
  and Soviet parallel, 149
pricing system, CMEA, 47 49-53
privatization
  Czechoslovakia, 9
  Poland, 136
PRON, *see* Patriotic Movement for National Revival
Public Against Violence (Slovakia), 150
PUWP, *see* Polish United Workers' Party

Radmilovic, Stanko, 114
Rakowska-Harmstone, Teresa, 20, 23
Rakowski, Mieczyslaw, 133
Rapallo Treaty (1922), 99
raw materials, Soviet, 48, 114-15
reactionary coup, Bulgaria
  possibility of, 195
Reagan, Ronald, 210
Red Army, 21
  components of, 59
  cuts in, 68
  Czech hostility to, 157
  in Moldavia, 75
  and anti-Russian danger of, 76
Red Army, withdrawal of, 59, 68, 71, 75, 76; *see also* Soviet military, Soviet troops, USSR military
reforms gestures, Albania, 210, 213
reforms pressures, Poland
  sources for, 130
reforms, East-Central European, 126-7
  Czech resistance to, 149
  as postcommunist models, 11-12 18
regional cooperation, East-Central European countries, 179
"rejoining Europe," 169-70
Renovica, Milanko, 108
republics, Soviet, 157
  increased power of, 157
  trade in, 173-4
republic to republic contacts,
  Czechoslovakia, 161
  Yugoslavia, 114-5

Republikaner, 90
revolution (1956), Hungarian, 167, 170, 176,
revolutions, Central European, 125-127, 129
Romanian-Soviet relations, 234-5
Robejsek, Peter, 175-6
Roman, Petre, 241
Romania, 2, 5
  autonomy of, 24, 229-30
  and China, 229
  and EC membership, 5-6
  and Germany, 230
  "hijacked revolution" of, 10
  MFN status of, 230
  as regional power, 243
  and the USSR, 229, 230, 231
  as WTO member, 243
Romanian Communist Party, 30, 229
  Congress (14th, 1989), 232-3
Romanian foreign relations, 232
Romanian government, and Bessarabia problem, 238, 239, 242
Romanian-Hungarian relations, 180, 232
Romanian military, 70
Romanian revolution (1989), 180
Romanian-Soviet relations, 229, 230
  economic, 243
  importance for Romania, 243
  low priority of, 240
  prospects of, 239
  reversal of, 231
Romanov empire, 21
Round Table Agreements, 5 April 1989, 28, 137
  discussions of, 133
ruble, 46, 173
ruling communist parties, November 1957 meeting of, 105
Russia, "sovietization" of, 22
Russian Communist Party, 21-2,
  renunciation of CPSU role of, 31
  and Yeltsin, 31-2
Russian Federation, 182
Russian officers, 31, 33
Russian Orthodox religious dissidents, 23

Index

Russian Republic
  anti-Soviet elements of, 24
  and Hungary, 166
  separate communist party establishment of, 30-31
Russian soldiers, 18
Ryzhkov, Nikolai I., 110, 111
Sakharov, Andrei, 23
Sarbanes, Senator Paul, 218
Securitate, 230, 233
security, 61
  alternatives for East-Central Europe, 71-75
  incresed need of, 61-2, 69-70, 74-5
  search for, 61-66
security concerns, 74
  in Bulgaria, 196
  change in, 168-9
  in East-Central European countries, 60-61, 71
  in Hungary, 168-9,
  and Romania, 240
  in USSR, 240
security strategies, 128
SED, *see* Socialist Unity Party
self-determination, Poland, 17
self-management, Yugoslavia, 105
Sergeenko, I., and IECO, 6-7
Shafir, Michael, 149
"shared fate," Yugoslavia-USSR, 113
Shatalin, 500 day plan, 103
Shehu, Mehmet, 127
Shevardnadze, Eduard, 26, 32, 60, 92, 171
  Belgrade (June 1987), visit of, 108
  Bucharest visit of, 238
  and foreign policy "new thinking," 26, 29
  and Soviet military in Afghanistan, 29
  and "Two plus Four" plan, 89
  on united Germany, 83, 94
  Yugoslav diplomacy of, 112
Shiriaev, Iurii, 45
Shishlin, N. V.
  and USSR stagnation, 5
Shliaga, Colonel General Nikolai I., 112
"shock therapy, Poland, 9, 12, 19, 135-36
Shumi Maritsa, 196

Sigurimi, 210-11
Sitarian, Stepan A., 109
Skubiszewski, Krzysztof, 138
Slovak National Party, 182-3
Slovene separatism, 9
Smirnova, Nina D., 204-5
Sobchak, Anatolii, 31-32
Sobell, Vladimir, 39
social internationalism, new interpretion of, 128
socialism, 2, 3
"socialist commonwealth," 24, 25, 125
  demise of, 17
  dilemmas of, 19-26
  myth of, 20, 22
socialist countries, 203
  and Marxist ideology, 203-4
  Hungary, 166-67
"socialist realism," 23
Socialist Unity Party (SED), 30, 87
  spurn of reform by, 84
Solidarity, 28, 129
  divisions in, 134
  in government, 126, 141
  independent stance of, 30
  influence of, 129
  legalization of, 130, 133, 137
  as opposition, 130
  and the 1989 Polish elections, 2, 28-29, 126
  success of, 129
Solidarity negotiations (1989), 132
Solzhenitsyn, Alexandr, 23
"Sovereignty and Independence" declaration, Yugoslavia, 104
Sovetskaia Rossiia, 191
Soviet control, on East-Central Europe, 66
Soviet debt, to Yugoslavia, 109-10
Soviet decision making process, 157-8
Soviet economic support, Bulgaria, 188
Soviet economy, 38
Soviet empire, 21
Soviet foreign policy, Poland, 136
Soviet Germany policy, 95-6
Soviet hegemony, 24, 33
  challenge to, 104-5

Soviet influence
  in Albania, 207
  on Bulgarian society, 190
Soviet military, 21
  and constitution article 6 removal, 30, 31
  and the CPSU, 31
  Main Political Administration role in, 31
  multinational nature of, 18, 21, 31, 33
  and Solidarity coalition government, 28
Soviet military guarantee, 29
Soviet military intervention, 29, 30
  and Baltic secession attempts, 32;
  see also Red Army, Soviet troops, USSR military
Soviet Moldavia, and Romanian minority, 235, 239
Soviet oil, 43-45
  CMEA countries supply of, 43
  and world market prices, 177
Soviet oil supply, 45-46
  to Bulgaria of, 196
  to Czechoslovakia, 161
  to GDR, 84
  to Hungary of, 173
  to Poland, 138
  to Romania, 234
  price of, 234
  and Soviet payment demand, 138
  Yugoslav dependence on, 107
Soviet policy changes toward Eastern Europe, 176-78
Soviet power, 22, 106
Soviet republics, and Hungary, 171-2
Soviet security, 75
  and East-Central European security efforts, 75-76
Soviet trade
  Germany, 97
  with Hungary, 172-73
Soviet troop withdrawal, 7, 154
  Czechoslovakia, 153-4
  Hungary, 167-8, 179
  Poland, 138, 139-40
  see also under Red Army, Soviet military, USSR military
Soviet-Albanian rift, 208

Soviet-American strategic weapons agreement (1991), 20
Soviet-East-Central European economic relations, 53-54
Soviet-Yugoslav rapprochement, 207-8
  see also under USSR entries
Spain, 195
Stalin, Joseph, 3, 23, 33, 84, 104
  influence in the Balkans, 206
  and the nationalist threat, 24
  and Volga Germans, 98
Stalinism, horrors of, 20-21
Stanculescu, Nicolae, 70
state socialism, 126
Stefani, Simon, 217
  reform gestures of, 210-1
Stelmaszuk, Zdzislaw, 69
strikes, Poland, 136-137
students demonstrations, Albania, 211, 212
  Shkoder, 213-4
Sudeten Germans, 151

Talyzin, N. V., 39
Teltschik, Horst, 88
Thikat (Knives), 211
threats, to East-Central European countries
  external 63, 66, 67
  internal, 63, 66, 67
Thurmer, Gyula, 3
Tikhonov, Nikolai A., 107
Tisza-Carpathian Group, 169
Tito, Josip Broz, 105-6, 208
  revolutionary ambitions of, 104
Tozaj, Neshat, 211
trade
  Czechoslovakia, 155, 156
  Hungary, 173-4
  Poland-USSR, 138
  economic reorientation of, 156
transformation
  price of, 181-2
transition, East-Central Europe, 5, 159
  Bulgaria, 196
  Czech features of, 159

Index

Transylvania, and Moldavia linkage, 237, 238
Treaty of Final Settlement (12 September 1990), 95
truck and taxi strikes, Budapest, 52
Tsipko, Aleksandr, 5
Tudjman, Franjo, 117
Tvardovsky, Aleksandr, 23
Two plus Four" Accord, 67, 95, 97, 138
    James Baker plan of, 89
"two-camp theory," 104
Tygodnik Solidarnosc, 134
Tyminski, Stanislaw, 19, 135

U.S. Arms Control and Disarmament Agency (ACDA), 8
UDF. *see* Union of Democratic Forces
Ukraine-Moldavia problem, 241, 242
Ulc, Otto, 49
umbrella organizations, Poland, 132
unemployment
    in Albania, 210
    in Hungary, 210
unification, Germany, 87, 89, 95
    and USSR attitudes, 85
Union of Democratic Forces (UDF), 74, 194-5
Union of Soviet Socialist Republics, *see* USSR
United Democratic Left (EDA), Greece, 208-9
united Germany, NATO membership of, 90, 92
    Soviet objections to, 90-91
United Nations, 196
Usanov, Vladimir, 51
USSR, and German unification, 88, 90-1, 92, 96, 97
USSR conservatives, 99
    influence on Bulgaria by, 195
USSR economy, and East-Central Europe, 37-38
USSR foreign policy, changes in, 128
USSR military 24, 242-3
    intervention possibility, 242-3
    and East Central European communist parties, 24
    see also under Red Army, Soviet military, Soviet troops
USSR, 12, 127, 181-2
    and the Balkan agenda, 223
    CMEA trade of, 50, 170
    and Czechoslovakia to, 151
    ethnic conflict threat in, 24
    and Finland relations, 2
    policy reversal, 126
    strategic interest, 131
    see also under Soviet entries
USSR State Bank, Foreign Currency Economics Administration, 47

Vacek, Miroslav, 72, 153, 160
Vatra Romanesca, 182-3
"velvet revolution," 150, 232
Venizelos, Sophocles, 209
Versailles Conference (1918-1919), 30
Veterans Committee, 222
Vienna Institute for Comparative Economic Studies estimates, 51-52
Visegrad summit meeting (24-25 Feb., 1991), 6
Volgyes, Ivan, 22
Volksarmee, 93
Vorotnikov, V. I., 108

Walesa, Lech, 19, 141
    victory election of, 135
Walesa faction, Solidarity, 134, 135
Warsaw Pact, 7, 28
    and Solidarity coalition government, 28
    and threat of disintegration, 17, 25, 65, 97-8, 153, 154, 157, 165, 168.
    see also Warsaw Treaty Organization
Warsaw Treaty Organization (WTO), 7, 22, 43, 71, 140
    and Albania, 204
    and Bulgarian security, 188
    and a Common European Home, 26
    and German unification, 88, 90, 92
    membership loss of, 59-60, 137, 166
    membership renewal of, 107

Political Consultative Committee meetings, 2, 152
and socialist commonwealth survival, 24
and Soviet hegemony, 59
and Yugoslavia, 105
Warsaw Treaty Organization Committee of Foreign Ministers
Warsaw (1989 October) meeting of, 29
Warsaw Treaty Organization forces, 26
and East Central European communist parties, 24-5
and military intervention, 29
and the USSR military, 25
withdrawal of, 7
see also Warsaw Pact
West German credits, 5
West Germany
and Gorbachev, 84
and GDR relations, 5
and Soviet military security guarantee, 25
Western aid, to USSR, 5, 32
Western diplomacy, 91-2
Western trade, and CMEA, 44
Western visitors, Albania, 216, 218
White generals, 21
Workers' and Peasants' Red Army, 31
Workers' Defense Committee (KOR), establishment of, 130
World Bank, 50, 51
USSR membership of, 97
world market, and CMEA goods, 48
WTO. See Warsaw Treaty Organization

Xoxe, Koci, 208

Yeltsin, Boris N., 114, 182
and Baltic policy, 18
defection from CPSU of, 31-2
electoral victory of, 115
and Gorbachev, 115-6
and independent post-communist republics, 32
Yugoslav army, 116, 117
Yugoslav changes

reasons for, 113
as model for USSR, 113
prospects of, 113-120
Soviet interest in, 110
Yugoslav economic crisis, 107, 109
Yugoslavia
and the Balkans, 196
divisions in, 9, 116-17
independent communist party of, 23, 24, 105, 112
and the Stalinist interstate system, 104, 105
Yugoslav "revisionsism," 107
Yugoslav road to socialism, 105
Yugoslav trade surplus, in USSR, 108, 109
Yugoslav-Soviet relations
acceptance of Yugoslavia in, 106
and changes, 104-113,
cooperation, 108-9, 112
possibilities of, 117-20
republic to republic negotiations, 107

Zhdanov, Andrei A., 23, 104
Zhelev, Zheliu, 10, 74
address to the U.N., 196-7
on all-European security system, 72
UDF leadership of, 194,
view of totalitarianism, 195
Zhivkov, Todor, 74, 187, 188,
and conservative communist governments, 191
fall of, 2, 30, 192-93
Gorbachev criticism of, 181, 191
and invasion (1968) of Czechoslovakia, 191
isolation of, 192
Khrushchev's backing of, 188
and Nina Andreeva letter, 191-2
and post-Brezhnev Soviet relations, 189
and reforms, 191
society's challenge of, 192
of Tiananmen Square crackdown, 191
Zhivkova, Liudmila, 190
Zolnierz wolnosci, 69

Security in Europe's Eastern Half

From where do threats arise? They are both internal and external, and a comprehensive treatment is beyond the scope of this paper. But the ways in which postcommunist and posthegemonic East-Central European systems may become endangered are not difficult to identify. Control over their own affairs, and ultimately the state system or government, is imperiled by old and new internal threats including:

- heterogeneity, especially ethnonationalism exacerbated by socioeconomic inequalities among strata and regional disparities;[12]
- the antipathy or active opposition of the old *nomenklatura* and secret police;
- a questionable loyalty among senior military officers and an uncertain relationship between civil and military authority;[13]
- an antipathy among unemployed workers, demobilized troops, and others whose social welfare expectations are disrupted (at least in the short term) by marketization;[14]
- and the antipolitics politics—the mix of anger at *all* politicians with a purposeful apathy—that has already appeared in Polish and Hungarian elections.[15]

To these internal fault lines one must add an ample and growing inventory of external threats:[16]

- Germany and Poland: Issues include ownership of property in Poland once held by German citizens and conflicting claims by the two states about rights in the Baltic. Although the *Bundestag* has given assurances about postwar borders, and a bilateral treaty officially recognizing the Oder-Neisse frontier was completed in November 1990,[17] nothing can forever set to rest issues that have transcended several centuries.
- Poland and Belorussia, Ukraine, and/or Lithuania: The Bug River became Poland's eastern border at the end of World War II. Polish nationalists are unlikely to rest quietly throughout the 1990s concerning the territories they lost after that war and about minorities scattered throughout the territory of the now unraveling USSR. However, other nationalists, from these increasingly independent republics, reject Polish claims and raise their own.
- Hungary and Romania: Far from dissipating, once communist regimes were toppled, these two states remain enmeshed in a bitter dispute with murky origins and a cloudy prognosis. Hungary claims, with justifica-

tion, that ethnic Hungarians in the Romanian territory of Transylvania have been denied economic and political rights and is highly critical of Romania's slow and painful transition from communist dictatorship.[18] Romania not only denies this but, also with some justification, claims that Hungary is attempting to interfere in Romanian affairs. Competing historical claims to Transylvania turn on arcane sources of information regarding who was there first, and on interpretations of the 1920 Treaty of Trianon that took Transylvania from Hungary. Nationalists on both sides have been vituperative in their attacks on one another, and calmer individuals may not always be able to diffuse the situation.

- Albania and Yugoslavia: For the Albanian state, the Serbian hard-line leadership of Slobodan Milošević has undertaken a concerted campaign to deny any rights to the ethnic Albanians in Kosovo (90 percent of the province's population). Tirana claims that the Yugoslav federal authorities and the army have done nothing to protect Albanians against Serbian political attacks and vigilante violence. The predominant attitude in Serbia is highly antagonistic toward Albanians and toward the neighboring Albanian state, which Serbs view as conspiring to absorb or annex Kosovo were the majority to have its way. The clashes in Kosovo have left scores dead since mid-1989 and continue to make this one of the more volatile disputes between the Baltic and Bosporus.

- Bulgaria and Yugoslavia: Macedonia, the bane of Balkan stability, is once again returning to confound rational policy-makers. Bulgarians are suspicious of a nationalist organization in their midst, among people who identify themselves as Macedonian. A part of the Bulgarian state would, presumably, be claimed by any revanchist Macedonian state, and the 1990 reemergence of a nationalist movement called *Ilinden* leads the Bulgarians to infer Serbian encouragement or sponsorship. Accusations have been made that Yugoslav authorities have provided financing for *Ilinden,* and there are unsettling implications for future acrimony.

- Greece and Yugoslavia: Athens refuses to acknowledge that a Macedonia or even Macedonians exist. Border incidents occurred in 1990— detention by Greece of individuals with passports identifying themselves as Macedonian, fearing that among those crossing the border were some trying to foment anti-Greek sentiment.

- Greece and Albania: The Greeks refer to that part of Albania, wherein a sizable Greek minority (Athens claims almost 300,000) lives, as

Northern Epirus. This population and overlapping minorities, e.g., Albanians in northern Greece, make this a troublesome border as well. Signs of this tension occurred in the latter half of 1990, when Tirana launched a media attack against anti-Albanian rhetoric in Greece, and when two ethnic Greeks trying to flee from Albania were killed by Albanian border guards and their bodies displayed publicly—acts that elicited strong warnings from the Athens government.[19]

- The USSR and Romania: Violence has erupted inside the Moldavian Soviet Socialist Republic—Bessarabia to the Romanians.[20] The Romanian ethnic majority of the Moldavian SSR strives for independence from Moscow, and nationalists on both sides of the Prut River demand a unified Romanian-Moldavian state. But the Russian minority in the union republic, plus Turks and other groups, want nothing of such a reunification. Fighting between ethnic groups within the Moldavian SSR necessitated the deployment of Soviet MVD (internal affairs ministry) and some regular USSR troops in late October to early November 1990, and continued unrest is more likely than not.

- Bulgaria and Turkey: There is a very large Turkish minority concentrated in the northeast and southeast of Bulgaria. Between 10 and 15 percent of Bulgaria's population, depending on the source of population data, is ethnically Turkish and/or religiously Muslim (Bulgarian Muslims are called Pomaks). There are, moreover, many other smaller minorities. The former communist regime tried forcibly to assimilate the Turks, leading to violence and police repression, especially during 1984-1985 and 1989. With Turkey's attention drawn elsewhere, this had become less of a critical bilateral issue in early 1991. But, within Bulgaria, tensions were high, in part due to efforts by hundreds of thousands of Turks who fled Bulgaria in 1989 to return and resume their past occupations and retake their possessions. Ankara's attention to Bulgarian Turks would quickly heighten, if renewed violence took place.

- Bulgaria and Romania: Part of the friction between Sofia and Bucharest has to do with irritations created by past communist governments, e.g., the egregious pollution of Bulgarian towns like Ruse by Romanian industry in Giurgiu across the Danube. Territorial disputes, however, are also present and pose long-term difficulties. Dobrudja, a territory adjacent to the Black Sea, is divided between Romania and Bulgaria, but Bulgarians sometimes observe that all of it ought to be united within Bulgaria. A not insignificant Bulgarian minority resides in the Romanian part of Dobrudja and made its presence felt in 1990.

This litany of extant bilateral disputes is not exhaustive and omits problems that may erupt as Yugoslavia fragments, or as Turkish-Greek animosity escalates because of some confrontation in the Aegean.

Yet, there is no doubt that these interstate flash points will become *more dangerous* in the early 1990s than they have been for decades. By no means does this imply imminent warfare on any of these frontiers. The artificial and onerous weight of Soviet hegemony and the ironclad constraints of East-West competition during the Cold War, however, are gone. Without a multilateral treaty organization—even one that was imposed by a hegemon—the possibilities of armed conflict are greater. Prior to the outbreak of any armed conflict, these same disputes could engender trade wars or migrations of people fleeing either persecution or what they judge to be imminent violence. Refugees, once streaming across borders en masse, will themselves constitute a security danger for all the political systems involved,[21] and their plight will heighten ethnonationalist anger on all sides.

For all that was reprehensible about Soviet control, such an ominous presence, coupled with the political and economic dependence of communist regimes on Moscow, *dampened* the antagonisms that have long resonated throughout Europe's eastern half. As noted elsewhere, "Driven by the visceral issues of peoples and borders, not by the strategic goals of an alliance, individual states may find it difficult to resist the tug of nationalism."[22]

The new political systems in postcommunist East-Central Europe, and the nascent parties and governments attempting to extrude in various regions from a dangerously weakened central authority in the USSR, thus live in a threat-filled environment. Internally and externally, these challenges are real and present dangers to control over their own affairs, to the vitality of the political system, and sometimes to the existence of the state.

How, then, is security being sought under such conditions? Particularly in countries between the Baltic and Bosporus corridor, can the capacities of states, systems, and governments be reinforced against evident threats? Can the threats, themselves, be mitigated by multilateral, bilateral, or intrastate measures? From where will these increments to capacities or reductions of threat be derived?

NEW THINKING ABOUT OLD DILEMMAS[23]

For each state of what had been the "Soviet bloc," a truly *national* security policy is being fashioned. Implicit to such a process are new assessments of